*Religion and Aging in the Indian Tradition*

*McGill Studies in the History of Religions,*
*A Series Devoted to International Scholarship*
*Katherine K. Young, Editor*

*SUNY Series in Aging*
*Sheldon S. Tobin and Edmund Sherman, Editors*

# *Religion and Aging in the Indian Tradition*

*SHRINIVAS TILAK*

*Foreword by Katherine K. Young*

STATE UNIVERSITY OF NEW YORK PRESS

*Published by*
*State University of New York Press, Albany*



*Printed in the United States of America*



*For information, address State University of New York*
*Press, State University Plaza, Albany, N.Y., 12246*

*Library of Congress Cataloging-in-Publication Data*

*Tilak, Shrinivas, 1939–*
*Religion and aging in the Indian tradition / Shrinivas Tilak.*
*p. cm.—(McGill studies in the history of religions) (SUNY series in aging).*
*Bibliography: p.*
*Includes index.*
*ISBN 0–7914–0044–1.—ISBN 0–7914–0045–X (pbk.)*
*1. Old age—India. 2. Aging—Religious aspects—Buddhism. 3. Aging—Religious aspects—Hinduism. 4. Aged—India—Social conditions. I. Title. II. Series: Suny series in aging.*
*HQ1064.I4T55 1989*
*305.2'6'0954—dc 19* *88-30583*
*CIP*

*10 9 8 7 6 5 4 3 2 1*

*Dedicated to the memory of my parents*
*Radha and Gopal Tilak*

# *Contents*

# *Foreword*

If aging is a biological process, old age is a construct of culture. So important, so difficult, and so delicate is the task of investing life with purpose and meaning at the time of perceived decline that the measure of a culture's sophistication and health may reside precisely in its creative imaging of the dignity of old age. It may also reside in its ability to inspire the "courage to be"—to borrow Paul Tillich's now famous phrase—despite the stress of aging, the impinging sense of loss and the awareness of approaching death (for the individual, family, and society).

Dr. Shrinivas Tilak in this pioneering study of traditional Indian views on aging and old age invites entry into a civilization's rich reflections on and constructions of a liminal zone of human experience. He has looked at the topic with care and insight through the dialectical relation of Vedic religion, Buddhism, and Hinduism as nuanced by the different historical periods and the concerns of the various genres of texts. He has also analyzed his data from the perspective of modern gerontology with reference to theories of engagement, disengagement, and differential disengagement. He finds the traditional Indian approach to be close to the latter.

According to the differential disengagement theory, one should selectively cast away some of the norms and values of middle age and take on a role more suited to old age. The Hindu view of the stages of life (*āśrama*) attempts to overcome the extreme opposition between this-worldly life (*pravṛtti*) and renunciation (*nivṛtti*)—which threatened the very fabric of Indian society in the 6th century

B.C.E.—by incorporating the positive features of both. Hindu thinkers analyzed, for example, the basic types of experiences in men's lives related to family, society, and religion and created appropriate categories such as the stages of life to characterize these experiences. They assigned to these stages of life attendant duties and goals to provide, concurrently or serially, experiences of this-worldly life and renunciation. And they correlated these stages with the aging process so that by the end of a lifetime a man's experience would have incorporated the poles and made possible, upon deep reflection, their ultimate integration.

Accordingly, the *āśramas* have a distinct order or rank. The first stage is studentship, which provides the seeds for this-worldly life: the student is educated for his future occupation and the skills of living in this world as a householder. The first stage also provides the seeds for renunciation for the student is trained in discipline, concentration, and chastity in a peaceful place outside the city in order to develop the initial taste for renunciation. The second stage of married life brings to fruition the occupational training and the duty to produce children. While the training in renunciation moves to the background, there are periods of the day or days of the year for the practice of withdrawal such as during morning prayers and yogic exercises, vows and pilgrimage. The third stage involves withdrawal from family obligations, a move to the forest, and the practice of chastity, thereby relegating the householder stage to the background (even though husband and wife may withdraw together) and bringing renunciation to the foreground. The final stage of complete renunciation proper, which may be postponed for future lives, completes the experience of renunciation by total withdrawal from society, enforced by being casteless and by constantly wandering or meditating in an isolated place.

Since the stage of renunciation in old age provides the freedom and calm to contemplate the experiences of life, it allows for mental integration of all phenomena and ultimately the experience of oneness. This mental integration has incorporated but ultimately transcended the original opposition of this-worldly activity and renunciation. Hence, in Hindu terms, there is the experience of the fullness of life leading to the realization of Brahman.

Now we are in a position to see how this ideal plan of life expresses a kind of differential disengagement that is distributed albeit with escalation throughout the life time and prevents any need for sudden withdrawal or perception of the meaninglessness of life. In the context of gerontology, worldly life or *pravṛtti* may be understood as engagement and renunciation or *nivṛtti* may be understood as disengagement. The subtle interplay of engagement and disengagement as found in the Hindu stages of life is a middle path between the two extremes and may be viewed as the Hindu equivalent of differential disengagement.

It is difficult to know to what extent precept became praxis in ancient India. Certainly the renunciation advocated as the fourth stage was such a dramatic and categorical step that most men may have postponed it until another life. Study of ancient Indian literature suggests that husband and wife withdrawing to the "forest" together as a type of modified renunciation may have been more common. Other accommodations of the *āśrama* model may have been prevalent. My own study of Śrīvaiṣṇava pilgrimage in Tāmilnāḍu today suggests, for example, that many elderly couples withdraw from their homes to travel about to the various sacred places (*divyadeśas*) during the festival season. Their extended pilgrimage over several months is akin to the wandering of the ascetic proper. Then, too, I have met many retired gentlemen in India who may practice other forms of renunciation that do not involve movement without as much as movement within: that is, the journey is viewed as a spiritual one involving some kind of scriptual study, yogic discipline and silence. Such individuals may set aside portions of the day for the pursuit of renunciation and may even withdraw from most domestic activities or the home proper to a simple hut on the family property.

While the *āśrama* model was elaborated mainly with reference to men, we do have some examples of female ascetics in ancient India. Generally, however, the woman accompanied the husband to the "forest." Should he die before her, the official options for the high caste woman were self-immolation on the funeral pyre of her husband (*satī*), which was rare, or widowhood, which was common. The culturally prescribed behavior for the latter has also many analogues with renunciation (the widow was to eat simple foods, forego all luxuries, dress in a plain saree often ochre in colour like the ascetic's garb, shave her head like the ascetic, etc.) though such renunciation was viewed as a kind of penance to expiate her bad *karma* believed to cause the husband's death and to ensure her reunion with him in the next life rather than as an expression of a spiritual path. That widows often go on pilgrimage or live at a sacred place mutes, however, the boundary between the phenomenon of asceticism proper and the forced renunciation of the widow.

That the Hindu woman throughout life performed vows (*vratas*) which involved some form of renunciation (usually of food) and a kind of yogic discipline suggests that for the woman, too, there was a kind of differential disengagement built into her life-plan though it was to be focused more on the husband than on spiritual goals per se. While the model for widows is not acceptable to many Hindu women today, given its negative imaging and its enforced hardship—which is not to deny its capacity in the past to provide meaning and purpose—women may now choose to practice differential engagement in the spiritual arena proper.

Dr. Tilak's research brings the textual sources alive to illumine the philosophical, religious and sociological dimensions of aging and old age in ancient India. It is worth pointing out that there have been few histories of ideas written on this scale in the field of Indology. Scholars have had a tendency to stay with a particular text, period or genre and have not often looked at the history of an idea as molded by the social and historical vicissitudes. In part, this is because of the sheer abundance of texts in the ancient and classical periods and because of the difficulty of reconstructing Indian history. It is to Dr. Tilak's credit that he has attempted a comprehensive study of traditional Indian views of aging and old age where others may have been deterred by the scope necessitated by such a study. The task was particularly painstaking because the passages were scattered throughout a range of texts in Sanskrit and Pali, perhaps numbering over a hundred volumes, and were found in philosophical works, dramas and poetry, epics, and medical texts.

The author has steered a middle course in this study by seeing patterns—which bring order to the enormous and, on first view, conflicting detail of his sources—yet by resisting the tendency to oversimplify his findings. The result is a technical work of interest to the specialist of ancient Indian thought and culture but also accessible to others in the fields of cultural gerontology because of the constant attempt to find bridges of discourse with others in gerontology, anthropology and hermeneutics.

In short, this book is a mature product of scholarship that represents extensive research and a long incubation of thought of both Indian textual sources and Western theoretical concerns. It makes a good case for the relevance of religion and Indology for the study of cross-cultural gerontology, and it promises to be a major contribution to the discussion of what is universal when the topic is old age.

More importantly, few Indian social scientists today have access to the vast texts of Indian thought and culture because they lack the knowledge of Sanskrit. Yet few Indologists and Sanskritists have combed the traditional materials to address topics of contemporary concern to social scientists. In recent years the field of traditional Indian medicine—because of its links to Āyurvedic medicine still practiced in India and because of its interests for those in the medical humanities—has begun to receive some scholarly attention. The present book will contribute to the latter and recover for Indian social scientists views of aging and old age found in Indian texts. Because these views are often still found in popular practices, they may help inform the analysis needed to create a culturally nuanced gerontology for modern India.

The present work, then, has relevance for contemporary Indian society as well as for cross-cultural studies in gerontology.

Katherine K. Young

# *Acknowledgments*

This study was made possible by a generous two-year fellowship from the Shastri Indo-Canadian Institute (1981–1983) for research in India. A six-month fellowship in 1984 from the Social Sciences and Humanities Research Council of Canada enabled me to complete the project in Canada. Finally, the preparation of the manuscript for publication was greatly facilitated by the two month Lawrence Research Fellowship offered by the Institute for the Advanced Study of Religion, Stony Brook, New York, U.S.A. in 1988. Thanks are also due to William Eastman, Director of SUNY Press, for his enthusiastic support.

I must record here a deep debt of gratitude to Professor Katherine Young, Faculty of Religious Studies, McGill University, Montréal whose own work in the field of Indology inspired me to undertake this study in the first place. I am grateful to Dr. G. K. Gurjar, formerly Head of the Sanskrit and Saṃhitā Department, R. A. Poddar College of Āyurveda, Bombay, India, with whom I read the relevant Āyurvedic texts in Sanskrit. Professors S. Baliah Naidu of the University College of Cape Breton, Sydney, Nova Scotia, and André Couture of Laval University, Québec, critically read the final draft and made many perceptive suggestions, which I have duly incorporated. Dr. Bernard Guay MD, a close friend, also made useful comments. Needless to say, I alone am responsible for the final version of this study.

I also wish to thank Donna Runnalls, Dean, Faculty of Religious Studies, McGill University, Montréal, for kindly providing me with office facilities. Heidi Furcha deserves thanks for her help in clarifying practical problems of word processing.

Finally, my wife Vidyā and daughter Manālī have graciously borne my long absence from home during the writing of this work, for which I am much obligated to them.

# *Abbreviations*

| | |
|---|---|
| AV | *Atharva Veda* |
| BAU | *Bṛhadāraṇyaka Upaniṣad* |
| BC | *Buddhacarita* |
| BCE | Before Common Era |
| BDS | *Baudhāyana Dharma Sūtra* |
| BSB | *Brahma Sūtra Śāṅkara Bhāṣya* |
| Ca | *Caraka Saṃhitā* |
| Ca.ci. | *Caraka Saṃhitā* "Cikitsā Sthāna" |
| Ca.ind. | *Caraka Saṃhitā* "Indriya Sthāna" |
| Ca.ni. | *Caraka Saṃhitā* "Nidāna Sthāna" |
| Ca.śā. | *Caraka Saṃhitā* "Śārīra Sthāna" |
| Ca.sū. | *Caraka Saṃhitā* "Sūtra Sthāna" |
| Ca.vi. | *Caraka Saṃhitā* "Vimāna Sthāna" |
| CE | Common Era |
| CU | *Chāndogya Upaniṣad* |
| DN | *Dīgha Nikāya* |
| GDS | *Gautama Dharma Sūtra* |
| KS | *Kāma Sūtra* |
| KU | *Kauṣītaki Upaniṣad* |
| MB | *Mahābhārata* |
| MN | *Majjhima Nikāya* |
| MS | *Manusmṛti* |
| MU | *Maitrī Upaniṣad* |
| RV | *Ṛgveda* |
| Rām | *Rāmāyaṇa* |
| ŚB | *Śatapatha Brāhmaṇa* |

| | |
|---|---|
| SD | *Saundarananda* |
| SN | *Saṃyutta Nikāya* |
| Su | *Suśruta Saṃhitā* |
| Su.ci. | *Suśruta Saṃhitā "Cikitsā Sthāna"* |
| Su.śā. | *Suśruta Saṃhitā* "Śārīra Sthāna" |
| Su.sū. | *Suśruta Saṃhitā* "Sūtra Sthāna" |
| SU | *Śvetāśvatara Upaniṣad* |
| VDS | *Vasiṣṭha Dharma Sūtra* |
| VP | *Vākyapadīyam* |
| YS | *Yoga Sūtra* |
| YB | *Yoga Sūtra Bhāṣya* |
| Ysm | *Yājñavalkyasmṛti* |
| YV | *Yogavāsiṣṭha* |

# *Introduction*

The present study is undertaken with the assumption that in India's literary heritage there is a wide range of attitudes to and images of old age and aging which, if identified and expressed from a gerontological perspective, could substantially contribute toward the development of a contemporary Indian gerontology that is also culturally nuanced. As a first step toward this future enterprise, the present study is concerned with the origin and development of the meaning and significance of aging and its medical and metaphysical dimensions with reference to selected Vedic, Buddhist and Hindu texts.

Given the relative lack of historical records in India, studying an aspect of Indian social and cultural history based on textual sources is neither unusual nor unreasonable. Decades ago the social anthropologist Irawati Karve (1965, 23) observed that a people's literature has a peculiar relation to its social institutions. In one type of literature the social institutions are idealized, in another they come in for ridicule, in a third the depiction is starkly realistic. This interrelation of the written or oral literature and the actual social institutions as lived by people makes for a fascinating study. Such an enterprise, to paraphrase Karve again, need not be construed as a nostalgic dip into a vanished past but rather as a tryst with the past that lives in India's present, vividly, obstinately and obtrusively. It must be studied by those who are interested in India's present and future.[1] I hope, then, that the findings of the present study, when checked against the growing epigraphic and archaeological evidence, will advance the understanding of old age and aging in Indian tradition.

## *Process of Aging*

Although in the popular sense aging has to do with the elderly only, aging is actually a lifelong process and an integral part of living. Circumscribed by birth at one end, aging is terminated at some point by death. Death, too, therefore, has a rightful place in any study of human aging. In fact, both aging and death are inherent in conception and begin at the same time as birth. Changes engendered on and within the body by the aging process are quite rapid in infancy and childhood and even more so in the fetus. Conception initiates a truly marvelous set of life events. Never does one age so rapidly again as in one's embryonic development whereby one ages, it is said, the equivalent of two billion years in less than a period of nine months.

Biologically, aging is a progressive and irreversible changing of the structures and functions of the living organism. Though deadly and stressful from the individual perspective, aging and death are nonetheless inevitable for the continuation of the species and life in general. The etiology of aging has not yet been scientifically explained nor is there a definite answer to the question of what is essential and primary in the decaying process of involution.

In the past, however, the causes of aging, the stress it generates, and death were understood in three basic ways. One view traces them to the gradual loss of an *élan vital* that is important for the maintenance of life. Senescence and death are natural processes inherent in the body cells; they are to be explained as due to the gradual loss of the energy stimulus which is supplied to the developing (and aging) organism at the moment of fertilization. Bodily growth and differentiation over time continue to take place in the organism until finally no energy is left and the organism dies of old age. The second view attributes aging and death to the gradual accumulation of a toxic substance in the body. Constant readjustment among the bodily humors necessary for human survival, according to the third view, renders the body susceptible to aging. Aging, therefore, is a stressful process. Like a mechanical device gradually worn out with use and the passage of time, the individual grows more and more inadequate to carry out the vital functions and eventually succumbs to death.

Notwithstanding the historical controversy regarding the etiology of aging, it is generally recognized that the process of aging incorporates within itself two simultaneously existing components: while there is growth and development of the body, there is also continued decline and atrophy of the body. In early life the growth aspect of aging masks and overwhelms the potentially degenerative process. The rate of aging, whether as development or decline, varies greatly from one individual to the next depending upon the bodily constitution. Again, in any single individual the aging process may appear to occur more rapidly during one period of life than another and at a greater rate in one organ than another (Hall 1984, 5). Not surprisingly, various meaningful ways of learning to live and cope with the stress of aging have been devised in different traditions.

The above observations on aging lead us to the discipline of gerontology which may be seen as a set of systematically argued beliefs and values concerning aging and the human response to it. The activity theory (Gubrium 1976), for instance, suggests that the aging individual actively aspires to extend the norms of middle age as long as it is physically and mentally possible to do so. The rival disengagement theory (Cumming and Henry 1961) posits that with age every individual comes under increasing pressure to cede control and power to the younger members of the family/community. As a cultural system, therefore, gerontology is the organization of concepts, theories and normative practices concerning both aging as a process and the aged. As an adaptive cultural response to the stress of aging and its consequences, it overlaps religion, which too, is concerned with providing meaning to life, aging and death.

Accordingly, though aging is a biological process, attitudes toward aging, the treatment the aged receive, the evaluation of the status of the aged, and the roles considered appropriate for them are as much matters of religious and cultural tradition as of physics or biology. This fact helps explain why aging has been infused with differing meaning and significance in terms of symbols and images in various traditions.

The process of aging, though occurring independently within a single body and mind is, therefore, to be appreciated as also taking place between individuals, and in culturally and religiously defined patterns. Together they provide clues to the meanings of aging since the self, body and world (or even cosmos) are bound to each other, not only in their implications for each other but in their fundamental structure by a symbolic reality formed by the acquisition of language and systems of meaning. Not surprisingly, the manifestations of stress precipitated by the aging process and responses to it are culturally determined and mandated. Each distinct culture tends to introduce a unique set of stresses in the aging individual and his/her family and community with respect to age-specific roles, norms, statuses and social worth. But at the same time the aging individual is also taught culturally sanctioned and defined defense mechanisms to cope with the stress of aging.

Relevant socialization and acculturation take place through the internalization of symbolic reality by suitably orienting one's inner world. That is, symbolic reality enables individuals to make sense out of their inner experience. It helps shape personal identity in accordance with existing cultural, religious and social norms. Symbolic meanings influence basic psychological processes such as the state of consciousness, cognition, memory and through them various bodily functions. If it is accepted that language is a cultural system linking thought and action, then gerontology, too, may be considered a cultural system linking aging and the human response to it. Both are forms of symbolic reality in that both are anchored in cultural beliefs and social roles as well as in individual behavior and experience.

The age-related characteristics of any social organization tend to be universal in scope. After Cowgill and Holmes (1972), they may be identified as follows:

1. Aging tends to precipitate the formation of a class of 'old people' in the society who are so identified by appropriate labels and nomenclature.
2. Most societies develop some system of age-grading which classifies individuals by age and sex, ascribing differential statuses and roles in terms of this classification.
3. At a certain phase in life, the aging individual is shifted to more sedentary and advisory or supervisory activities often involving psychological or spiritual pursuits rather than physical exertion.
4. Cultures and communities value life and seek to prolong it even in the face of aging. Accordingly, they have sanctioned a widespread search for elixirs, talismans, and charms to protect health and prolong life until the advance of death seems to outweigh the burdens of life.
5. Most societies have designed set patterns of behavior to meet death with honor and dignity.

These universal features of the aging process suggest that any meaningful quest of the 'why' of aging would involve the investigation of the semantic, physical and metaphysical dimensions of the 'what' of aging. The body is the means through which individuals act and react with the surrounding world. The self is not just in the body or attached to it. The body may be regarded as an object, but if it is treated merely as an object part of the selfhood is lost. The process of aging is potentially disruptive of this coherent trinity of the self, the body and the world. Aging invariably precipitates a series of losses on all these three levels. As such, aging is too vast and complex a subject to be left solely to biological or social scientists.

Because aging is at once a uniquely personal as well as universal experience and because one measure of the humanness of a cultural and religious tradition is its understanding of the aging process and its treatment of the aged, the humanities have a vital contribution to make in the interpretation of this phenomenon. Aging has only recently engaged the attention of humanists (that is, those interested in the philosophy, religion, literature, art and history of a given people). In the exploration of attitudes, aspirations and cultural practices underlying the ineluctable facts of aging and old age in the past, therefore, humanists can play a vital role. Indeed, it may be that our perception of past reservoirs of knowledge will provide the possibility of imagining a meaningful and human future for the aged. Until we know what we have been, we cannot know what we can or should become.

## *Setting of the Problem*

It was not until the demographic realities of the growing numbers of elderly men and women in modern India confronted Indian social scientists that they 'discovered' the elderly. Academic humanists in India have yet to realize that aging is going to be an all-important phenomenon in modern India in the coming decades. Demographers arbitrarily define the population of a country as 'young' if the percentage of persons above the age of sixty-four in the population is less than four, as 'mature' when this percentage is between four and seven, and as 'aged' when it exceeds seven percent. By that reckoning, the population of modern India was still 'young' according to the census of 1981. However, in absolute numbers the population of persons aged sixty and above reached thirty-three million. By 2000 CE, it is expected to top the sixty million mark (Sahni 1981).

There is, therefore, growing interest in and concern with the problems of the elderly. The welfare-oriented liberal policies of successive governments in India since 1947 have improved public health programs, hygiene and education. These policies also promoted industrialization, modernization and urbanization all over India; this has contributed to the burgeoning elderly population. There is, thus, an urgent need to evolve the science of gerontology in order to begin elderly health-care and welfare programs directed at this growing age-homogeneous group. The question, then, is no longer whether Indian religions, philosophy, literature and arts can provide source material for a variety of humanistic perceptions in the investigation of aging, but more to the point, in what ways can humanists conversant with Indian traditions produce a fund of knowledge upon which the science and art of gerontology may be initiated by those qualified to do so?

One of the obstacles to the proper, indigenous development of gerontology in modern India is that the collection and treatment of gerontologically significant data is informed and guided by Western notions and hypotheses on aging. Whenever these are reformulated to suit the Indian context and purpose, they tend to be discontinuous with Indian tradition at large. Rarely has reference been made to traditional, indigenous material on aging.

In fairness to Indian social scientists trained in modern gerontology, however, it must be pointed out that to date no full-length monograph on the subject of aging in relation to culture and religion in Indian tradition has been published. It was only recently (1985) that a special issue by the *Journal of the Indian Anthropological Society* published seven articles on the situation of the aged in India. Over the last two decades only a handful of short monographs or articles have appeared dealing with the conditions of the elderly in modern India. Desai and Naik (n.d.), Soodan (1975), and de Souza (1982) have published surveys on the problems of the urban elderly; Hiebert (1981), Vatuk (1975, 1980), and Maduro (1981) have contributed studies on a particular aspect of old age in contemporary India. The situation is no better with respect to cultural gerontology. Ramacandran (1985) has published a three page article on gerontology in Āyurveda, and Comfort (1985) has a brief note on geriatric medicine in Indian tradition. Finally, Kurian published a brief article (1972) on aging in India and Canada from a comparative perspective, and Mehta (1978) translated a few verses on old age from the Sanskrit wisdom literature. Not surprisingly, in a national seminar on aging held in Bombay in 1981 (Desai 1983) and attended by the present writer, hardly any of the papers suggested much familiarity with the relevant data that lie buried in the religious, medical and literary texts dating from the ancient and classical period.

Yet, like many contemporary intellectuals the world over, Indian social scientists, too, tend to engage in the cultural devaluation of the past. They trivialize it by equating it with outmoded social and/or religious practices. Endeavors to draw on the past in looking for solutions to current problems are often resented. Any such reference to the past itself is regarded as an expression of romantic nostalgia or reaction.

Nevertheless, the works of Christopher Hill (1961), for instance, suggest that even radical movements draw strength and sustenance from the myth or memory of a golden age in the distant past. At a more individual level, this observation is reinforced by the psychoanalytical insight that loving memories originating in the past constitute a valuable psychological resource and strength in one's mature years. The belief or the hypothesis that in some ways the past may have something meaningful to contribute to the resolution of current problems by no means rests on a sentimental illusion. As Lasch (1978) has observed, a denial of the past superficially couched in 'progressive' rhetoric may, on closer analysis, turn out to embody the despair of a generation that cannot face the future.

If the test of the hardiness and vitality of any cultural and religious tradition is its capacity to draw on the resources of its own symbol system to meet the challenge of new circumstances, then one way to examine the usefulness of the Indian religious tradition as a basis for the proper evaluation of human aging is to explore how that very tradition drew upon its resources in similar circumstances in the past in order to understand aging.

The focus of the present work, accordingly, is on the recovery and reinterpretation of the relevant material from those Vedic, Buddhist and Hindu texts which may help enhance our understanding of the meaning and significance attached to the process of aging in traditional India. In scope, this inquiry extends to the following issues:

1. What are the typical Vedic, Buddhist and Hindu responses to aging? Can they be attributed to religious and doctrinal differences?

2. How is aging related to life and death in the classical Hindu medical texts? What are the suggested mechanisms to manage and cope with the stress produced by the experience of old age and the approach of death?
3. What metaphysical significance and meaning is attached to aging in Hindu and Buddhist myths?

Examination of these issues constitutes the subject matter of the next five chapters.

The first chapter, on historical dialectic, traces the evolution of the typical but differing views about aging held in Hindu and Buddhist traditions in India. It begins by arguing that early Vedic texts maintain a somewhat simplistic, naive but fond attitude toward life. There is a desire to live a long, healthy life into ripe old age. Buddhist texts provide an important critique of this lust for life, arguing that aging is evil and a source of suffering. Hindu texts such as the Dharma Śāstras, having the advantage of hindsight on the two opposing views, provide a balanced and accommodating account of the aging process and its role in the creative unfolding of the potential for development in persons.

The second chapter, on "growing old", discusses the Vedic, Buddhist and Hindu understanding of the various phases and signs in terms of which the aging human body is perceived.

The third chapter, "Between Life and Death" posits aging as a process mediating between the two structural polarities of life and death. It also analyses the role allotted to time (*kāla*) in connection to aging and then seeks to explain the process of aging in terms of change and mutation (*pariṇāma*).

The fourth chapter, on "coping with stress" discusses the mechanisms suggested in the classical Hindu medical texts to cope with and manage the stress of aging based on the concepts of *vāja* (rejuvenatory and revitalizing force) and the code of moral behavior (*sadvṛtta*).

Despite sophisticated attempts at providing a physical and empirical explanation, aging still remains an enigma and a predicament. The fifth chapter, "Interpretations", analyzes various Hindu myths that seek to interpret aging and its etiology in terms of two important cultural constructs—deeds (*karma*) and desire (*kāma*).

The conclusion critically reviews the contribution of the Indian tradition to the understanding of the process of aging, its relevance to the development of gerontology in modern India and its significance for cross-cultural studies.

In the debate regarding the nature of aging in Indian tradition, three principal streams may be isolated:

1. The Vedic stream stemming from the revealed (Śruti) texts, which generally evaluate aging in positive terms.
2. the Buddhist stream, which generally evaluates aging negatively as an impediment to spiritual liberation.
3. the Hindu stream, which emerged as the compromise resulting from the dialectic interaction between the first two.

This broad categorization, though convenient, is not without hazards. For example, there are strong and definite differences of opinion regarding aging in texts belonging to various schools categorized within any of the three traditions. Even within a single school major controversies may be detected on a given age-related question. The purpose of producing a representative overview of traditional Indian understanding of aging may, therefore, best be pursued by examining relevant texts belonging to all three strata.

## *Texts Consulted*

It is essential to remember that gerontology *per se* is not the subject matter of any of the Indian texts used as source material. Since there are no formal statements on aging or old age, any relevant information occurring therein is incidental and often couched in symbolic or mythical forms, thereby eluding the casual reader. Mundane ideas dealing with human birth, growth, decay and destruction, for instance, are also found inscribed at the cosmic level in terms of composition (appearance) and decomposition (disappearance).

In certain myths a fundamental consubstantiality is posited whereby one entity may be created out of the material substance of the other, which then undergoes dissolution. The two, then, are understood as *alloforms*, alternative shapes or forms, of one another. Human beings and the material universe are viewed as alternate moments in a continuous process, whereby one is continually transmuted into the other.[2] To understand specific events in the human lifecycle, therefore, one must also examine their cosmic counterparts. Our texts, accordingly, deal with subjects of a truly metaphysical nature such as the immutable and autonomous self contrasted with the mutable (or aging) and contingent human body, and the 'short-comings' of this-worldly life characterized by disease, old age and death.

Since Indian textual material is enormous, the amount of such incidental and symbolic information on aging is vast. Selected texts, therefore, were first sifted for promising passages which were then examined from the gerontological perspective. Many of these texts are elegantly composed and are justly prized for their literary beauty and quality. In some instances their stylistic and literary traits are relevant for the purpose of the present study, a fact which will become apparent in the chapters that follow.

Again, one must also bear in mind that in these texts the problem of human life and aging is dealt with from different perspectives and at different levels.[3] This typical Indian tendency to examine any problem from various angles and levels simultaneously is at once a strength and a weakness. One has to be constantly aware of and on guard for shifting premises and hypotheses, as well as the fact that the arguments keep oscillating between levels abruptly and often without warning.

A relevant instance is the discussion regarding the nature of the embodied self in an early medical text called *Caraka Saṃhitā*. While in the "Sūtra Sthāna" chapter the discussion moves at the physical level, the "Śārīra Sthāna" chapter treats it at the metaphysical level. Thus, we are inevitably drawn back to the ontology of the problem; while the question of what aging *is* is dealt with at the physical level, its etiological presuppositions hover at the metaphysical level. This is because in the larger Indian scheme of the theory of knowledge, the two problems are, in fact, a single problem: physics is the shadow of metaphysics.

From the Vedic stream, the texts principally consulted are the two compilations in verse (Saṃhitā)—the *Ṛgveda* (ca. 1500 BCE) and the *Atharva Veda* in Śaunakīya version (ca. 1200 BCE). The *Ṛgveda* (RV) comprises principally hymns of invocation and prayer to the gods and goddesses—Indra, Agni, Aśvins, Soma, Uṣas, Vāc—who are supplicated to bestow long, healthy and happy life unto ripe old age. The *Atharva Veda* (AV) contains speculations on the source of being, creation and the relation of the embodied self to the supernatural and the cosmos. Hymns grouped under the categories of *āyuṣyāṇi* (long life) and *bhaiṣajyāṇi* (medicines) are particularly relevant for this study. The Brāhmaṇas (ca. 1000–800 BCE) are voluminous tomes dealing with the Vedic rituals (*yajñas*) in their relationship to the potent, unseen forces at work in the cosmos.

From among these, the *Śatapatha Brāhmaṇa* (ŚB), in particular, was found to contain much relevant information pertinent to the present inquiry.

In the Upaniṣads (ca. 800–600 BCE), the interest in sacerdotalism begins to recede, and the attention of the thinkers and hermits to whom this class of texts is attributed is focused instead on the person in relationship to the ultimate and irreducible principle within (*ātman*). For our purpose the following Upaniṣads warranted particular attention: the *Bṛhadarāṇyaka* (BAU), *Chāndogya* (CU), *Śvetāśvatara* (SU) and *Maitrī* (MU).

The principal texts consulted from the early Buddhist stream (ca. 500 BCE–200 BCE) include the Nikāyas: the *Dīgha Nikāya* (DN), *Majjhima Nikāya* (MN) and the *Saṃyutta Nikāya* (SN), the *Dhammapāda* and the *Sutta Nipāta*. The *Milindapañha* is a record of the dialogues between King Menander (ca. 140–100 BCE) and Nāgasena the Elder (Thera). Though post-canonical, it nonetheless provides useful information, particularly on the topics of time (*kāla*) and action (*karma*) as understood in early Buddhism.

Hindu and Buddhist literature in Sanskrit composed according to the rules of the Pāṇinian grammar begins to appear between 600–300 BCE and attains its golden age in the period between 400–800 CE. Two Sanskrit works from the early classical period (400 BCE-200 CE) of considerable interest to us are the epics *Mahābhārata* (MB) and *Rāmāyaṇa* (Rām). The genre of literature known as Kāvya arose in the early centuries of the common era as court poetry. Composed at urban centers and patronized by princes and merchants, it is distinguished by a refined style and erudition. Of this material, special attention is paid to the two Mahākāvyas of Aśvhaghoṣa: the *Buddhacarita* (BC) and *Saundarananda* (SD) as well as the Mahākāvya of Kālidāsa *Raghuvaṃśa*. Both poets skillfully depict the extremes of lifetimes in their portrayals of the elderly and the young who interact frequently. But whereas in the works of Aśvaghoṣa the two generations are in conflict, in Kālidāsa they coexist in harmony, as balancing and necessary components of the total human experience of aging (see chapter one).

The class of texts known as the Dharma Sūtras (ca. 300 BCE) and Dharma Śāstras (ca. 200 BCE–100 CE) were compiled by the brahmin priests in order to provide a ritual framework for the precepts and practice in accordance with the lifestyle allegedly laid out in the Vedas to legitimate the moral and legal rules of behavior under which every individual of a given class (*varṇa*) and age-specific stage of life (*āśrama*) is expected to live. While the Dharma Sūtras are in the form of aphorisms (*sūtras*)—short, pithy sayings which may be easily committed to memory—the Dharma Śāstras are a later and more developed form of literature in verse. The principal works belonging to this class used here include the *Manu Smṛti (MS) and the Yājñavalkya Smṛti* (Ysm).

Āyurveda, the science of surviving to a ripe old age, traditionally revered as one of the subsidiary limbs of the Vedas, is obviously indispensable for the present study with the works of Caraka (Ca) and Suśruta (Su) supplying relevant source material. While the former is placed by scholars ca. 100 CE, the latter is to be dated ca. 400 CE.

Almost all the major religious systems of India incorporate some form of the spiritual discipline generically known as *yoga*. Though there are various forms of *yoga*, the classical type is that associated with the philosophy called Sāṃkhya and expounded by Patañjali in a compilation known as the *Yoga Sūtra* (ca. 100–200 CE). The *Yoga Bhāṣya* (ca. 400–600 CE) of Vyāsa is the earliest commentary on the *Yoga Sūtra* and is of considerable aid in providing a clearer understanding of the notions of time and change, which are only tersely outlined in the *Yoga Sūtra*. The *Tattvavaiśāradī* (ca. 800 CE) of Vācaspati Miśra seeks to elucidate both the *Yoga Sūtra* (YS) and *Yoga Bhāṣya* (YB).

Sāṃkhya-Yoga is a great expository metaphysics explaining the origin of the cosmos and of the human personality through images of change. The three *yoga* texts cited above also deal at length with the constitution of temporality as well as subjective experience originating in the temporal order. For this reason, they have been utilized here for the purpose of explaining the physical and philosophical basis of the aging process as change and mutation.

The Purāṇa (ca. 300–800 CE), the ancient lore, is a group of eighteen texts, which like the Dharma Śāstras, seek to perpetuate the lifestyle allegedly first outlined in the revealed literature of the Hindus (Śruti). Some of the Purāṇas provide a valuable source of information on aging which is couched in the form of myths. The principal Purāṇas which are of engaging interest are the *Brahmavaivarta*, the *Padma* and the *Bhāgavata*.

The *Yogavāsiṣṭha* (ca. 800) is yet another equally relevant *yoga* text, centered on an incident in the life of Rāma (the hero of the epic *Rāmāyaṇa*). It is in the form of a long dialogue (with over 27,000 verses) between Rāma and his preceptor, the sage Vasiṣṭha wherein it is asserted that the universe is nothing but a mode of the consciousness of self. As O'Flaherty (1984, 131) suggests, the *Yogavāsiṣṭha* (YV) may be viewed as a metatext dealing with metaphysical issues not discussed in the epic *Rāmāyaṇa*.

Translations of the citations from the *Ṛgveda* and *Atharva Veda* are based on the works by Geldner and Whitney respectively. When warranted, Sāyaṇa's commentaries (*bhāṣyas*) on them are also taken into consideration, since they make available alternative interpretations based on traditional grammar, etymology, myths and legends. References to Buddhist canonical works allude to the translations sponsored by the Pali Text Society. Unless otherwise indicated, renditions of the passages from the classical Sanskrit texts are by the author.[4]

# 1

# *Historical Dialectic*

The course of the historical dialectic on aging in India runs parallel to the development of Hindu ideal views on life and its organization from the time of the Veda (represented by the term *ṛta*) to the formulation of the moral digests known as the Dharma Śāstras, (represented by the term *dharma*), that is, from about 1500 BCE to 200 CE. For the purpose of the present study this period may further be divided into six subperiods dominated by the emergence of one or the other genre of texts sacred to Hindus or Buddhists, each genre emphasizing unique and often contradictory or competing views on human life and, by implication, on aging. It should, however, be stressed that this periodization is for heuristic purposes only and that there is considerable overlapping of ideas propounded in different periods:

1. The Saṃhitā period (ca. 1500–1000 BCE), during which the compilations of the four Vedas including the *Ṛgveda* and the *Atharva Veda* took place.
2. The Brāhmaṇa period (ca. 1000–800 BCE), which gave rise to the Brāhmaṇa texts dealing with the theoretical and practical details of Vedic sacrifice (*yajña*).
3. The Upaniṣadic period (ca. 800–200 BCE), which is marked by the rise of speculative and metaphysical texts on topics such as the self and being.
4. The period of emergent Buddhism (ca. 500–400 BCE), which saw the beginnings of the compilation of Buddhist canonical texts such as the *Nikāyas*.
5. The Dharma Sūtra and the Pali Canon period (ca. 400–200 BCE), which is characterized by the emergence of the Smṛti literature of the Hindus and the formation of the Pali Canon of the Buddhists.
6. The Dharma Śāstra period (ca. 200 BCE–200 CE), during which the very influential *Manu Smṛti* as well as the two important works of Aśvaghoṣa (the *Buddhacarita* and the *Saundarananda*) were composed.

## *Vedic Vision*

Since the verse compilations (Saṃhitā) of the Vedic texts incorporate the earliest documented views on human life, aging and death in Indian tradition, it may be useful to begin our survey with the discussion of the *Ṛgveda* and the *Atharva Veda*. The Vedic philosophy of life revolves around Vivasvat, the ancestor of humankind and his son Yama, the god of death. Under the protection of Vivasvat, the Vedic Indians hoped for a life as long as possible and a natural death as late as possible. With Yama's favor they hoped for as happy an after-life as possible in the world beyond (AV 18:3.13).

That Vedic culture was life-affirming with a distinct this-worldly emphasis on material prosperity, longevity and progeny is clearly discernible in numerous hymns of the *Ṛgveda* and the *Atharva Veda*. The primary desire and hope expressed in these early texts is to acquire and enjoy full life within the confines and bounds of a homestead economy in the company of sons and grandsons (RV 10:85.42). Prayers for a longer life also abound in the *Ṛgveda* as in 10:18.5, which features a prayer to Death:

> As the days follow in order, as the seasons faithfully follow the seasons, so *order* their lives, O Regulator, that he who comes after may not abandon him who went before!

Ṛgveda 9:113.7 includes a prayer to Pavamāna (god Soma) in which the poet requests to be placed in that deathless, undecaying world, wherein the light of heaven, and everlasting luster (*Sonne*) shines. In another hymn the poet pleads:

> Never may we suffer want in the presence of the sun and, living happy lives, may we attain old age (RV 10:37.6).

The seer (*ṛṣi*) of the hymn to the Aśvins (the twin physicians to the gods) is the old maiden Ghoṣā, daughter of King Kakṣīvān. Suffering from an incurable disease, she invokes help from the Aśvins by reminding them that:

> You made Cyavana, weak and worn with length of days, young again, like a chariot, that he had power to move . . . You gave vigor of youthful life to the sage Kali when old age was approaching (RV 10:39.4, 8).

Ghoṣā then begs the Aśvins to cure and rejuvenate her also.

The *Atharva Veda*, on its part, includes various magical and medical charms similar to the ancient German medical charms or Russian oaths (Gonda 1975a, 278–279), spells and prescriptions for long and healthy life (*āyuṣyāṇi* and *bhaiṣajyāṇi*). Usually these treatments are a matter between the priest and his clients, who ranged from the chaplain to the king. Intended to assure this-worldly pleasures and long life, the *Atharva Veda* constitutes a manual for the laity, the warriors and the kings wherein an important motif is to avoid death before old age as exemplified in AV 5:30.17. Another hymn to the fire god (Agni) is a prayer for the welfare and long life of a young child:

> O Agni, having partaken of the sweet, pleasant clarified butter of the cow, do you now protect this boy, as a father his sons, up to old age.
> Nourish this one . . . with your splendor, render him one to die of old age; let there not be a premature death for him (AV 2:13.1, 2).[1]

*Atharva Veda* (2:28.1, 4, 5) is a eulogy for long life for a child. It is to be invoked by the parents in praise of old age personified as deity (Jariman):

> Unto you alone, O Jariman, let this one grow; let not the other deaths, that are a hundred, harm him; as a thoughtful mother in her lap a son, let [the deity] Mitra protect this one from harm that may come from a [treacherous] friend.
> Let sky and earth [Dyauḥ as the father and Pṛthivī as the mother respectively] make you reach old age.

*Atharva Veda* (3:11.5, 6, 7, 8) is a prayer addressed to various deities on behalf of a sick person asking for relief from disease and for a long life.

> Enter in O Prāṇa and Apāna (the two vital breaths), as two draft-oxen a pen; let the other deaths go away, which they call the remaining hundred.
> O Prāṇa and Apāna . . . carry his body, his limbs unto old age again.
> Unto old age do I commit you [the sick one]; unto old age do I instigate you; may old age, excellent, conduct you; let the other deaths go away, which they call the remaining hundred.[2]
> Let old age bind you as a cow with a rope . . . let Bṛhaspati with the two hands of truth release the fetters by which death had bound you at birth.

Though it begins with a salutation by the priest to Death on behalf of a young boy, hymn 8:1 of the *Atharva Veda* is really a salute to life (Ayuḥ Sūkta). While pouring consecrated water on the young boy, the priest touches the boy's navel and recites a prayer for the boy's living unto old age. He supplicates various medicinal herbs and their king (Soma) to infuse long life into the boy. *Atharva Veda* (8:2.8) is a prayer expressly addressed to Death wherein he is requested to grant long life up to old age (one hundred years) with eyesight, hearing capacity and other bodily members in good health.

*Atharva Veda* (7:53.5, 6) again supplicates the two vital breaths (Prāṇa and Apāna) to enter the body in the manner of the oxen entering their pen (*vrajam*) and adds:

> Let not this treasure of old age be reduced; let it increase. I instigate Prāṇa in you and drive maladies away. Let this superior fire god (Agni) grant us long life of all kinds.

This desire and will to live for one hundred years and the lust of life is variously expressed in the Atharvan hymn (19:67) to the Sun god (Sūrya) in the form of the refrain "May we see a hundred autumns", and reiterated six times with the original use of the verb "see" (*paśyema*) successively substituted by the following verbs:

| | |
|---|---|
| Wake | (*budhyema*) |
| Grow | (*pūṣema*) |
| Adorn | (*bhūṣema*) |
| Live | (*jīvema*) |
| Prosper | (*rohema*) |
| Be | (*bhavema*) |

Similarly, in the hymn "To the Waters for Long Life" (AV 19:69), the act of living is mentioned four times with four different propositions:

> *Living* are you; may I live; may I *live* my whole life time.
> *Living on* are you; may I *live on;* may I live my whole life.
> *Living together* are you; may I *live together* my whole life.
> *Lively* are you; may I be *lively.*

These prayers suggest that in Vedic society death must have been more commonly associated with youth and vitality than with old age and decrepitude. Indirect evidence for this hypothesis is discernible in the frequent use of the Sanskrit compound meaning "death in old age" (*jarāmṛtyu*) in these prayers. Life in reality usually ended suddenly due to disease or war rather than fading out by degrees in old age.[3] There was, therefore, no necessary or compelling reason for the Vedic people to connect death and sickness with old age or to assume its inevitability.

However, by the time of the Brāhmaṇa period Vedic society had overcome, at least partially, its early irrational fear of the afterlife so graphically depicted in the *Ṛgveda*. Awareness of and contact with death were now integrated into everyday life since death (particularly violent or premature death) no longer held mythical power over the living (the Brāhmaṇa texts vouch for that).[4] There was no reason to fear any potential revenge from old or dead people.

In early Vedic society demographic, social and cultural factors combined to permit limited differentiation of the lifespan, which tended to be relatively short. Accordingly, the distinction between childhood and adulthood remained blurred in that the two major adult roles—parenthood and gainful work—generally stretched over the lifespan, whatever its duration. The integration of economic activities within the family unit also provided continuity in the usefulness of the older Vedic male. Old females on their part also contributed to the family-oriented economic unit by engaging in spinning and weaving. People generally tended to be preoccupied with material pursuits, and even the brahmins were more priestly in their outlook than mystical or philosophical.

The foregoing demonstrates the life-affirming, this-worldly hopes and aspirations of the Vedic Aryans. The Vedic literature reveals a certain adulation and fondness for old age and old people bordering on a gerontophilia. But this in no way indicates that the Vedic people lived a long life. The individual life course was still not marked by phases; the metaphor of the cycle or the circle to describe lifespan was not in vogue. And different age groups were still not completely segregated in accordance with their functions. Unlike modern times, when parents generally complete their child-rearing tasks with almost a quarter of their active lives still ahead, in Vedic India parenthood probably stretched to the end of life, given the fact that life expectancy was short.

In addition, marriage and the family unit were frequently broken by sudden and/or premature death attributable to warfare, natural calamities and diseases. Not surprisingly, the question of the *why* of aging is thematically avoided or perhaps does not arise in the Saṃhitā or the Brāhmaṇa periods, since few if any lived long enough to experience old age at first hand. Speculating on old age would not, therefore, be a meaningful enterprise.

However, toward the end of the Brāhmaṇa period and certainly by 600 BCE a major shift and movement away from the Vedic *weltanschauung* had begun, which, in fact, was the reflection of very important changes in the political, social and economic conditions of north India.[5] The lust for life that characterized the early Vedic lifestyle was gradually transformed into weariness of life and gerontophilia was replaced by gerontophobia. The frontier spirit, pioneering economy, robust optimism and premium on a happy, healthy and long life was replaced by a disenchantment with active, this-worldly pursuits (*saṃsāra*) and a longing and urge for a quiet, contemplative life in the forest away from the dust and din of the city.

There was, thus, a growing cleavage of ideas concerning the old Veda-inspired and controlled ideal life and its organization. This break has been traced to different factors—establishment of autocratic, centralized political units and the ensuing institutionalization of injustice and violence; increasing industrialization, modernization, urbanization and mobility; and over-population, famines and foreign invasions. The growth of towns and commerce and the organization of trade and craft into guilds made the north Indian social landscape quite distinct from the earlier Vedic one (Lannoy 1971, 215; Thapar 1978, 211–239).

The older Vedic gods and sacrifices as conceived in the Saṃhitās and the Brāhmaṇas had reflected a rural and pastoral economy. In the face of the new urbanizing and changing world of 600 BCE, much of the symbolism and rituals originating in natural and pastoral functions and phenomena began to appear irrelevant (Pande 1974, 262–265). With doubt and skepticism in the air, sensitive and reflective individuals began to look beyond the old ways of life, seeking to replace or infuse them with new meanings and attitudes. In this enterprise they were supported both by the newly urbanized populations increasingly alienated from nature, and by social discipline, which called for new productive techniques and implements.

It is to this class of reformers and thinkers who came from both orthodox (brahmin) and heterodox (Śramaṇa)[6] circles that the unique ideas concerning spiritual liberation, whether understood as *mokṣa* or *nirvāṇa,* enshrined in the Upaniṣads and Buddhism may be traced. In the context of the history of aging it would seem that these post-Vedic thinkers asking ultimate metaphysical questions about the "why" of aging entertained three fundamental assumptions:

1. There is something or somebody responsible for aging.
2. Aging belongs to the realm of intelligibility and as such, one need not remain helpless in the face of aging.
3. Suffering and anxiety resulting from aging can be eliminated.

The stimulus for redefining the inherited Vedic worldview and the meaning of life may be traced to the developing polarity in the Upaniṣadic period between this-worldly suffering on account of repeated births (*saṃsāra*) and the aspiration for a liberation (*mokṣa*) which would transcend the condition of human aging altogether. Although few Vedic passages specifically denigrated the process of decay in old age, the fear of it lurks beneath some of the passages therein as evidenced in the *Ṛgveda* (1:89.9)[7] and the *Atharva Veda* (12:2.24) where death is feared as evil.

But it is in the Upaniṣads, such as the very influential *Bṛhadāraṇyaka* (for instance 3:1.3, where Yājñavalkya is the instructor), that old age begins to be seen as diminishing human strength and powers. Old age is now projected as unavoidable and incurable. The desire to be free from death, therefore, begins to be accompanied also by the desire to be free from old age. The term denoting one who is deathless (*amara*) almost becomes synonymous with the term for one who is ageless (*ajara*) or one who is free from old age (*nirjara*). A new coordinative compound meaning one who is ageless and deathless (*ajarāmara*) is also formed, elevating old age to the rank of death in importance (*Chāndogya* 8:1.5; *Kaṭha* 1:3.12). Though it claims to be a continuation of the old exegesis of the Veda, in effect, the Upaniṣadic thought constitutes a break with that tradition as far as the understanding and meaning of human life is concerned.

This is clear from the number of disturbing insights that certain Upaniṣads begin to provide into the process of aging, paving the way for a vision of the essentially painful nature of the processes of human life here on earth. The nature of sorrow attributable to old age is radicalized to such a degree that the only resort is escape into another form of lifestyle or organization in the forest leading to liberation (*mokṣa*). Certain common traits nonetheless seem to run through both the early Vedic and the Upaniṣadic views. First, no fundamental *ontic* distinction is posited between spirit and matter. Though the Upaniṣadic quest seeks to go beyond the life of worldliness and ritualism centered in ritual action, it does not advocate the radical renunciation of a life of action as will be later counseled by the Buddha. Nor does it condemn the world as a vale of tears (see Heesterman 1982).

The Upaniṣads recommend a life of meditation and contemplation of the great truths in the later years of one's life, but they do not emphasize withdrawal from the mundane pursuits of a householder's life (this is evident from the fact that Yājñavalkya renounces the world in his old age and King Janaka was a householder). There is occasional disgust expressed at the contemptible nature of worldly existence, but it stops short of advocating total withdrawal from the alleged sorrowful and evanescent nature of mundane life. On the question of aging and its sorrow, the Upaniṣads consider sorrow as originating in the aging condition of humans and yet as being capable of awakening them to their transcendent nature. Anxiety caused by the recognition that suffering is inherent in old age is believed to drive the sensitive thinker to break out of his/her condition of being human and transcend it (CU 8:1.4,5; 8:4.1).

On the question of the dreadful consequences of aging, Upaniṣadic reflection opens up a new perspective, pointing out that the evil of old age does not in reality consist so much in this or that sickness, handicap or loss sustained as a consequence of old age, but rather the very fact that the human being is destined to grow old and decrepit and ultimately to die. The optimism of the Vedic compilations (Saṃhitā) is replaced by an acute awareness of the decaying body as the unavoidable factor in human life, which cannot be miraculously cured or prayed away (Panikkar 1977, 465).

This is evident from a passage in *Bṛhadāraṇyaka Upaniṣad* (4:3.35–38), which features a dialogue between Yājñavalkya and King Janaka regarding the status and nature of the self (*ātman*) in its various states such as sleep, dream and death. Yājñavalkya explains that with age the person is burdened as if by a heavy load and is gradually reduced to bone and skin. All organs, which were so prompt to serve in youth, cease their service. That decay of the body is one of the main reasons for disenchantment and anxiety within oneself is also discernible from the beautiful legend involving Indra (king of all Vedic gods), Virocana (the demon) and Prajāpati (the father of all beings).

After thirty-two years of apprenticeship by Indra and Virocana as students, Prajāpati declares to them that the self (*ātman*) is nothing but the person and its body image in the mirror. But Indra is not satisfied. He doubts that the body—subject to injury, decay and old age—is the self. Unlike Virocana, he is not satisfied with the explanation that the body is identical with the self (*dehātmavāda*). Prajāpati then provides alternative explanations of the self. But Indra is not satisfied by them. It is only then that Prajāpati reveals to him the truth that the body is not the self, because it is mortal and that the desire for the ageless state free from decay is nothing other than the search for the self (CU 8: *Khaṇḍas* 7–12).

It was pointed out above that in the Saṃhitā period the course of human life was characterized by a relatively short and homogeneous lifespan. Accordingly, major life events such as marriage, parenthood and retirement were not structured into distinct stages. The Upaniṣadic period, in contrast, recognizes two distinct phases in life (as against one in the Saṃhitā period) identified as the sacrificing householder and the hermit practicing austerities in the forest. But the relation between the two phases is still ambiguous. They are perceived as being neither consecutive nor interrelated. The stage of studentship is presumed to be a preparation for either or both. The stages are not known by the distinct names they acquire in the later Smṛti works such as the *Manu Smṛti* and the *Yājñavalkya Smṛti.*

This is evident from a passage in the *Bṛhadāraṇyaka Upaniṣad* (3:5.1ff) attributed to Yājñavalkya where he somewhat hesitantly identifies the important stages in the ideal life as being 'sage,' 'child,' 'silent ascetic' and 'married priest.' He rates the brahmin 'sage' over the rest as the highest stage.[8] In summing up, it may be argued that in the Upaniṣadic period, for the Vedic Aryan, life in community and life in the forest constituted two alternating poles in terms of rituals based on the concepts of sacrifice (*yajña*) and the sacred fire (*agni*) respectively, wherein the fundamental ontic unity between spirit and matter still remained intact.

## *Buddhist Challenge*

Buddhism, which was one of the major protest movements of ca. 600 BCE along with those of the Ājīvikas and Jainas, eventually broke apart the two poles of spirit and matter, precipitating a structural hiatus in the old Veda-inspired and controlled worldview and lifestyle. The ideal of *nirvāṇa,* originating in the world-negating mode of life (*nivṛtti*), emerged as the competing ideal to the this-worldly and life-affirming (*pravṛtti*) ideal here on earth and subsequently in the other world. Various verses (*suttas*) in the *Majjhima Nikāya* bear testimony to these trying times of social ferment and change. In fact, in the words of a disgruntled brahmin recorded in the Pali Canon, the Buddha instituted the dispensation of renunciation (*pravrajyādhikaraṇa*) in place of the dispensation of sacrifice (*yajñādhikaraṇa*). This succinctly summarizes the shifting world view (Pande 1974, 325).[9]

Further, under the impact of continued industrialization and demographic changes in the period identified above as that of emergent Buddhism, a gradual differentiation in age groups and age-related specialization in function began to emerge, although it was by no means complete towards the Dharma Sūtra period (300 BCE). A significant consequence of this development was the apprehension of aging, which was dramatized in the newly evolving attitudes toward the treatment of the young and the elderly.

As inscribed in the Pali Canon the newly emerging ascetic world view held that one must renounce the world in quest of spiritual liberation while still in youthful vigor. It is however silent on the question of whether youth has any ethical or familial responsibility toward society. It believed that elderly people have neither the energy nor the right aptitude for undertaking the arduous task of the spiritual quest. To those belonging to the orthodox social order, however, the physical infirmities and the inevitable end associated with old age did not present an imminent danger to society and did not, therefore, provoke the degree of anxiety produced by problems vis-à-vis the young in whose social control much lay at stake.

Traditional Vedic society nevertheless tended to regard undisciplined and unsocialized youths as potentially disruptive of social organization. The control and orthodox socialization of the young was deemed essential to prevent their growing into socially unacceptable and potentially destructive non-Vedic adults who might be lured by powerful and influential heterodox teachers, such as the Buddha or Mahāvīra. This concern for social order is evident in the arguments of the brahmin mathematician Moggallana (see "Gaṇaka Moggallana Sutta", *Majjhima Nikāya* 3:1–7). But it was Gośāla, another brahmin thinker and contemporary of the Buddha, whose ideas on evolution in relation to education, desire, knowledge and spirituality seem to have provided an antecedent to the formulation of the age-specific life stages (*āśramas*) of later times (Barua 1970, 313).[10] It is conceivable that the Buddha's alternative doctrine of eight higher spiritual ranks (*aṭṭhapurisa puggalā*) was designed in light of the brahmin Gośāla's ideas.

The contrast between the two competing views of Gośāla and the Buddha is nonetheless important, for it suggests a historical shift from a biologically and socially determined view of life events to a morally and spiritually determined one at the hands of the Buddha. That these developments precipitated a growing conflict and chasm between the orthodox brahmins and the heterodox teachers such as the Buddha is indicated by a reference to it in Patañjali's *Mahābhāṣya* on Pāṇini (2:4.9) which observes that the orthodox brahmins and the heterodox ascetics had separate orders which were in permanent opposition to each other. The division is also referred to in the inscriptions of King Aśoka.

People of the Magadhan-Mauryan era witnessed an increasing lifespan beyond that of the early Vedic period.[11] In part, this may be attributed to the continued advances being made in the field of medicine (Āyurveda). The *Suśruta Saṃhitā,* for instance, confidently asserts that those familiar with the *Atharva Veda* saw a hundred and one deaths, but only one of them is a death in due course of time. The rest are adventitious and presumably avoidable (Su.sū. 34:6). The number of persons succumbing to degenerative diseases attributable to old age, accordingly, must have become considerably more than those dying of infection, trauma, snake bite and childbirth. As the result of increased life expectancy, death was now also perceived as the inevitable consequence of growing old. The theme of aging accordingly began to be treated with dread and avoidance as revealed in certain Upaniṣadic and Buddhist texts. This was a radical departure indeed from the Vedic period when aging was prized because lived experience of aging was so rare!

Canonical Buddhism, by contrast, would make aging (and its inevitable consequences—disease and death) the cornerstone of its doctrinal and soteriological edifice. It is, therefore, not unreasonable to argue that, at least in part, the rise of Buddhism may be understood as one attempt to deal with the problems created by more people living long enough to fear old age and its unhappy consequences. Advances in medical technology assured more numerous first-hand experiences of old age and consequently of sickness and dying as well.

Indirect linguistic evidence backing the hypothesis of the increased life span is available in the *Aṣṭādhyāyī* of Pāṇini, whose date is by no means certain though it is generally accepted that he must have flourished between 600–300 BCE. In his discussion of the institution of lineage (*sapiṇḍa*) Pāṇini points out that a great-grandson is called *yuvan* if a more elderly *sapiṇḍa*, that is, either his uncle or grand-uncle, is alive (4:1.165). In addition, he suggests the terms *vaṃśya* (4:1.163) or *vṛddha* (1:2.65) to designate the male head of the family and *yuvan* for junior members. The head of the family, for instance, is to be distinguished from the junior members by affixing specific suffixes such as l) *garga*, 2) *gārgi*, 3) *gārgya* and 4) *gārgyāyaṇa*. Here *garga* denotes an ancestor who started a line of descendants. As such he is a *saṃjñākārin* (who gave his name to the family or started a lineage). His son would be known as *gārgi* (*antarāpatya* in grammar). The grandson of *garga* and the son of *gārgi* would be *gārgya*.

According to Pāṇini 4:1:162, all other descendants numbering a hundred or even a thousand would be called *gārgya*. Thus, while *garga* would denote the patriarch, *gārgyāyaṇa* would denote his juniors. These distinctive titles were of relative value. A *gārgya* as patriarch, for instance, represented his family in the social assemblies.

A junior member such as *gārgyāyaṇa* would be given the nomenclature *gārgya* only when the former was admitted to the headship of the family in the absence of *gārgya* the elder (Agrawala 1963, 86).

Agrawala (1963, 94) has also observed that the term *sapiṇḍa* is peculiar to the post-Vedic literature and is not found in the Saṃhitās, Brāhmaṇas or Upaniṣads. But such later texts as the *Manu Smṛti* (5:60) explain *sapiṇḍa* as blood relations up to the seventh degree on the father's side and fifth on the mother's side.

The coining or at least the legitimation of these terms by Pāṇini suggests that by his time many were living long enough to be called grandfathers and founded lineages that were named after them.[12] It would appear that a number of such lineages were established in the Dharma Sūtra period with significant political implications (Thapar 1984). Death of the patriarch must have been preceded by a relatively long ambulatory period imposed by old age in contradistinction to the early Vedic era when sudden death in early life was more frequent. These changes are mythically and symbolically documented in the Pali Canon as well, for example, in the creation myth of the world, humans, and society in the "Aggañña Suttanta" of the *Dīgha Nikāya* (3:80–98) or in the legends describing young Siddhārtha's confrontation with the phenomena of disease, decrepitude and death (see below).[13]

It is in this context that one must understand Kane's observation (1974, 2:1,2) that the earliest mention of the four life stages (*āśramas*) occurs in the Dharma Sūtras. The *Gautama Dharma Sūtra* (3:2), one of the earliest, lists them as student, householder, wandering beggar and hermit respectively (*brahmacārin, gṛhastha, bhikṣu* and *vaikhānasa*). But the *Āpastamba Dharma Sūtra* (2:9.1) provides different names and a different order for the same four stages—*gārhasthyam, ācāryakulam, maunam* and *vānaprasthyam*. The *Vasiṣṭha Dharma Sūtra* (7:1.2) has *brahmacārin, gṛhastha, vānaprastha* and *parivrājaka* (Young 1981). The much later (ca. 500 CE) *Kūrma Purāṇa* curiously changes the order, and the terms once again are *gṛhastha, vanastha, bhikṣuka* and *brahmacārin* (1:2.39).

The foregoing suggests that the plan of age-specific life stages was in the air by the time of the Dharma Sūtras, but the structure, sequence and details were still in flux. Gautama (GDS 3:1) and Vasiṣṭha (VDS 7:1.3) concede that the choice of the mendicant (*bhikṣu*) stage is optional. This reflects the inroads made by the ascetic and renunciatory tendencies in the realm of the Vedic ideal life and its organization (*dharma*). As Olivelle (1978) argues, such inroads caused a radical change in the notion of Vedic concept of righteousness (*dharma*) by introducing an element of choice and alternatives to the socially fixed and immutable *dharma*.

But one must also remember that an equally fundamental change was taking place in the Buddhist ideal of ascetic life. The early ideal of the solitary life of a wandering *bhikṣu* in the forest was replaced by a sedentary life in the monastery (*saṃgha*). The *Sutta Nipāta* is full of praise for solitary living like a rhinoceros in the forest. Now this gives way to the organized and relatively comfortable life in the monasteries where the motto was "blessed is the unity of *saṃgha*, blessed is the exertion of the united (Misra 1972, 117). The lure of the secure life in monasteries, away from the travails of the family duties and obligations in society, began to attract a number of young men and women to Buddhism. Many took to ascetic garb in order to escape physical labor, hardships or poverty.

The *Mahāvagga* refers to Magadhan soldiers (who were ordered to quell rebellions on the frontier) and debtors taking refuge in the monastery (Misra 1972, 35). Many members of the warrior class (Kṣatriya), feeling the pull of class (*varṇa*) loyalty, were drawn to monasteries founded by a member proud of his warrior class. Following Young (1981), one may therefore, conclude that the ideal of life stages as elaborated in the Dharma Sūtras represents the brahminical resolution of the conflict between the competing ideals of renunciation in young age and the moral responsibility of discharging the three debts incumbent on each Ārya.

It was during the reign of King Aśoka (ca. 300 BCE) that emergent Buddhism—originally limited to meditating monks in the forest or the monasteries—was transformed into a popular religion of the masses. Under the sponsorship of King Aśoka, the long process of reformulation and codification of the principal tenets of Buddhism was begun, resulting in the establishment of the Pali Canon. The loss of political patronage under the Śuṅga dynasty—which succeeded the Mauryas in the Magadha—was compensated to an extent in Northwest India in the Buddhist kingdoms of Kaniṣka and Milinda (ca. 100 BCE–100 CE).

Doctrinally, canonical Buddhism as then formulated was distinguished by the twin concepts of the wheel of ethical life (*dharmacakra*) and the wheel of biological life (*bhavacakra*) based on the doctrine of dependent origination (*pratītyasamutpāda*, see chapter two). The explanatory model of the aging body, which is implicit in the Pali Canon, seems to be patterned after the analogy of a machine. The world is understood as a *sui generis* circular machine composed of discrete parts (cogs) moving through time and space pivoted by the fundamental law of *karma*.

Although aging in the organism appears to be qualitative (since it is said to revolve around the different phases of childhood, youth and old age), it is really quantitative, that is, an impersonal flow of discrete moments (*kṣaṇa*). Put differently, in contrast to the traditional Vedic atemporal account of human existence, early Buddhism proposed that any authentic understanding of human existence must fully recognize life's temporal contingency and its resolute encounter with old age, disease and death.

It is in the first part of the *Dīgha Nikāya* and the whole of the *Majjhima Nikāya* in the Pali Canon that one comes across the earliest cogent and organized exposition of the fully fledged and typically *Buddhist* meaning and interpretation of old age. It is not clear whether the Buddha himself meditated and reflected on the facts and evils of old age; certainly, however, it is in the Pali Canon that one begins to come across the picturesque legends of the young Siddhārtha being introduced to the triple evil of old age and so forth (see below). The Nikāyas (MN 2:75; 3:179) refer to old age (perhaps sarcastically) as one of the three divine messengers (*devadūta*).

In the "Mahānidāna Suttanta" of the *Dīgha Nikāya* (2:55–71) is to be found the full explanation of the doctrine of dependent co-origination and its role in the phenomenalization of birth (*jāti*), old age (*jarā*) and death (*maraṇa*). The thread of this argument is taken up again in the "Nidāna Saṃyutta" of the *Saṃyutta Nikāya* (2:1–133) where we find the Buddha teaching to the monks that the chain of causation begins with ignorance and ends only in old age and death. The "Mahāparinibbāna Suttanta" of the *Dīgha Nikāya* (2:72–168) records the last message of the Buddha in these words:

> Age (aging) is inherent in all component things. Work out your own salvation with diligence.[14]

This teaching, it may be argued, is the keynote of early Buddhism and neatly summarizes the early Buddhist understanding and evaluation of the aging process.

The Pali *Dhammapāda,* which contains the most sublime statements of early Buddhism, is placed by Barua (1970, 41) in 300 BCE. Chapter eleven of this test entitled *Jarāvagga* (section on old age) records the early Buddhist understanding of aging as primarily a biological process that wastes the human body which itself is conceived as a heap of corruption and an abode of old age, death, pride and deceit. Similar ideas are also put forth in the "Vijaya Sutta" of the *Uraga Vagga* and the "Jarā Sutta" of the *Aṭṭhaka Vagga* of the *Sutta Nipāta* which Barua (1970, 238) describes as one of the oldest books of the Pali Canon.

In several accounts in the Pali Canon, the future Buddha (and current Bodhisattva) expounds on the three evils of suffering (old age, disease and death). Indeed, as recorded in the *Aṅguttara Nikāya* (1:3.4.1–6), he recounts to the monks the dialogues wherein Yama, the god of death, chastises three mortals for 1) failing to live the pious life and 2) not recognizing old age, disease and death as the three evils.

This episode involving young Siddhārtha's encounter with disease, old age and death is retold in elegant Sanskrit in Aśvaghoṣa's *Buddhacarita*. The variations from the original account in the Nikāyas tell us much about the shifting spectrum of the Buddhist understanding of old age and aging in this period (ca. 100 CE) when the model of the life stages (*āśrama*) in its final mold had already appeared in the Dharma Śāstra texts such as the *Manu Smṛti* and which as such appears as the premise to be refuted (*pūrvapakṣa*) in the *Buddhacarita*.

The reflections on aging put in the mouth of the Buddha and other monks suggest a new point of reference in uncovering a significance and meaning to the losses engendered by old age and so forth. This seems to go beyond an exclusively negative appraisal of their impact. The questions and doubts that arise in the agitated mind of Siddhārtha (BC 3:28) are pregnant with new answers and meanings. Is aging a predetermined process? Is it caused by an external agency? Are aging and old age accidents in that they happen to some unfortunate individuals? Are others spared from this evil? If old age is an accident, can it be avoided? Or is it an intrinsic, natural condition in human beings unfolding itself with the passage of time? Is there a permanent, immutable self (substance) that does not age but appropriates the experience of aging suffered by the body?

The initial brahmin-endorsed explanations of old age and aging as furnished by the charioteer fail to satisfy Siddhārtha thereby setting him on a spiritual quest (BC 3:33). After he attains *nirvāṇa* and becomes the Buddha (the awakened one), Siddhārtha begins to insist upon the need for living fully *now* with attention to the immediacy of lived experience. In order to realize this fullness in the present, he institutes a spiritual discipline composed of eight stages. For that purpose, one is asked to remove oneself from the centers of power divesting oneself of external social roles and relations; one is to turn away from the world's claims while still young rather than waiting for old age and infirmities to force one to do so. The constant refrain of the evils of old age is essential to remind us to live fully *now* so that the losses suffered due to old age can be viewed as vivid reminders of human finitude.

This line of thought and reflection is conspicuously absent from Vedic revelation and Upaniṣadic reflection.[15] Buddhism is not content with a lifestyle where the "facts" of birth, growth, old age and death are nonchalantly accepted as given. Their presence in human life cannot be simply passed over in silence. Canonical Buddhism accordingly directed its indignation against the Vedic familism, an expression of sexuality in the guise of a conjugal relationship, and the brahminical *karma*-oriented social ethics and philosophy (see BC 6:44–47).

The most characteristic and surprising expression of Buddhism in this period as recorded in the works of Aśvaghoṣa is the campaign against aging and old age which held a special terror to early Buddhism. It is likely that with the increasing proportion of old people in the population, the problem of old age attracted attention of the anxious monks.[16] The mythical versions of the episode of the young Siddhārtha's awakening to the human condition suggest some idea about the psychological temperament and anxious personality of the Buddha himself and others like him. It is a sensitive mind that detects the all-pervasiveness of sorrow in the old man, sick man and the dead man where others before him failed to see it. He was able to extract and extrapolate the subtle meaning underlying these common, everyday phenomena. His preoccupation with suffering originates in a metaphysical vision and existential condition of humankind (see below chapter 5).

That awareness may have been brought into a sharper focus to him in ca. 600 BCE by the changing political, economic and social conditions of his time.[17] The Buddha's doctrine of suffering (*duḥkhavāda*) is a philosophical worldview symbolizing demographic, political and economic vicissitudes. As Eliade (1969, xvi) has pointed out, it is the human condition, and above all the temporality (and aging, shall we add?) of the human being that constitutes the central problem of Indian thought. India, therefore, has not been unaware of the relation between illusion, temporality, and human suffering as a "becoming" conditioned by the structures of temporality (Eliade 1969, xviii).

Anxiety, then, is the impelling basis of human existence. The Buddha sought a way out of this predicament by positing a theory and practice of spirituality that was erected on the denial and neutralization of the idea of self. The ego is the root of all human anxieties and fears (*duḥkha*). The Buddha was led to these conclusions, because he was dissatisfied with the Vedic ontology that he had inherited, an ontology which took for granted the view that time is a kind of vessel in which events take place. Persons exist in this vessel as a substratum that subsists through time.

The Buddha found this analysis unconvincing, because it ignores the temporal, contingent aspect of human beings, and results in the supposition that beings and time are inseparable. He argued that the belief in human existence as an immutable substance, separated from the progression of time (see chapter three), is only a protective shield against anxiety, resulting from the awareness of the inevitable human destiny.

There is no apparent causal relation nor perhaps *any* relation between the eightfold spiritual discipline he proclaimed and the facts of aging, disease and death. The only probable rational connection between these two is the possible emergence of the psychological feeling of security and assurance resulting from the rejection of the duties and responsibilities, as well as the pleasures and comforts, of the life of the householder. As portrayed in the *Buddhacarita,* the Buddha repeatedly argues that the uncertain and accidental character of death provides the justification of the passionate urgency with which spiritual liberation has to be worked out in youth, before old age takes its inevitable toll.

This characteristically Buddhist stance is also clear from the response of the monk Nāgasena to King Milinda's query: "How does he who orders his life aright realize *nirvāṇa*?"

> He who orders his life aright grasps the truth as to the development of all things (*saṃkhārānām parattam sammāsati*) and when he is doing so he perceives therein birth, he perceives old age, he perceives disease, he perceives death. But he perceives not therein either happiness or bliss (dilemma 81, *Milindapañha*).

Within this mechanistic-sounding interpretation, human development and aging are seen as consisting of discrete elements. Such a model features prominently in the Buddha's sermon on dependent co-arising, which hypothesizes the relation of antecedent to consequent as the fundamental explanation of human life and its development from birth through death. Human growth and aging is a continuous series in that it is reducible to or predictable from pervious antecedents. From the moment of inception, aging is continuous with suffering and remains so till death.

With its emphasis on unique particulars (*svalakṣaṇas*) rather than on universal sequences, life events including aging are understood as specific causes of specific events with specific outcomes. The task, accordingly, is to identify the cause-effect relations and the variables which mediate or interact with them.

Early Buddhism, therefore, is relatively unconcerned with the collective or cultural factors surrounding the process of aging *per se;* although identified with suffering, aging does become the very raison d'être of the Buddha's life and mission. The age of the Buddha was replete with conflict between young and old. Those who endorsed the path proposed by the Buddha sought to transcend the preoccupation with retaining or regaining their youthful vitality and vigor in the manner of their Vedic predecessors. Rather, they longed to escape what they believed was transient and impermanent.

The Buddha was certainly interested in enjoying long life and satisfying desires if only in good health and in the absence of old age (BC 4:86). This explains, in part, why he refused to die though urged by Māra (the personification, at once, of desire and death). As a mere process, aging is reducible to time which itself is a chimera and causes nothing. The same general processes or mechanisms underlie the apparent growth and decay of the body in its various phases. Thus, as a focus of attention, aging deserves to be relegated to minor status. There is really no need to explain aging and differences caused by aging. The task at hand is to eliminate aging.

Consequently, any doctrinal discussion of age-specific social and ethical duties at the individual level (*āśramadharma* or *svadharma*) is avoided in the Pali Canon.[18] This is because, *prima facie,* these texts are intended for the benefit of the members of the religion of renouncers who have left society and its norms behind them. To be sure, a Buddhist layman (*upāsika*) or a laywoman (*upāsikā*), who has not yet left society behind him/her, does have duties deriving from his/her station in life—whether he/she be king, queen or outcast—but these are not duties *qua* being a Buddhist, that is, these duties are not a function of the Buddhist dogma.[19]

## *Hindu Compromise*

After the demise of King Aśoka, the Maurya dynasty weakened and royal support for Buddhism also declined. When the Śuṅga dynasty replaced the Mauryas, the stage was set for the revival of brahminical orthodoxy (ca. 200 BCE). The horse-sacrifices of King Puṣyamitra and related gifts to the brahmins replaced the charities which Aśoka had lavished on monks and their monasteries. This return to orthodoxy also affected linguistic, social and cultural fields. The rivalry between the newly invigorated brahmin orthodoxy and the still influential Buddhism must have forced rival thinkers to modify and develop their religious and social ideas in order to win and maintain popular support. In the process the principal tenets of the two contestants acted and reacted dialectically upon each other till some sort of a middle ground tacitly accepted by both emerged.[20]

Consequently, as far as the brahminical side was concerned, after much ferment and speculation, the reification of ideas regarding the stages of life came about so that by the time the influential and authoritative *Manu Smṛti* (100 BCE–100 CE) was compiled, the ideal framework of organized life in terms of age and class specific duties (*varṇāśramadharma*) was formalized with the four life stages identified as celibate studenthood (*brahmacārin*), householder (*gṛhastha*), hermit (*vānaprastha*) and wandering ascetic (*yati*) (MS 6:87, 137).[21]

The awareness of and the need for structuring the steadily extending lifespan in terms of institutions, norms, roles and values to deal with them had already begun (as pointed out above) in the Dharma Sūtra period. However no age-specific stages with clear boundaries for them had been demarcated. It was only when the Dharma Śāstra texts began to be written that interest in the 'middle years' as a distinct segment of adult life arose out of the need to differentiate social, psychological and spiritual concerns of 'middle' age from 'old' age.

The social and cultural conditions of the beginning of the common era contributed to sharpening and demarcating the boundaries between various age-specific stages. In gerontological terms, two of the most important changes were the increasing association of function with age and the formation of segregated, age-based peer groups (for instance, education with childhood). This segregation by age occurred first in the brahmin class and was only later (perhaps grudgingly) extended to other classes.[22]

In later centuries (ca. 300 CE on), the Purāṇas tried to distinguish additional phases in adult life, but it is doubtful if they were ever developed into heuristically useful concepts. The *Nārada Purāṇa* (2:61.55b–56a), for instance, observes that it is not the soul but the gross elements (constituting the physical body) that attain the seventh stage (old age) before ceasing to exist. Similarly, Nīlakaṇṭha, a medieval commentator on the *Mahābhārata* identified the following ten stages of human life:

1. The stay in the womb.
2. Birth.
3. Infancy up to the age of five.
4. Childhood up to twelve years.
5. Stage of pre-puberty (*pauganḍa*).
6. Youth.
7. Old age.
8. Decrepitude.
9. Suspension of breath.
10. Death (Tagare 1981–1982, 2:903).

From the text of the *Manu Smṛti* it is clear that old age by then had come to be ideally recognized as a specific period of late adulthood with a formal ritualized beginning at the age of seventy-five. This stage was also institutionalized by the prescription of appropriate norms, duties and rites of passage. A sizeable portion of each Dharma Śāstra manual, accordingly, is devoted to a structural-functional explanation of this human relationship between long life and old age in terms of the stages of life model whereby the entire system of life comes to be structured on the triad of class, duties and stages.[23]

The Upaniṣadic and the Buddhist insights were accommodated in these Smṛti texts as developmental devices whereby the other-worldly ethics and ambitions (*mokṣa* and *nirvāṇa*) preached therein were harnessed and harmonized as age-specific norms and duties to be taken up in the later part of life with this-worldly ethics encapsulated in the concept of *dharma*. This synthesis was worked out on the basis of the hermeneutic principle of the three debts already in vogue in Vedic circles:

1. Knowledge given by the seers (*ṛṣi*).
2. Gift of life received from the ancestors (*pitṛ*).
3. Gifts received from the deities (*devatās*).

These debts are to be repaid by 1) learning as a student in the first quarter of life, 2) procreating a son in the second quarter, and 3) offering specific prescribed sacrifices in each of the first three quarters. In this manner, the authors of the Smṛti texts tempered the excessive zeal of the Vedic this-worldliness and the ascetic other-worldliness by predicating aspirations of both as age-related tasks spread evenly over the entire lifespan. In Hindery's (1978, 93) words, the Vedic world-lust and the ascetic world-disgust are replaced with world-concern for planned and ordered growth and development.

The *Kāma Sūtra,* a text attributed to Vātsyāyana and extolling the satiation of desires, was compiled at the height of the Indian Golden Age (400 CE). It begins by providing a tightly knit, clear, and explicitly age-specific evaluation of the first three goals of life (*puruṣārthas*) spelled out in the Dharma Śāstras.[24] Yaśodhara's gloss (*Jayamaṅgalā*) on these verses of the *Kāma Sūtra* succinctly summarizes its this-worldly attitude in these terms:

> Let one enjoy or give unto whatever is produced—in its proper time and age—discharging duties, acquiring wealth and satiating desires until one becomes exhausted [with age].[25]

Allusion to the direct, functional link between age and a particular sphere of activity is also provided (from a perspective different from that of the *Kāma Sūtra*) by Śaṅkara while commenting on the *Bṛhadarāṇyaka Upaniṣad* (6:2.15). He observes that while the householder is bound to *karma (karmasambaddha)*, the hermit and the ascetic are bound to the forest (*āraṇyasambaddha*). Similarly, Yājñavalkya's announcement to Maitreyī of his projected departure to the forest as recorded in (BAU 2:4.1) is paraphrased by Śankara as:

> Desirous of going beyond the order of the householder . . . I will break off the bond [with the household].[26]

In the *Upadeśa Sāhasrī* ("Gadyaprabandhaḥ" 21), a didactic tract again attributed to Śaṅkara (ca. 700 CE), the teacher—when instructing the disciple on the relationship between the various age-specific sacraments (*saṃskāras*) and the four stages of life—points out that by the sacrament of the tying of the sacred thread, one acquires the title of the chaste student (*brahamcārisaṃjñā*). By the sacrament of the tying of the [husband's] body to the wife, one acquires the title of the householder (*gṛhasthasaṃjñā*). The same body acquires the title of the hermit (*tāpasasaṃjñā*) by the sacrament of the forest. Finally the same body acquires the title of the wandering ascetic (*parivrāṭsaṃjñā*) by the sacrament of disengagement from acts.

Towards the middle of the first millennium, classical Hinduism (Purāṇic, Epic and Tāntric) came to recognize old age as horrible and wicked, yet accepted it as an inevitable and integral part of the human condition. In this manner it tried partially to reconcile the lived experience of old age with the fundamental Vedic desire for a healthy, happy and long life. The Dharma Śāstras such as the *Manu Smṛti* or the *Yājñavalkya Smṛti*, written in verse, are much more extensive than the other Dharma Sūtras and consecrate a larger number of pages to the elucidation of rules and norms of a juridical, this-worldly character (*vyavahāra*) in addition to the brief discussion of the duties of the classes and stages.[27]

Thus, chapter six of the *Manu Smṛti*, dealing with the last two stages of hermit and wanderer (*vānaprastha* and *yati*), is the shortest of them all with just ninety-seven verses with the final two verses reiterating the eulogy of the superiority of the stage of the householder. Anyone who would seek to become a hermit or an ascetic without paying the triple debt, that is without living out the order of the householder, is threatened with hell (MS 6:35).[28] But according to Manu as soon as he observes the birth of his grandson or when his hair turns grey, the householder should distribute his property among his children and with or without his wife renounce the world and enter the forest in order to undertake the prescribed tasks of the third order (*vānaprastha*) (MS 6:2). The *vānaprastha* is explained as one who is established in the forest (*vane pratiṣṭhita iti vānaprastha*). His other epithet is *vaikhānasa* (Govinda's gloss on BDS 2:6.16).

Furthermore, the householder's key duty is the practice of five kinds of austerities (*tapas*) so as to divest his body and mind of all attachments and passions so that there does not remain in him even the remote possibility of the appearance of pride (see Vijñāneśvara's gloss *Mitākṣarā* on the *Yājñavalkya Smṛti*, 3:4.56, 57).

Then, with his body rendered parched by the practice of harsh austerities, he should contemplate retiring from the stage of the hermit and enter the final stage of the wandering ascetic (*yati*). Baudhāyana (BDS 2:10.6) states that renunciation (*saṃnyāsa*) is advised when one has passed beyond the age of seventy. He then describes the formal ritual ceremony to enter the stage of the wandering ascetic (BDS 10:17, 27). The *Yājñavalkya Smṛti* (3:4.56, 57) advises such an individual to stop the performance of the fire sacrifices and internalize them in the self to mark his entry into the order of the ascetic from that of the hermit.

Verses 6:76, 77 in the *Manu Smṛti* are intended to cultivate disgust and revulsion toward the body in the mind of the wanderer.[29]

> He is to be consciously aware of his [aging] body as a storehouse of urine and fecal matter . . . [realizing which] . . . he shall discard the body which is the abode of material substances, that is, a product of earth, in the form of fat, urine, semen and blood. Such an entity cannot be the abode of the self.

MS 6:78 further develops the figure of the defiled body with reference to the simile of the bird leaving the tree. But this does not mean that the body should be deliberately killed off, for instance, by entering into the fire. The idea, rather, is that one should not persist in one's attachment to the body. One should let the body fall off by itself by the exhaustion of the karmic residuum, just as the tree on the bank of a river falls off. However, if one has realized the inner light and withdrawn from all manifestations of illusion, then one may voluntarily drop off the material body in the manner of the bird taking off from a tree.

Ideally, then, such an individual has attuned his mind and body to be receptive to spiritual enlightenment. He must not engage in any kind of productive activity. As the *Manu Smṛti* (6:26, 29, 31) states, such a person is to wander alone, without any companion, fully realizing that the solitary individual who neither forsakes nor is forsaken, attains the desired end. He shall neither tend the ritual fire nor maintain a permanent dwelling. Indifferent to everything, firm of purpose, he shall concentrate and meditate for the sake of realizing the supreme reality (*brahman*).

By not injuring any creatures, by detaching the senses (from their objects of enjoyment), by the performance of rites prescribed in the Vedas, and by rigorously practicing austerities, the state of ultimate reality (*brahman*) is reached even in this world. This reformulation of the model of the wandering ascetic (*yati*) is noteworthy in that wandering and begging is the final duty in life, and as such equivalent to the highest aspiration in life *mokṣa*.[30] But at the same time, exclusive emphasis on any single goal in life (*puruṣārtha*) is studiously avoided. The *Manu Smṛti,* in fact, ends its discussion of the section on the wandering ascetic by once again reiterating that the stage of the householder is the best. Though they institutionalize the model of the wandering ascetic, the writers of the Dharma Śāstras never tire of reminding us that the householder is the source of all other orders, feeding and sustaining them all.

Winternitz traced the etymological meaning of the term *āśrama* to signify "religious exertion" on the part of the Śramaṇas and observed that the brahmins named even a life of householder as *āśrama* so that, through this designation, they placed the householder's lifestyle in line and on a par with the other three orders (Upadhyaya 1979, 190).[31]

The focus of the stages of life model, nevertheless, is the twice-born male. Members of the servile (Śūdra) class and women of all the classes do not come under its purview. The *Manu Smṛti* deals with the duties of women at the end of chapter five after discussing various precepts regarding food. This would drastically reduce the scope of the model of the life stages. The apparent absence of women from the age-homogeneous organization may be attributed to the practice of integrating women into domestic and familial roles. The kinship ties affecting women are designed to stress *vertical* family bonds rather than the horizontal bonds of age.

The stages of life model, it may be argued, posits the ties of age as a balance to kin bonds. The bond developed with a fellow male hermit in the forest is designed to substitute or replace the bond of kinship developed in the context of the family. While kinship *ipso facto* is perceived to be a source of conflict, the organization by age is viewed as a harmonious counterweight.

The formal organization by age is presented as a channel for avoidance or management of conflicts stemming from the parent-child knots in the rope of generational succession. From that perspective, the age-homogeneous residence of the aging adult as a hermit in the forest is likely to serve as a tension deflector. Spatial separation from home probably provided insulation from the worries of succession. It is for these reasons that women who were expected to stay within the domestic sphere, therefore, were also less likely to participate in formal age groups such as that of the student, hermit, or the ascetic wherein men's lives and duties would be played out in the public arena and where principles other than kinship would operate. Aging, therefore, does not seem to have had the same meaning or involved the same circumstances for men as for women.

The great difference in the reproductive potential of the two sexes also seems to play an important role. While men are deemed to be capable of siring offspring when they are well into their seventies or eighties (see chapter four dealing with rejuvenation and revitalization therapies), after menopause a woman is no longer considered to be a person with sexuality. In many ways the status of an aged woman is not unlike that of a prepubescent girl. Both are relatively free of many repressive sex-taboos and regulations imposed on the young and middle aged woman. As she begins to take on the signs and the qualities of senescence—wrinkled skin, greying hair, and so forth—there is a noticeable change in her manner of approach to others. Aging essentially brings out (and permits) relaxation and warmth in her social interaction with the old and young of both sexes according to the Dharma Śāstra texts.

Symbolically, this is reflected in the fact that she no longer has to lower her gaze when in the presence of males. But though more highly esteemed with advancing age, a woman is always subordinate to the male, except perhaps during the early socialization stages of her sons. Again, directly or indirectly, her role is invariably associated with sexual reproduction and food production and preparation. To that extent certain age-specific norms for women (*strīdharma, patnīdharma*) are closely tied to equivalent male norms.

Occasionally, woman is eulogized as the root and support of the order of the householder (*gṛhasthadharma*), which in itself is praised as the source of *all* the *āśramas*. Like a root, the wife sustains and nourishes the householder and his obligations, which entail sustaining and nourishing all the members belonging to the remaining three orders. The order of the householder, thus, is the very pulse of the orthodoxy which can be so only with the participation of the housewife (MS 3:77–80).[32]

The roles prescribed for various stages of life as envisaged in the Smṛti works appear to be normative, ideal constructs created by intentional intensification or exaggeration of a cluster of traits, and by the synthesis of a number of discrete phenomena based on individual characteristics. In their conceptual purity, therefore, the ideal role models of the student, householder, hermit or wanderer would not be approximated in reality. This is evident from Śaṅkara's gloss (*bhāṣya*) on the *Brahma Sūtra* (3:4.40) that the norms of an individual are determined on the basis of the relevant revealed injunctions (Śruti), not on the basis of the capacity, ability, predilection or the expertise of an individual for successfully carrying out a particular duty. It would, therefore, be hazardous to imagine social reality through the precepts laid down for various orders.

It is not, therefore, surprising that there is no evidence that the theory of the stages of life ever became a total and practical reality—that is, that any considerable number of the twice-born or even the brahmins among them, for that matter, actually carried out the tasks of the stages in the course of the ideally prescribed duration and in the prescribed order. The number of such persons must have been small. Many were content to spend their last years in semi-retirement in a small hut erected not far from the habitation of their family members. This practice is legitimated in the *Manu Smṛti* under the category of *vedasaṃnyāsika*, an ideal which, strictly speaking, lies outside the stages of life scheme.[33]

It is likely that the optional model of a semi-retired elderly male was more popular among the warrior classes (Kṣatriyas). As rulers, ministers and generals who had disengaged from active duties in old age, they settled into a more quiet lifestyle in a modest retreat usually situated within the confines of a palace or a mansion they previously possessed.[34] As such they would be readily available as consultants when called upon by the younger, inexperienced members of the family in charge of worldly affairs.

## *The Stages of Life: A Gerontological Reappraisal*

Our survey of the relevant Vedic, Buddhist and Hindu texts suggests that from around 500 BCE Buddhism challenged and sought to replace the then prevailing Vedic vision of life and culture (to the extent it differed from the similar Upaniṣadic critique from *within* the Vedic tradition) and almost succeeded in that endeavor during the reign of Aśoka (ca. 200 BCE). But the brahmins mounted a spirited counteroffensive of their own and eventually gained the upper hand by reformulating the Vedic principles of ideal life and by accommodating the Buddhist ideas on renunciation. The Hindu literature and ideals may, therefore, be taken to represent the consummation of the combined Vedic and Buddhist views on the philosophy and culture of life.

On the practical side the Dharma Śāstra's consolidation and endorsement of the stages of life model meant the triumph and continuity of the positive Vedic ideal of a long, healthy and this-worldly lifestyle tempered by a good dose of detachment. It is not clear whether the Buddhists ever developed a similar social philosophy of the stages of life for the benefit of the lay Buddhist. There is, however, evidence to suggest that the life of the monks and nuns in the monasteries was organized and graded according to age.

Wayman (1984, 48ff), after scrutinizing the available relevant evidence, concludes that the argument that the Buddhist "going forth" (*pabbajā*) resembles the Hindu hermit (*vānaprastha*) stage and the full ordination of the Buddhist monk/nun (*upasampadā*) is equivalent to attaining the stage of the wandering ascetic (*saṃnyāsa*) of the Hindus, is not valid. He points out that the Buddhists did not recognize the requirement to be a householder. He therefore takes the Buddhist novice as equivalent to the Hindu celibate student (*brahmacārin*) and the fully ordained monk/nun to be roughly equivalent to the forest-hermit.

With the disappearance of Buddhism as a social philosophy in India by about 1200 CE, the stages of life model emerged as the dominant ideal of life and culture and even today most Indians are familiar with its basic postulates and tacitly endorse them. For this reason, it would be instructive and relevant to provide a reappraisal and an evaluation of the meaning and significance of aging as it is anchored in the Indian psyche from the classical times onwards.

The basic presupposition of the Dharma Śāstras is that the world of human beings is living and active, deriving its meaning from its organic wholeness and cosmic identity. The human organism, a reflection in miniature of the cosmic organism, is an active and growing entity, both qualitatively and quantitatively. Organic synthesis rather than cold philosophical reflection on discrete, physical entities (*skandhas,* on which see chapter two) as in Buddhism is taken as the guiding principle of the theory of aging.

It is held that although efficient causes may have effect on various quantitative and qualitative changes on the body and the mind, the fundamental cause of aging is teleological. That is, though destructive and harmful at the physical level, the change engendered by the aging process works for the better at the metaphysical level of the self set against the backdrop of the law of *karma,* the doctrine of transmigration (*saṃsāra*), and the theory of the threefold character based on the concept of *guṇa* (see chapter three). One ripens, matures and grows progressively from the first student stage through the householder stage and so forth, to the final stage of the ascetic.

The Buddhist mechanistic model of aging as noted above stresses the analysis of the lifespan as a discontinuous, discrete flow of unique moments and seeks to explain the lifespan as a result of the relation of antecedent to consequent (*krama*). Life events are seen as potential stressors, as a source of suffering. In fact, aging, as a visible image of the discrete, flowing moments, *is* suffering.

The Hindu thinkers, therefore, are careful to steer clear of both the negative and the false, positive visualizations of aging. Instead, they struggle to state what a genuinely positive meaning of aging ought to be. They realize that both the Vedic and the Buddhist views on aging are limiting. While the former hopelessly overvalues it, the latter goes to the other extreme. For the negative view, the realities and the facts of human aging spell the doom of the human being; for the stay-ever-young-and-healthy Vedic view of aging such realities and facts are nonexistent.

The writers of the Dharma Śāstras, therefore, sought to map out a middle ground where human growth is to be appreciated as coeval with aging and as occurring from the moment of conception till death.[35] They recognized, it may be argued, that aging in human beings reflects diverse changes at the physical and psychological levels which can be catalogued and labeled (as the different names for different stages suggest) and readily distinguished. The wooden chariot, too, changes and ages with the person sitting in it, but this happens ever so slowly. Compared to the diversified changes that take place in the lifespan available to humans, this change is monotonous.

Early Buddhist metaphysics, as documented in the *Abhidharma*, seems to have failed to take this fact into account, equating the human being with a chariot by not distinguishing between their differing aging patterns. To the writers of the Smṛti texts, to grow to maturity means to learn to accept the real human predicament. The purpose of self-reflection is, they argue, not, first of all, to deny or confirm the Buddhist claims that there is no being, that to become is to age and that all aging is suffering. One must not deny the fact of aging as characteristic of existence; rather, one must devise ways to *cope* with this unique dynamic feature of the human condition (see chapter four).

On the other hand, they also recognize that one cannot grow indefinitely either, as the Vedic texts had proclaimed. The blossoming life, like the morning dew drops, cannot last forever. Humans must be consigned to decay and the eventual falling apart of the different constituents of the body in death. The Vedic seers had entreated the gods for a long life without caring to reflect upon the travails of aging that inevitably accompany late life. One must now develop a clear appreciation of late life that is inseparable from the phenomenon of old age, of development and aging as inextricably bound in an organized complexity.

As the instigator of development and growth, aging precipitates significant structural changes spread over three or more phases or time periods. This development, in the classical Hindu view, is partly continuous and partly discontinuous in that future development is not completely reducible to previous phases as the Buddhists are prone to do; yet future growth potential is predictable from the past phases.

In other words, growth in the householder phase is not reducible to that in the student phase; but the potential of growth that would take place in the hermit or wanderer phase is, at least partially, predictable from the growth accomplished in the student phase. Despite their unique identities, the stages of life and the associated values, goals and duties are not mutually inconsistent. Further, the succeeding stage is not necessarily superior to the preceding one in terms of associated values or goals. Human aging, therefore, is understood to be *goal directed*. The emphasis, however, is on the universal typology of growth and development taking place simultaneously with advancing age rather than on individualized and particularized aspects of aging and development.

From this Hindu perspective then, life events are to be understood as components of an organized complexity rather than as specific causes. Events in a particular life are important, but examination of them in isolation will not explain the nature of aging; one must focus on the underlying human structure in which individual life events are reflected.[36]

The stages of life model suggests that epistemological, emotional and ethical developments in the human being occur during the entire lifespan, conveniently segmented into four stages. Manu and Yājñavalkya (perhaps in the manner of Plato and Schopenhauer) consider the highest stage of human development to be of epistemological order and attribute it to old age. It is the aged wandering ascetic (*yati, saṃnyāsin*) who is in a position, at least potentially, to attain that true insight into the nature of the ultimate reality (*brahman*). Advancing years bring with them increases in the understanding of this metaphysical truth spelled out in terms of the knowledge of ultimate reality.

It is only in the second half of life that a follower of the Vedic view develops cognitions that meaningfully relate tasks accomplished in the early years of life to those to be accomplished in the later half. The cognitive shift that usually takes place toward the midpoint in the lifespan alone facilitates the true understanding and ability to effectuate the transition from the householder stage bound to deeds (*karma*) to the hermit and/or wanderer phase bound to knowledge (*jñāna*).

The stages of life model thus sees the later years of life as an integrative period continuous with the early years in some ways and yet distinct from them in others. The task of meaningfully integrating and relating one's life as it has been lived and the final acceptance of one's own death are specific concerns of later existence. To deal with them is the great task in old age. In terms of the goals in life (*puruṣārtha*) to be striven for, it is essentially different from the tasks of infancy, youth and middle age where the concern is with fulfilling the worldly ends in life, which, following Edgerton[37] may be described as the ordinary norms compared to the extraordinary norm of spiritual liberation (*mokṣa*) to be attained in the final years of life.

The norm of liberation makes relatively higher demands of a metaphysical and ethical nature on its aging practitioner (hermit) beyond those required of the young student and the middle-aged householder. The philosophy and practice of abandonment implicit in the spiritual norm of *mokṣa* is negative or disengaging compared to the usual worldly norms. But as Herman suggests (1976, 270), it is the direct consequence of a metaphysical understanding realized in later years. What the elderly wandering ascetic learns in the course of the final stage in life is to draw the existential consequences ensuing from this deepened understanding.[38]

To that extent, the stand taken by the writers of the Dharma Śāstra texts in promoting the stages of life model vis-à-vis the early Buddhist view of ideal lifestyle and its principal task of attaining *nirvāṇa* appears at once more realistic as well as ambitious in that it prescribes with equal care and consideration the tasks to be accomplished in one's early as well as later years. This stand is further supported by an adequate analysis of various functionally age-related aspects of life which are evenly spread over the entire life cycle. In addition, it is also harmonized with the view that the psychodynamic unfolding of the potential of the mind is a function of advancing age.[39]

Creatively incorporating relevant insights both from the Upaniṣads and Buddhism, the model of life stages focuses on the innate need as well as desire on the part of sensitive and attuned individuals to fulfill human potential through striving for liberation (*mokṣa*). Human life has, it is consciously recognized, an implicit goal and sense of direction to achieve its full potential. Our bodily sense is a lifelong anchor as well as a pointer of the self within and its awareness.

That awareness has to be amplified by reducing our concerns with the gross body. In the second half of life, therefore, one must reduce preoccupation with the gross body by cultivating the feeling of disgust (*jugupsā*) toward it (see chapters three and four). The emphasis, thus, is on both becoming and growth. The continuity of life is predicated on the sequential fulfillment of different ends (*puruṣārthas*) changing with age. Implicit in this is intentionality and projection into the future. This, in turn, is based on the realistic acceptance of temporality and the relationship and continuity between its phases conceived as the past, present and future (see chapter three for a more detailed discussion of these modes of time and their relationship to the aging process).

The Dharma Śāstras make only guarded and qualified reference to the series of losses attributed to aging and documented *ad nauseam* in the early Buddhist texts. They readily admit that aging in its wake does unleash such losses in every member of the body and the mind, but they also stress that these 'losses' of the later years also have the potential for unfolding new creative developments in the person's selfhood. One must, in fact, rejoice in the realization that with age the bonds of the embodied self are coming loose, creating favorable conditions for eventual liberation in the near future. The focus, therefore, must not be on vain and futile attempts to deny or avoid aging but rather on the growing awareness of the widening opportunities for self-realization offered by the aging process.

The writers of the Dharma Śāstras also discount the Buddhist claim that dispassion is the general personality disposition that can be easily cultivated so that the virtues of poverty, continence, homelessness, and solitude can be developed by anybody at any stage in one's life (preferably in youth).[40] Instead, they stress that personality formation and behavior are situational and age-specific, evolving gradually over the entire lifespan from experiences of socialization and roles beginning with the first stage in life to culminate in the last.

As if anticipating developments in the modern humanistic psychology (Maslow 1970), it is argued that the desire and motivation for attaining liberation will only be felt after basic needs for physiological wellbeing, love and belonging have been met. The hermeneutic concepts of the three debts and the four ends in life are envisaged for just that purpose. Since the embodied individual self is inextricably bound with other embodied selves, fulfillment of the basic needs for affection and affiliation are, it is believed, an essential ground for future liberation understood as self-realization.

The Hindu thinkers detect a logical inconsistency in the Buddhist teaching, which conceptually appeals to *self*-realization, while at the same time striking at the foundation of *self-hood* in family, society and culture. With the Buddha, the purpose in this life is clearly stated in terms of the self-legislating individual. Ethical justification of one's quest for spiritual liberation is to be found within one's own self in the application of one's own reason. From the contemporary Vedic socio-ethical point of view, this was not an acceptable ideal, however praiseworthy it may have been from a purely egotistic point of view. And unless it can be represented as an ideal in some way superior to the prevailing Vedic ideal, the Buddhist model of the self-centered 'young renunciate' is without relevance. This is because it amounted to what Coomaraswamy has called the practice of "premature revulsion" toward the body, family and society, premature in that it was to be cultivated in young age.[41]

It may be argued that this practice must have created serious problems of a psychological and social nature in many of the young disciples of the Buddha. Forcing oneself prematurely to a life of a meditating mendicant in the forest before youthful desires and needs have been successfully fulfilled must have generated disturbing and distracting psychological and familial problems. Aśvaghoṣa has forcefully depicted them (albeit as the premise to be refuted) in his portrayals of the young Siddhārtha and Nanda in the *Buddhacarita* and *Saundarananda* respectively.[42] Young Nanda, for instance, resents being ordained, against his will, by the Buddha.

Citing instances from history and legend, he affirms the power of youth and love and justifies his resolve to return to married family life:

> Therefore while my *guru* [The Buddha] is away begging, I will discard the mendicant's robe and return home presently from here [the monastery]; for the person who carries the noble signs with wavering mind and confused understanding and with impaired judgment, has nothing to expect in life and has no part even in this world (*Saundarananda* 7:52).

Here one must take into consideration the legacy of pre-Buddhist notions of renunciation, the Buddha's own reformulation of that ideal, and the practice of renunciation as institutionalized in the Hindu stages of life model. Only then may one be able to appreciate and understand the moral dilemma faced by Nanda as it is depicted in the *Saundarananda*. The writers of the Dharma Śāstras would not see any moral difficulty in the ideal of renunciation *per se*, since they respond to a recognized and much lauded practice of the pan-Indian social ethos. But they would locate it securely within the Vedic this-worldly ethos.

By contrast, the selves of young Buddhist monks or nuns must be projected into their behavior towards the lay householders who sustain them. Accordingly, they must be willing to pay a high price for opting for the spiritual quest in youth. The episode of Nanda is selected by Aśvaghoṣa to dramatize the need and reason, as perceived by the Buddha, for abandoning the familial, social and ethical responsibilities at a young age for greater self-development and realization of *nirvāṇa*. Membership in the monastery would make him oblivious to the demands made upon him by the older surviving segments of his society—his family, city and republic.

The Dharma Śāstras, by contrast, view renunciation at a young age as antithetical to world acceptance and not as a life-ideal functioning at the same level as those of 1) teaching, 2) administration, 3) agriculture and commerce, and 4) service prescribed respectively to the four classes (priests, rulers, merchants and servants). This is consistent with their basic position that renunciation is compatible with and follows from attainment of the worldly goals of duties, prosperity and desires. One must rather rehearse the techniques of spiritual liberation such as meditation and its theoretical underpinnings from a qualified teacher in one's first quarter of life, reflect on them, prepare and purify one's body and mind in the second and third quarters of life, and then actively seek liberation in the final quarter after having successfully discharged the three debts (see above).

This ideal proceeds on the hypothesis that the degree of adaptation and adjustment that one must develop in old age depends on one's earlier life experience, especially the degree of relative isolation and physical deprivation (in terms of comfort and pleasure) that is expected of the seeker of liberation, whether in the Buddhist or the brahmin scheme of things, and to which he was exposed and trained in the formative period of early life (*brahmacaryāśrama*).

To recapitulate, the model of life stages, which emerges as a compromise between the Vedic and Buddhist dialectic on the meaning of life, posits a direct relation between age and the organization of social life guided by ethical reasoning. In gerontological terms, there is an attempt to avoid both the gerontophilia and gerontophobia discernible in the Vedic and the Buddhist texts respectively.[43] The ethic of Dharma Śāstra assumes aging as a process running parallel to the developing self whose intellectual capacities and ethical sensibilities are expected to grow, mold, and change with growing age. It seeks to propose an expanded and fuller humaneness with advancing age. The elderly hermit or the wandering ascetic is deemed to be more fully human (*mānava*), not solely for what has actually developed within, but also for potential spiritual development.[44]

As envisaged in the Hindu texts, the model of life stages embodies a system of vital social values, ethical principles, goals of life and ideals of conduct for structuring the life of society founded on the Vedic tradition. Like the Vedic *ṛta,* the concept of *āśrama,* too, has both physical and metaphysical dimensions, which are closely related.

Thus, according to Swāmī Nikhilānanda (1963, 16), the Vedas were arranged to conform to the four stages of life: the student studied the Saṃhitā portion, the householder followed the injunctions as laid out in the Brāhmaṇas, the hermit practiced contemplation according to the Āraṇyaka texts and the wandering ascetic was guided by the wisdom of the Upaniṣads.

Such a practice of harmonizing later historical developments with the revealed religious texts (a practice common in most traditions of the world) is consistent with the traditional Hindu view that all the four portions of the Veda were revealed simultaneously and have existed from the very beginning of the cycle. The model of life stages, therefore, is seen by most Indians as a continuation of the implicitly conceived Vedic norm of life, and thus rooted in Vedic tradition.

# 2

# *Growing Old*

It was pointed out in the introduction that the process of aging incorporates within itself two opposing polarities of development and decline. Just when and at what age the developmental phase stops and the decline of the body sets in is understood differently in different cultures. The present chapter seeks to examine the typical Indian ideas regarding human lifespan and the decline of the body attributed to aging in terms of the various age-specific phases and signs associated with them within the Vedic, Buddhist and Hindu perspectives.

Since the human body is both a system of meanings as well as a biological substance the semantic field of symbolic reality as it relates to aging may be seen as polarized according to 1) the physical and empirical dimension of aging (discussed in this and the next chapter) and 2) the transempirical or metaphysical dimension of aging (discussed in chapter five).

## *Embodiment*

As a physical and social object, the human body—in good health or ill, young or old, male or female—belongs to the world as well as to the self.[1] It is the face and front of the self toward the world and as such the most intimate connecting link between self and world. Repudiation of the body (because of its perishability) as a failed object or as an enemy would jeopardize this connection and would result in serious alienation. Existentially speaking, the frailty and the inevitable aging of the human body need not necessarily constitute a cause for despair, but neither are they to be celebrated in a 'cult of suffering'.[2] The aging body and the ageless, transcendental self embodied within it, should be seen in dialectical interaction; they contain the possibility for a meaningful life on earth.[3]

Such views are implicit in the traditional Indian belief that the human being is a dynamic entity possessing an ever-changing potential. The usual Indian exposition of the physics and physiology of the body accordingly begins with the assertion—generally shared by all the schools of philosophy including the Āyurveda—that as an aggregate being evolved out of the cardinal elements, the human body is the foundation of action, knowledge, life and death. But the schools differ widely on whether the individual retains his/her identity over time or is merely a succession of moments in a series.[4]

As the Indian tradition understands it, the process of aging is coeval with the transmigratory process, involving a circular movement (*saṃsāra*) from birth to death and birth again. In a given life cycle aging refers primarily to the perceivable evidence of physical and psychological changes which are construed both as positive and negative characteristics. We tend not to acknowledge the fact of aging until certain visible, external manifestations begin to appear on the body, even though subtle physiological processes that lead to these changes have been working their silent subversion long before they become externally visible.

The principal idea and the understanding of aging in Indian tradition is conceptually and implicitly tied to the imagery of the 'wheel of life', the idea that human life is encompassed within the cyclical rhythm of expansion and decline. The earliest documented evidence of the use of wheel symbolism to infuse life with meaning is present in the *Ṛgveda* (1:164.11–15). The seer of this hymn, Dīrghatamas, develops an extended metaphor of the human life span in terms of wheel imagery, which becomes archetypal for all subsequent speculation on the life course as lived out in Indian tradition.[5] The hymn is composed as a riddle (*brahmodya*) with the answer phrased punningly (*śleṣa*). It describes the ageless, cosmic wheel of order (*ṛta*) revolving continuously across the firmament. It is also homologized with time, involving three naves (seasons) and twelve spokes (months).

The speculative attribute of this cosmic wheel is that, though it turns constantly, it is not destined to age or decay or break up.[6] Thus, it is devoid of destruction and end. The world of people, mounted on the cosmic wheel, is also subject to rotations. But it is conditioned by aging and death. The recognition of the fact that human destiny is bound to death and mortality is expressed in the compound *mṛtyubandhu* (bound to death).

The Brāhmaṇa texts hold that dead persons, upon proper ritual cremation, would be taken by the god of fire (Agni) to the realm of the fathers and to Yama in the highest heaven, where, reunited with a glorious body, they would enjoy bliss (Johnson 1980, 115). But both the Upaniṣadic and Buddhist speculation replaced this naively optimistic view of lifespan, death and happy life in the hereafter with the notion of recurrent death (*punarmṛtyu*). Potentially endless life now became unremitting monotony and a dire fate. Though the metaphor of the wheel was retained, transmigration (*saṃsāra*) as the wheel of life became endless purgatory into which humans were repeatedly born to improve themselves in their ability to transcend the phenomena of life and death. Transcendence constituted the only end to endlessness.

The *Śvetāśvatara Upaniṣad* (1:6), for instance, refers to the great wheel of *brahman*, which is said to animate and envelop everything. A swan (symbolizing the individual self) rambles within that wheel erroneously imagining that it is the *pouvoir moteur* of the rotating wheel. Chapter two of the *Maitrī Upaniṣad* features a dialogue between certain bald-headed (Vālakhilya) sages and the sacrificing father of the universe (Kratu Prajāpati) on the embodiment of the self. Prajāpati explains how, as the immutable self (*ātman*), he enters the body to animate it in the manner of a potter activating his wheel.

Buddhism, the most influential non-Vedic soteriology, sought to transcend disease, decrepitude and death, which were identified as the chief features of the wheel of life (known technically as *bhavacakra*). Equated with becoming, the motif of the wheel of life inspired elaborate textual descriptions and visual images which were utilized by pious Buddhists for the purpose of meditating on the transient nature of life. In a grandiose manner, the *Majjhima Nikāya* equates the human life process with the wheel of suffering powered by the causative force of one's maturing deeds (*karmavipāka*) fostered upon the illusory substantiality of the body understood as the collection of five *skandhas* (see below). The *bhavacakra* unfolds itself from birth to death and from death to subsequent rebirth.[7] This illusion of life is sustained over twelve distinct co-arising causes (*nidānas*, note the numeric similarity with the twelve-spoked wheel in the *Ṛgveda*). Old age and death (*jarāmaraṇa*) constitute the last of the twelve causes determining the common destination of each future existence by rebirth, which is to travel again through the stage of "becoming" and through the process of decay (*jarā*) unto death.

The *karma*-formed and determined accumulations of passive impressions or residues (*saṃskāras*) act as the restarting impulse of the next life cycle. Thus, old age and death, ostensibly the last (twelfth) cause, is paradoxically far from that. The significance of death for life, like the significance of birth, lies in the fact that it has to be mediated again and again through old age, until the hidden self-winding mechanism of the maturing causality (*vipākahetu*), fueled by *karma* and pivoted on ignorance (*avidyā*), is destroyed by taking to the eightfold noble path advocated by the Buddha.[8]

The obsession with transmigration (*saṃsāra*) as the unending wheel of life at times becomes pathological in epic passages too. The *Mahābhārata* ("Strī Parva" 11:6.11, 12) develops an extended metaphor of the wheel of life (*saṃsāracakra*) wherein the old sage Vidura seeks to console his cousin—the blind King Dhṛtarāṣṭra—who is grieving the destruction of his one hundred sons (see below).

## Structure of the Body

### Vedic Perspective

A human being in the Vedic understanding may be viewed as a complex entity characterized by a structural unity of dynamic forces or elements (identified as *devatās* in AV 11:8.32) which are themselves cosmic in nature. But these forces are not blind mechanical forces; rather, they posses an inherent intelligence of different grades which favors the formation of functional units with inner and outer hierarchical structures, on both cosmic and individual levels. Thus, cosmos emerges out of chaos with the individual beings issuing out of the interplay of cosmic forces.

A hymn in the *Atharva Veda* (11:8) dealing with the cosmic forces identifies them with various physiological and psychological processes which dwell in the individual as cattle in their pens (11:8.32).[9] A person owes his/her individual existence to the highest principle in the universe and is identical with it. This latter is responsible for preserving the structural unity over a determinate period of time. *Ṛgveda* (10:16.4) calls it unborn (*aja*); it is not directly perceptible or evident in humans. Mind (*manas*), which directs and guides the phenomenal person, is linked with the unborn (*aja*) at a deeper level.[10] The individual's phenomenal being is further divided in two structural entities (bodies):

1. The gross physical body (*śarīra*, RV 6:25.4) comprised of material organs formed of the five cardinal elements which are returned to the cosmos upon the death of the individual (RV 10:16.1).[11] The gross body, however, is not the ultimate personality of the individual but the lowest visible level of existence which is mistakenly taken for the essential character of the human being.[12] In the classical Sanskrit literature the gross body is commonly understood to mean the perceivable human body which is subject to old age, decay and death. *Deha*, a synonym for *śarīra* and derived from the root *dih* meaning to plaster, fashion or mold, also has the extended meaning of body, form, shape, mass or bulk.
2. *Tanu* is the luminous likeness of the gross body or shape. It is the more subtle second unit which is comprised of mental faculties. It designates that luminous component in the individual with or without its gross body. Thus, when the fire god Agni is enjoined to burn the dead body (AV 18:3.71) but not to reduce it to ashes (RV 10:16.l), the term used in either case is *śarīra*. But when the departed one is asked to 'envelop' itself with a 'body', the word used is *tanu* (RV 1:188.2). It accordingly refers to the subjective form which cannot be burnt away like the physical sheath. As such, it is the Vedic expression for what was later to be called the subtle body (*liṅgaśarīra*).

The three distinct layers of the person (*aja*, *tanu* and *śarīra*) are said to correspond to the three cosmic levels of existence (*bhuḥ*, *bhuvar* and *svar*). Later developments envisaging multiple bodies, sheaths and layers (*śarīras*, *kośas* and *kāyas*) on the human as well as cosmic level, both in Hindu and Buddhist cosmologies, are elaborations of this basic Vedic notion of person and body (Werner 1978).

The *Chāndogya Upaniṣad* (8:4.1) stresses that self (*ātmā*, akin to the Vedic *aja*) is not cut down by the march of days and nights as are other transmigrating entities. At death the material component (*śarīra*) is dissolved into the five cardinal elements and the remaining structure is reconstituted in a finer, transfigured form. Depending upon personal merit, it goes to an appropriate world (*loka*) or ancestral or divine sphere (*pitṛyāna* or *devayāna*). In the context of prescribing the five important sacrifices to be performed by the orthodox, the *Śatapatha Brāhmaṇa* refers to the phenomenon of repeated death, which is only overcome by those who attain identity or community of nature with the ultimate reality (*brahman*, ŚB 11:5.6.9). These ideas of rebirth, of return and of successive lives whether on earth or elsewhere are expressed in different contexts in the *Ṛgveda* and were fully spelled out in the subsequent centuries.

The Vedic poets also made use of the sun as an image to evoke the meaning of the evolving, unfolding life as they understood it. The notion of cosmic law or order (*ṛta/dharma*), which in later centuries becomes an important hermeneutic principle underlying the ascription of meaning to different phases of life (see the discussion on the Dharma Śāstras in chapter one) is often equated with the solar passage. A Ṛgvedic hymn (1:152.6) to the gods Mitra/Varuṇa uses such solar imagery to penetrate semantically the dispensation of Mitra/Varuṇa, that is, the victory of order (*ṛta*) over chaos or disorder (*anṛta*).

Another solar deity Uṣas (dawn) is described as rising out of the implicit chaos of the night, spreading the light (of order) across the darkened universe. Dawn is followed by the sun whose ordered course across the firmament symbolizes the steady, orderly evolution and unfolding of the human lifespan across time. While the dawn suggests the inception and the development of order, the sun is its visible sign (see also Johnson 1980, 89).

The *Ṛgveda* (2:2.4) posits a close relation between the origin of life and the complex visible appearances embodied in the fire god (Agni) since both the principle of life (*hiraṇyagarbha*) and the fire god are made of gold. Both spring from the womb of the waters (RV 10:91.6). *Rasa*, an immanent force, exists in water and tends to be in its purest form in the sap of plants which are "the embryo of the waters" (AV 8:7.8). The sap of the Soma plant, in its strongest concentration, is the essence. The same substance is found in cow's milk, rain, dew, human seed and wine. All these things impart health, warding off sickness and old age.

A hymn from the *Atharva Veda* (10:2) describes the wonderful structure of man (*manuṣyamāhātmya*). The poet lists various body members and organs and asks which particular divinity (*devatā*) is responsible for the creation of which particular organ, and then provides the answers.[13] Another Atharvan hymn (11:8.13) declares that having poured together the whole mortal being, the gods entered it. Then sleep, weariness, dissolution, and deities named evil and old age entered the mortal body. *Brahman* (ultimate reality) was the last one to enter (11:8.23).

The meaning of life is made explicit by linking it with wind and breath both of which have movement as a common feature. Motion is the soul and essence of life. Wind is not just air; it is *moving* air. Breath is this moving air within living beings. Life is intrinsically movement, which fact is brought out in the fancy etymology of the embodied self (*puruṣa*) as that which constantly moves ahead (*puraḥ kuṣan*, see Pāṇini, *Uṇādi Sūtra* 4:74).

In the Upaniṣads, the principle of life (*hiraṇyagarbha*) is represented as the breath of life, indicating an interiorization of life experience and endowing it with an ontological basis. In sum, life in the Vedas is principally viewed as the biological fact of vital movement, growth and pre-reflective consciousness (*dehātmavāda*). In the Upaniṣads the embodied self ceases to be a passive participant in the cosmic process; rather, it becomes the focal point. Life now means the vital consciousness of self.[14] Life (*prāṇa*) is not that which gives form, but that which underlies existence (*prāṇātmavāda*). According to Panikkar (1977, 208–210), this *prāṇātmavāda* of the Upaniṣads supplants the *dehātmavāda*, the interpretation of the self in terms of the body, which was such a dominant theme in the Brāhmaṇas.[15]

The *Garbhopaniṣad*, of unknown date, also provides a fancy etymology of the gross body (*śarīra*) in physiological and ritual terms. The sage Pippalāda explains in verse 4 that because the three fires are located in the body, it is known as *śarīra*.[16] The text then goes on to elaborate a metaphorical description of the body and its functions in terms of the Vedic sacrifice (*yajña*) and its performance by fabricating numerous homologies. The body, for instance, is said to function like the sacrificial altar (*yajñavaṭī*).

As the substratum par excellence for the performances of sacraments (*yāgabhūmi*), it is one's sacred duty to keep the body healthy, happy and holy (ritually pure). This attitude of sacralizing the body is also apparent in the *Chāndogya Upaniṣad,* which metaphorizes human life as a sacrifice (*puruṣayajña*) and homologizes the three life stages (*āśramas*) with three different types of sacrifices to be performed during life.[17]

The same theme is also picked up in the *Mahānārāyaṇa* (verse 5) and *Prāṇāgnihotra* (verse 6) Upaniṣads. The centrality of the person and its body to the concept of sacrifice, which is deemed to be the integral human act, is once again brought out with imaginative metaphors. Each sacred duty of life coinciding with the changing age, is a sacrificial act. Death, the final act of life, is also the supreme purification as well as the ultimate human sacrifice (*śarīrayajña*). Panikkar (1977, 388–390) has argued that because of this identification of sacrifice with "man" (*puruṣayajña*), certain Vedic texts speak of human life in terms of a constitutive debt (*ṛṇa*), a kind of moral obligation or duty that man has to discharge when he sacrifices. This sacrifice is an act which entails the fulfillment of man's being. The *Manu Smṛti,* too, envisages it as the ideal to be striven for, that is, the body is to be so rendered as to be infused with the ultimate reality (*brāhmīyam krīyate tanuḥ,* MS 2:28).

### *Buddhist Critique*

In order to understand the distinct sense in which the human being grows old and ages in the Buddhist view, consideration must be given to the unique Buddhist ideas about the human body. These are significantly different from the earlier Vedic view. Although the *Sutta Piṭaka* and the *Vinaya Piṭaka* continued to use for didactic purposes the conventional Vedic terms to express their own views on being, person, mind, body and so forth, the later *Abhidhamma Piṭaka* shied away from utilizing them. Instead, it promoted new and typically Buddhist terms consistent with the fundamental Buddhist doctrine that there is no identifiable self within the body existing over a period of time. There are only physical and mental phenomena of existence (*nāma* and *rūpa*), which the ignorant construe as distinct units of personality and corporeality. The concept of the body, therefore, is to be admitted only provisionally, and for heuristical purposes. The Buddhist view of the body, its functioning, aging and the eventual dissociation, accordingly, is affirmed in terms of elements (*dharma*), mass or aggregate of elements (*skandha*), base of cognition (*āyatana*) and element-potential (*dhātu*). *Kāya* is the technical and global term representing these various units that make up the human body (see the chapters entitled "Dhammasaṅgaṇi" and "Vibhaṅga" of the *Abhidhammapiṭaka*).

A manual of metaphysics composed by Vasubandhu (*Abhidharmakośa*) expounds in a systematic manner the early Buddhist understanding of the body and its processes. "Lokanirdeśa" is a chapter devoted to clarifying the Buddhist idea that the universe is composed of innumerable worlds (*lokas*) and is inhabited by beings alternating between the three spheres of existence. The chapter entitled "Karmanirdeśa" deals with the doctrine of *karma* (see below) and its relation to the body and its processes.

The "Dhātuvibhaṅga Sutta" of the *Majjhima Nikāya* (3:237–247) posits the individual to be made of six aggregates (*khandhas*): earth, water, fire, air, space and consciousness. At any given time the person is but a temporary combination of these aggregates, for the *khandas* are subject to continual change.

The "Jarāsutta" in the *Aṭṭhakavagga* of the *Sutta Nipāta* (804), too, laments over this state of affairs in the following words:

> Short indeed is this life. Within a hundred years one dies, and if any one lives longer, then he dies of old age. A person does not remain the same for any two consecutive instants.

In this context Vasubandhu refers to the *Saṃyutta Nikāya* (13:21) and calls the preceding instant the "burden", and the following one the "carrier of the burden" (see Chaudhuri 1976, 230).

The "Khanda Saṃyutta" of the *Saṃyutta Nikāya* is more unequivocal and forthright on this premise:

> Those who are unskilled in the noble *Dhamma* wrongly conceive, "the body is mine", "consciousness is mine". He who clings to the *Khandas* is Māra's bondsman. Sorrow and despair arise in the body made of the *Khandas* owing to their changeful and unstable nature (SN 3:1–188).

Similar ideas are expounded in the "Rādha Saṃyutta" (3:188–201) and the "Diṭṭhi Saṃyutta" (3:202–224) of the *Saṃyutta Nikāya*, which are then clothed in metaphysical propositions in the "Dharma Skandha" of the *Abhidharma*. The early Buddhist view of the body and its lifespan then is based on the dual axioms that everything is both impermanent and suffering (*sabbam aniccam, sabbam dukkham*).[18]

It is further elaborated with reference to the triple nature of pain in the *"Saḷāyatana Saṃyutta."*

1. Pain gives rise to further pain, for instance, the direct contact of the senses with the sense objects causes an immediate unpleasant feeling. When the skin is cut, even the crudest mind becomes aware of this form of suffering (*dukkha dukkhatā*).
2. The second category of pain presents a contrasting phenomenon to the ordinary mind where even pleasurable feelings transform into suffering on account of their inherent transitoriness (*pariṇāma dukkhatā*).
3. This category of pain originates in the concept of *karma*. Actions are ever in search of opportunity—like a core of flame hidden under ashes that catches fire whenever it comes into contact with inflammable material (*saṃsāra dukkhatā*) (SN 4:1–204).

Being subject to this triple pain, the human body can never be the abode of anything but evil. A final deliverance from all bodily life, present and to come, is the greatest of all blessings. The body is the sphere of suffering and the origin of suffering. Subjectively understood, suffering is desire (*tāṇhā*). Objectively, it lies in embodiment and matter. The Buddha systematized his response to the suffering of old age by a set of presuppositions, which cannot be justified on logical or rational grounds.

By identifying old age with suffering, instead of with the sources of suffering, the Buddha merely revealed his intense anxiety and disgust with respect to the phenomenal existence of the person and his/her life experiences, including aging. The disgust with the perishable nature and the aging of the body (*nibbidā*) as set forth in the "Vijaya Sutta" (11) in the *Uragavagga* of the *Sutta Nipāta* also is a reflection on the worthlessness of the human body:

> The body which is put together with bones and sinews, plastered with membranes and flesh, and covered with skin, is not seen as it really is. In nine streams impurity flows always from it; from the eye the eye-excrement, from the ear the ear-excrement . . . And when it lies dead, swollen and livid, discarded in the cemetery, relatives do not care [for it].
>
> The *bhikkhu* (monk) possessed of understanding in this world, having listened to Buddha's words, certainly knows it [the body] thoroughly, for he sees it as it really is.
>
> As this [living body is] so is that [dead one]; as this is so that

> [will be]; let one put away desire for the body, as to its interior and as to its exterior. (Fausböll 1973, 32–33).

Both Hindus and Buddhists believed in the existence of a unique type of life between death and the impending rebirth. The theory of such an intermediate state (*antarābhava*), however, was a disputed point among the early Buddhist sects (Wayman 1984, 251). In the third chapter of his own commentary on the *Abhidharmakośa*, Vasubandhu argues that an intermediate state (*antarābhava*) separates death and rebirth, but he denies that it is the same as the self (*ātman*) of the brahminical system. The process leading to rebirth is explained by him in a thoroughly oedipal manner:

> Driven by *karma*, this *antarābhava* goes to the place where rebirth is to take place. Possessing a divine eye thanks to its *karma*, it looks for its future parents in the act of sexual intercourse. If male, it is smitten with desire for its potential mother and vice versa. Stirred up by this passion, it attaches itself where the sex organs of the couple are united. Thus does the body composed of the five *khandha* arise in the womb. One's appearance, constitution and the length of life are determined by the combined result of the *karma* done in the past (McDermott 1980).

Though post-canonical, the *Milindapañha* (ca. 100 CE) is still authoritative and throws important light on the Buddhist understanding of the body and its aging. Dilemma 57 in this text poses a question that is of great gerontological significance: When king Milinda asks, "Why have those who attain *nirvāṇa* (Arhants) no power over the body?", Nāgasena replies that there is one kind of pain only, (*dukkha dukkhatā* possibly? see above) which the liberated one (Arhant) suffers. He/she has no control over bodily pain and the ten qualities of the body: cold, heat, hunger, thirst, fatigue, sleep, old age, disease, death and voiding excreta. But he/she can train and master his/her mental processes.

This exchange suggests the presence of a realistic undercurrent in Buddhism which recognizes and accepts the inevitability of the aging process and the finitude of the human body.[19] To that extent Nāgasena's ideas closely echo the basic Āyurvedic views on aging when he declares:

> Just as the bull never forsakes its own stall, just so . . . should a strenuous *Bhikshu* (monk), earnest in effort, never abandon

> his body on the ground that its nature is only the decomposition (aging) of that which is impermanent (dilemma 38, Rhys-Davids 1969).

Dilemma 80 describes the nature of *nirvāṇa* in quaint terms which, nonetheless, are of gerontological relevance:

> As medicine puts an end to diseases, so does *nirvāṇa* put an end to grief . . . as food is the support of the life of all beings, so is *nirvāṇa* when it has been realized, the support of life, for it puts an end to old age and death (RhysDavids 1969).

Being a Buddhist text the *Milindapañha* duly records its disgust and contempt toward the body. But this is accomplished in a restrained and balanced manner without sacrificing or compromising the underlying doctrinal or soteriological motivation. This is clear from the following exchange between King Milinda and Nāgasena the Elder. The context is the Buddhist dogma that the body is to be regarded as an impure thing and foul (*pūtikāya*):

| | |
|---|---|
| Milinda: | Is the body, Nāgasena, dear to you recluses? |
| Nāgasena: | No they love not the body. |
| Milinda: | Then why do you nourish it and lavish attention upon it? |
| Nāgasena: | Is the wound [suffered in a battle] dear to you that you treat it so tenderly and lavish attention upon it? |
| Milinda: | No, [the wound is dressed so that] the flesh may grow again. |
| Nāgasena: | Just so, with the recluses and the body. Without clinging to it do they bear about the body for the sake of righteousness of life (RhysDavids 1969, 1:115). |

From the gerontological perspective, then, the basic credo of early Buddhism may be restated thus:

> To be, in fact, is to become and age, and to age is suffering. We are never free of temporality and its bodily analogue, aging, which constantly reminds us of our ultimate condition: death. Joyous moments of life are but beguiling shadows of inevitable old age and its accomplices: disease and death. Old

> age and the consequent bodily suffering is the destiny of the human beings in this world.

The "Raṭṭapāla Suttanta"[20] of the *Majjhima Nikāya* links this suffering with other losses incurred by the human beings:

> Misfortunes arising out of old age (*jarāhāni*), fatal disease (*vyādhihāni*), loss of fortune (*bhogahāni*) and loss of relatives (*jñātihāni*) impel one to adopt monastic life (MN 2:54–74).

The second noble truth affirms that there is a cause of suffering (identified with aging). By stopping the operation of the causes and conditions that generate suffering, it is possible, as affirmed in the third noble truth, to uproot suffering. The fourth noble truth delineates the method and technique one has to adopt in order to achieve complete freedom from suffering.

The Buddha's replacement of the Vedic notion of being by that of becoming and his assertion that the universe is but an uninterrupted and unmanifest stream of momentary particulars prompted his followers to elaborate a systematic technique of eliminating suffering understood as decrepitude-disease-death (*jarā-vyādhi-maraṇa*) based on the doctrine of momentariness (*kṣaṇikavāda,* see below). Thus, the idea of emancipation from the suffering of old age in early Buddhism is that this suffering is endured both by the body and the mind. The suffering will cease when both cease to be. Both must be blown out (*nivṛta*); anything less will not lead to *nirvāṇa*. The suffering of old age—which is real and coterminous with dependently originated existence and lived experience is to be eliminated by means of a meditative self-effort (*dhyāna*) (Pande 1974, 186).

*Hindu Response*

The Āyurvedic exposition of the body, which may be taken as the representative Hindu response on the subject under discussion, unfolds within the parameters of the ideas derived from the Sāṃkhya, Vaiśeṣika and Vedānta presuppositions of the physical universe. Following Larson (1987) these may be stated as follows:

1. The genetic body born of father and mother is a collection of gross physical constituents, either as atoms (*aṇu*), substance (*dravya*) or gross elements (*mahābhūtas*).

2. The mind or psychic apparatus is made of the same stuff as the body though a subtle manifestation of the gross elements (*tanmātrās*).
3. This psychic apparatus along with the subtle body made of karmic reservoir (*karmāśaya*) and residual dispositions (*vāsanā*) and so forth, transmigrates from one life to the next. Though it animates the physical body, it is construed to be quite distinct from genetic inheritance. That is, in any given life an organism is determined *both* by its genetic, physical heritage and by its psychic heritage.
4. Ontologically, both the physical body and the psychic apparatus evolve out of the threefold subtle matter understood either as *guṇa* (in the Sāṃkhya scheme of things) or *dravya* (in the Vaiśeṣika scheme of things).

The *Caraka Saṃhitā* (sū. 1:41) states that Āyurveda as the science of life is concerned with defining the happy and unhappy conditions of life and its span. Life (*āyus*) is a productive and dynamic aggregate of sense organs, mind, body and self, held together and maintained over a definite period of time by the power of *karmas* performed in the previous lives (Ca.sū. 1:42; śā. 1:53). By nature, human life is unstable and volatile since the body, its principle component, decays with every passing moment. This evanescent characteristic of the body, and therefore of human life, is reflected in the different synonyms given to it.

Life is known as *dhāri* (support) because it is supported and sustained by the three humors (see below). *Jīvita* (lively) is another synonym for life because it is animated by the vital principle (*prāṇa*). 'Ever moving forward' (*nityaga*) and 'bound to other bodies or *karmas*' (*anubandha*) are two unusual synonyms of life, found only in the medical texts.[21] Made up of the five cardinal elements, the body also serves as an abode of enjoyments and/or suffering produced by actions. It is formally defined as that which is subject to decay and degeneration (*śarīra*). Because of the evanescent characteristic of its constituent elements (*nityaga dravya*) the body undergoes mutations at every moment.[22] It can only digest, assimilate and absorb those nourishing articles of food which share the body's physico-chemical composition (*samayogavāhi*).

The modifications (*vikāra*) of the body are attributable to imbalance among the three humors. When dynamic balance is held between them, it is in a state of good health (*prakṛti*). But modifications, which equally affect the body and the mind, lead to pain (Ca.sū. 9:4). Because of its mutating nature, the body of childhood is different from that of middle age. Nothing about the body ever remains the same; everything, in fact, is in constant flux. The body is produced anew every moment, yet the similarity with the old body gives the apparent impression of persistance (Ca.śā. 1:46).[23]

The day-to-day normal functioning of the body and its maintenance and welfare as well as pathological changes (e.g. aging) culminating in death are explained in Āyurveda in terms of the concepts of bodily humors (*doṣas*) and elements (*dhātus*). The humoral theory of Āyurveda postulates the existence of three humors in the body which are the three supportive as well as pathogenic factors responsible for the sustenance, ill health, decay and death of the person. They are known as *kapha* (derived from the cardinal element water), *pitta* (derived from the cardinal element fire) and *vāta* (derived from the cardinal element wind), and are recruited from the food eaten, digested and assimilated. Thus, they sustain life and its smooth functioning.

The bodily humors have their homologue at the cosmic level. The relation between the macrocosmic and the microcosmic aspects of the three humors is posited by Suśruta in the following manner:

> Just as the moon, sun and wind uphold the world by their action of release, absorption and dissemination respectively, even so do *kapha*, *pitta* and *vāta* act with regard to the body.[24]

The humors are in continuous flux, possessing definite circadian rhythms. Under the influence of the yearly solar cycle (divided in six seasons) and the monthly lunar cycle, the relative proportions of the three humors constantly undergo decrease or increase. They may also remain in a state of dynamic equilibrium (Ca.sū. 17:114). The humor of wind, for instance, prevails at the end of the day, in the rainy season and in old age (Ca.ci. 30:308–311). Normally the variations in the relative strengths of the humors remain within tolerable limits, but under the influence of culpable insight (*prajñāparādha*), seasonal variations (*pariṇāma*) and uncongenial interaction between senses and the sense objects (*asātmyendriyārtha*), they cross the limits, giving rise to pathogenesis that includes premature as well as timely aging (Ca.vi. 6:6).

The humors are so called because they are liable to become morbid (the equivalent Sanskrit verb is *duṣ* from which the substantive *doṣa* is derived) by the wrong kind of nutrition, behavior, seasonal variation, or by internal factors such as emotions or restraint of natural urges. Once rendered morbid, they, in turn, vitiate the seven bodily elements (*dhātus*). In their balanced state the humors are also known as the supporting elements of the body (*dhātus*), but for the sake of convenience of exposition and uniformity of application, they are separately identified as humors (*doṣas*) even in that benevolent condition.

The relative prevalence of a particular humor in the body provides important clues to the typology of the human constitution. Thus, due to the stabilizing property of the humor of water (*kaphadoṣa*), the subject dominated by it is immune to sudden changes of mood and pathological conditions and, consequently, ages relatively slowly (*mandajaraḥ*, Su.ci. 31:56; Ca.vi. 8:111). Due to the heat inherent in the humor of fire, (*pittadoṣa*), the subject dominated by it is prone to premature aging and wrinkles (Ca.vi. 8:97[1]). On account of the swiftness of the humor of wind (*vātadoṣa*), the subject dominated by it is liable to sudden variations of moods and pathological changes (Ca.vi. 8:98).[25]

The Āyurveda also posits the human being as the product of a nutrient fluid (*rasa*) generated by the activities of the three humors. One must, therefore, preserve it with care and effort.[26] The postulation of the concept of a nutrient fluid thus serves as yet another meaningful link between the individual and the cosmos. It is also seen as the first among the seven manifest elements (*dhātus*) of the body, namely:

nutrient fluid (*rasa*)
blood (*rakta*)
flesh (*māṃsa*)
fat (*medas*)
bones (*asthi*)
marrow (*majjan*)
semen (*śukra*)

These constituents evolve progressively one out of the other, starting with the nutrient fluid. While homologous environmental factors maintain health; any variation in them adversely affects health.[27] Some of the more important among these factors include:

Time or climatic seasonal environment (*kāla*).
Intelligence (*buddhi*).

Sense objects including items of diet and pleasures of senses (*indriyārtha*).

According to another important interpretation of Āyurvedic theory based on the philosophy of Sāṃkhya-Yoga, life is also a coproduct of the conscious monad or self (*puruṣa*),[28] and the primordial materiality (*prakṛti*) made up of three material constituents (*guṇas*):

The subtle matter of pure thought (*sattva*).
The kinetic matter of pure energy (*rajas*).
The reified matter of inertia (*tamas*).

The *puruṣas* are ubiquitous (Ca.śā. 1:80) and conscious monads (Ca.śā. 1:76) with each occupying a separate gross body (Ca.śā. 1:81). But there is only one primordial, unconscious and material substance (*prakṛti*). Both are without a beginning and end (Ca.śā. 1:82). Influenced by the metaphysics of the Vedānta, the *Caraka Saṃhitā* also states that the individual is an epitome of the macrocosm and ultimate reality (*brahman*), which, in turn, is reflected in the empirical self (Ca.śā. 1:155; 4:13).[29] Also known as *ātmā*, the *puruṣa* is changeless, transcendent and becomes the cause of consciousness when brought in contact with the mind, the senses and the sense objects. But despite this association with the perishable body, the self itself remains untouched by all pathogenicity, [including aging] (Ca.sū. 1:56 and Cakrapāṇi's gloss on it).

The three material constituents (*guṇas*) dialectically interact with each other to generate the manifest world of subjective experience and objective existence. Objectively, the physical body evolves out of the five generic essences (*tanmātrās*) which are present throughout nature and which are transmitted genetically though the semen (*śukra*) of the father and the ovum and blood (*śoṇita*) of the mother. This understanding of human life serves the purpose of the psychic self (*ātman*) as well as a composite biological image of human being. Suśruta (Su.śā. 1.12) designates this composite product as the acting self (*bhūtagrāma*) which is the locus of medical and geriatric treatment. Āyurveda lays great stress on the embodied nature of the self claiming that the body is the very foundation of the human being (Ca.ni. 6:6). The desire for a long and healthy life is the first among the three basic desires (*eṣaṇās*) entertained by human beings (Ca.sū. 11:4). Before everything else, therefore, one should take care of the body, for in the absence of the body, there is total extinction of all that characterizes embodied beings (Ca.ni. 6:7).

The process of the embodiment of the self begins with the embryo and fetus which develops as a result of the successful union of semen and menstrual blood (*śoṇita, ārtava* and *rakta*). The "Śārīra Sthāna" section (chapters three and four) of the *Caraka Saṃhitā* describes in detail how the fertilization of the egg by the sperm sets in motion the development of the fetus. The fetus is said to be self-born (*ātmajaḥ*) and is known as *antarātman* (the equivalent of Vedic *tanu*) which subsequently becomes known as *jīva*.[30] The embodied self, as noted above, is eternal, without diseases, nonaging, immortal, nonperishable, nondivisible, universal, unmanifest, undying and without a beginning. Having entered the womb, it unites with the sperm and blood and generates itself through fertilization. Unborn (*ajāta*), the self generates the unborn fetus (*ajāto hyayam ajātam garbham janayati*).

The same fetus, with the force of time 'acquires' the various phases such as child, youth and old age (Ca.śā. 3:8) without undergoing real modifications.[31] The fetus is constituted by the modifications (*vikāras*) of the five elements: ether, wind, fire, water, earth. Consciousness (*cetanā*) serves as the sixth component Ca.śā. 4:6).[32]

A similar account of the genesis of the human body is also provided in early Buddhism in the "Yakkha Saṃyutta" of the *Saṃyutta Nikāya* wherein a celestial being (*yakṣa*) named Indaka observes:

> Form is not the living principle in the opinion of the Buddhas. How does the soul possess this body? Whence to soul does come the lump of bones and liver? How does this soul hide within the body? (SN 1:206–215).

The Buddha's explanation is that first the fetus in the primary stage of development (*kalāla*) emerges, and then undergoes successive developmental stages (such as *abbuda*, see Barua 1970, 164). In a similar vein Manu (MS 6:76, 77) also puts forth his understanding of the characteristics of the human body (*dehasvarūpa*). Generally his explanation closely follows the familiar ideas detailed in the Āyurvedic texts. Manu's intention, however, is to direct the aging person's energies to the cultivation of dispassion with respect to the transmigrating mundane world (*saṃsāra*) and the realization of liberation (*mokṣa*).

The body and mind are the abodes of diseases as well as of health. Right contact or interaction between the four factors, that is, time, mind, senses and sense objects, is responsible for good health and well being (Ca.sū. 1:54–55). Whereas the three humors in their morbid condition constitute the pathological factors at the somatic level, passion and delusion (*rajas* and *tamas*, see above) are the complex of pathogenic factors at the psychic level (Ca.sū. 1:57). When there exists erroneous, inadequate or excessive interaction among the above four factors, the result is ill health (psychic or somatic) and premature aging (Ca.sū. 1:54, see Cakrapāṇi's gloss). This imbalance in the elements of the body (*dhātuvaiṣamya*) also results from errors of regimen with reference to personal hygiene. It can, therefore, be rectified by careful observation of the norms of proper health and ethical behavior (*svasthavṛtta* and *sadvṛtta*). If the condition of the imbalance is allowed to progress further, it may lead to the vitiation of the humors.

Perhaps influenced by the Buddhist tendency to regard the body as an impediment to spiritual progress, the moral digests such as the *Viṣṇu Smṛti* (96:43–55) or the *Manu Smṛti* (6:76, 77) insist that one must recognize that this human frame consisting of seven constituents covered with a skin and having a foul smell is a receptacle of impure substances. Though surrounded by a hundred pleasures and though carefully sustained and nourished, the human body is subject to change (aging) and destruction. Covered by six skin layers, the body is kept together by three hundred and sixty bones.[33]

The description of the genesis, development and death of the body in the *Yājñavalkya Smṛti* (3:3.85–106) is considerably more vivid and detailed and provides a long account of the bodily functions also influenced by yogic and Āyurvedic ideas. Vijñāneśvara's gloss, *Mitākṣarā*, on these passages reminds us that the knowledge of the bodily functions and organs is for the purpose of cultivating dispassion. Furthermore, this knowledge is for the sake of discriminating the ephemeral from the eternal and to facilitate spiritual liberation. One particular passage strongly reminiscent of the *Caraka Saṃhitā* puts it succinctly:

> The beginningless self does not get embodied (*saṃbhūti*). It is the self within (*antarātman*) which occupies and pervades the gross body (*śarīra*) through the relation of inherence (*samavāya*). This comes about due to delusion, desire, repulsion and one's own *karma*. The body is ripened (*vipākaḥ*) by the power of the deeds committed in previous lives. Upon

> dissolution at death, it is reborn here on earth or elsewhere on account of the process of becoming (*bhava*, YSm 3:3.133).

The human lifespan is not determinate because otherwise none would seek longevity by Āyurvedic means such as the rejuvenation therapy (*rasāyana*). There is timely or untimely death, because there exist also timely and untimely dietary habits or leisure activities. The epic literature, too, reflects the familiar classical ideas of the embodiment of the self and the different structures and layers of the visible body enveloping it. Thus, in a dialogue in the *Mahābhārata* featuring the brahmin named Kaśyapa and a perfect master (Siddha) the former wants to know how the body disintegrates, how it is born and how it obtains release from worldly existence (*saṃsāra*, 14:17.2–3). The perfect master, in a long-winded reply (14:17.6–39), reproduces the standard explanation of the embodied self as elaborated in the medical texts (Ca. "Śārīra Sthāna"). Of a similar vein is Bhīṣma's discourse on the relationship between one's deeds and the condition of the body (MB 12:194).

In the *Rāmāyaṇa*, Rāma consoles his distressed younger brother Bharata—who is trying to persuade Rāma to abandon his exile in the forest and return to the capital city of Ayodhyā—by discoursing on the general nature of human life and body which has death for its substratum. Everything, philosophizes Rāma, ends in loss and falls to pieces. Just as a house, supported by strong pillars becomes old and falls down, so people consigned to old age and death fall down. Just as a reservoir of water is quickly dried up in summer, so are the lives of all creatures consumed by the march of days and nights (Rām 2:98.18, 19).

However, alongside statements of this kind are also to be found pronounced positive affirmations. The *Yogavāsiṣṭha* insists that to the spiritually blind the body is the source of suffering and pain; but for the sage it is the source of unimaginable bliss (4:23.2, 18).

## *Phases of Aging*

In Vedic society, when life expectancy was relatively short, the average lifespan was conceptually divided into two phases only: youth and old age (see chapter one). This primitive dichotomy is also discernible, in some measure, in Vedic language and literature. As the lifespan continued to increase with developing technology and improved health-care, it came to be further divided into three, four, seven or even ten phases. Such a restructuring of the lifespan in multiple phases is pictorially described and recorded through various symbols, metaphors and myths by identifying the phases of life with three sacrifices, four seasons, five cardinal elements etc. A hymn from the *Atharva Veda* (5:28.3), for instance, posits three phases of life—childhood (*bālya*), youth (*tārunya*) and old age (*vārdhakya*)[34] which are next said to be symbolized by the three strands of the sacred thread (*yajñopavita*) worn by all initiated males. Just as its three strands are made of the same material, says the hymn, so are the three life stages governed by one principle of righteousness (*dharma*) and animated by *one* being that is identical. Later Dharma Śāstra and medical texts replace this metaphysical visualization of the phases of life with a temporal and biological understanding. The *Caraka Saṃhitā* defines the age of a person as a condition of the body, which, in turn, is a function of the measure of time.[35] It envisages the typical male lifespan in three phases:

1. *bālyam:* the phase stretching between the ages of sixteen and thirty and dominated by the humor of water. The bodily constituents and vigor are not fully developed which keeps the body tender but unable to bear hardships. It is also characterized by the continued physical growth and maturity.
2. *madhya:* This middle phase is dominated by the humor of fire and runs up to the age of sixty. It is characterized by the full and balanced development of all the seven bodily constituents endowing the adult male with vigor, energy, manliness, heroism and the capacity to absorb, retain, recall and express knowledge.[36]
3. *jīrṇa:* This is the final phase, which in theory lasts until the age of one hundred and is dominated by the humor of wind. It is characterized by the depletion and/or loss of the developed bodily constituents, vigor of the sense organs, power, energy, heroism and knowledge.[37]

The lifespan and its phases, thus, are predicated on the basis of the bodily constitution and other signs of life (*āyurlakṣaṇas*) as outlined in Ca.vi. 8:95 ff. The condition of the semen and blood (ovum), fetal development through time, the condition of the parent in sickness and his/her diet and daily routine, seasonal modifications in the cardinal elements—all these are deemed to be the functions of the fetal constitution, which, in turn, is determined by the predominance of one or the other of the following—1) the three humors, 2) birth in the given clan, 3) habitat, and 4) time.

These factors render people genetically susceptible to a varying rate and pattern of aging with various environmental, nutritive, social and cultural conditions also acting as the predisposing factors. The basic constitutional disposition (*dehaprakṛti*) of each body in the first instance is determined by the respective constitutional peculiarities of the parents at the time of the fertilization of the egg by the sperm. The relative dominance of one of the three humors is determined by different factors in operation at the time of fertilization. These factors include:

1. The nature of the ovum and sperm.
2. The time and season.
3. Age of the parents.
4. Habitation.
5. The conduct, habits, and diet of the parents.

Individuals whose constitutional disposition is dominated by the humor of wind tend to possess low vitality, bear a smaller number of children, age faster and have a shorter lifespan. They are also prone to quick pathological changes in mood (Ca.vi. 8:98). When the humor of fire dominates the disposition, the individual tends to possess moderate vitality and medium lifespan. But the thermogenic nature contributes to premature grey hair, bald head and the appearance of folds of skin at various places on the body at a relatively early age (Ca.vi. 8:97). But individuals with a dominant disposition of the humor of water are gifted with good vitality, enduring capacity and long lifespan. Pathological changes and variations of mood are slower to develop in these individuals. Those who also possess the essence of all the bodily elements (*dhātus*), will age at a much slower rate (*mandajarasaḥ* Ca.vi. 8:111).

Caraka next argues that the temporal factor that brings about aging and death is also responsible for generating certain diseases specific to old age (Ca.śā. 1:115). These diseases are natural (*svabhāvaja*) and as such irremediable. Cakrapāṇi's gloss on this verse explains that natural diseases manifest themselves at appointed hours (*kālaja*). They are caused by old age or appear as premonitory conditions of death (*jarāmṛtyunimittajāḥ*) depending upon the normal span of life in a given age (*yuga*).

The natural manifestation of old age is irremediable in the sense that it cannot be treated by any therapy except the rejuvenation therapy, which does not, however, *cure* old age (Ca.vi. 3:32, and Cakrapāṇi's gloss on it). It merely serves as a prophylactic measure, delaying the onset of old age. Anyone who is familiar with the role that astrology plays in the life of the Hindus will not be surprised to learn that the phases of life are also controlled and superintended by the planets.[38]

Varāhamihira (ca. 600 CE) in his *Bṛhat Saṃhitā*, a work on astrology, rules that the phases of life in persons under the protection of the Moon, Mars, Mercury, Venus, Jupiter, the Sun and Saturn are said to be respectively those of:

Breast-fed baby: first year
Child: 2–3 years
Innocence (*vratasthita*): 4–12 years
Youth: 13–32 years
Middle age: 33–50 years
Old age: 51–70 years
Very old age: 71–120 years.[39]

*Spreading of Old Age*

In one short sentence Suśruta graphically describes the damage caused to the body and mind by the aging process. After the age of seventy, with each passing day, the seven body elements, sense organs, energy, vitality and enthusiasm become debilitated giving rise to wrinkled skin, grey hair, baldness, chronic cough and hard breathing. The aging individual's capacity to perform all kinds of functions is reduced progressively. Eventually, the person goes under, like an old home giving in after a heavy downpour (sū. 35:29).

Both Caraka and Suśruta provide a detailed account of how any disease, once it has found a home in the body, spreads through it gradually in clearly identifiable stages, eventually killing the body. Since they also regard aging and old age as a disease, it is possible to provide an analogical account of the aging process as it spreads to different parts of the body. The essential stages involved in this process may be presented as follows:

1. Accumulation (*samuccaya*) of the humor of wind. As explained earlier, the process of aging originates in the imbalance among the three humors and the resultant accumulation of the humor of wind. This is the first sign and symptom of aging.

2. Vitiation (*prakopa*). With the abnormal increase in its proportion, the humor of wind changes from its benevolent aspect present in the state of balance into a malevolent one on account of the imbalance. According to Caraka, this deranged humor stops circulating through its normal channels, forcing itself into the wrong ones (ci. 28:12).
3. Diffusion (*prasara*). The deranged humor begins to spread out of the areas of the body it had first struck into those immediately adjoining, picking up speed in the process.
4. Localization (*sthānasaṃśraya*). With increasing rapidity, old age undermines the entire organ or the physiological system which is liable and prone to aging. As Caraka puts it in a colorful metaphor, the humor of wind pours down its vitiating element wherever it finds a congenial site and causes disorder there just as a cloud showers down rain on a favorable spot (ci. 15:37). It strikes first in the urinary bladder, followed by rectum, waist, thighs and colon, in that order (Ca.sū. 20:8). According to Caraka these particular parts of the body are likely to age at a faster rate than others betraying the tell-tale signs of old age earlier than elsewhere in the body.
5. Manifestation (*vyakti*). Soon the calling card left by the process of aging becomes manifest and visible for all to see. The aging individual becomes aware and convinced of old age only when others confirm the signs of old age.
6. Rupture (*bheda*). The aging process effectively mediates between life and death. It begins the moment the body, sense organs, mind and the self are brought together as a life (*āyus*) and culminates in death whereby the composite being that had been held together by the factors of time, deed, desire, and nutrition is dissolved (Su.sū. 21:18–36).

In the classical literature, the spreading of the visible signs of old age is said to begin with the forehead. In one of the plays of Śūdraka entitled *Mṛchhakaṭika* (3:8), the hero Cārudatta, describing the phenomenon of sleep compares its onset to the process of aging:

> Here is sleep, approaching me as it were, from my forehead, overwhelming my eyes. Invisible in form and elusive, it gains strength like *old age*, overcoming the human vitality of a person.[40]

This simile is appropriate since it is believed that the first dozing impulse is felt in the region of the forehead. Similarly, old age is metaphorically said to approach a person from the forehead, because the sign of grey hair, its forerunner, is first observed on the temples. This imagery is also discernible in a verse from the *Subhāṣita Ratnabhāṇḍāgāra* (13):

> Old age, the messenger of death, approaching at the root of the ears says. . . .[41]

Kālidāsa resorts to similar imagery to describe how old age, as if apprehensive of Kaikeyī's evil designs, approached the aging King Daśaratha from behind his ear in the guise of grey [hair] and whispered, "crown Rāma [as the next king]" (*Raghuvaṃśa* 12:2).[42]

## *Signs and Symptoms of Aging*

Aging is a slow and continuous process of physical and psychological decline and deterioration in strength, initiative and energy. It has determinate incubation periods as well as specific modes of spread, manifestation and localization in every part of the body (*kriyākāla*). But aging occurs ever so imperceptibly that humans are convinced of the truth of old age only when they discover its manifest and visible signs and symptoms on the body and in the failing faculties of the mind. Caraka documents these changes in accurate and consummate detail:

> Bald head, receding hair line, greying hair, wrinkles on the face, emaciated, lean body, slowing down of the reflexes, debilitated vital physiological functions . . . (Ca.ci. 18:24–39, and Cakrapāṇi's gloss on them, Ca.Ni. 6:8).

Caraka judges (ci. 1:1.4 and Cakrapāṇi's gloss) old age to be a natural disorder or disease (*svābhāvika vyādhi*) which is responsible, among other things, for the vitiation of the semen (ci. 30:134–137) with the result that the aging man becomes aware of his flaccid sex organ and depleting semen (ci. 30:153–157) so that in advanced old age he becomes impotent (ci. 30:176–180).[43] The *Vāyu Purāṇa* (31:26.40, 45), with reference to the Yayāti-Puru dialogue (see chapter five), also describes old age as the destroyer of libido and enjoyments as well as of good complexion and beauty.

Such disorders of geriatric nature invariably accompany aging which the medical texts trace to the impairment of the seven bodily constituents. It is explained that with advancing age, first the nutrient fluid (*rasa*) becomes afflicted, with the result that blood turns acidic. Consequently, flesh becomes flabby and flaccid rendering the bones brittle and dry. Fat thereby gets distended, shrivelling up the marrow. Finally, the production of semen is reduced to a trickle so that the essence of all the seven constituents (*ojas*), is dangerously depleted.

Parallel pathogenic changes are brought about in the body of the woman. The menstrual discharge, which usually begins at the age of twelve, comes to a halt after the woman has reached the age of fifty. These impairments attributable to the aging process further give rise to the specific somatic and psychic disorders which are outlined in precise detail in the relevant sections of the *Caraka Saṃhitā* and the *Suśruta Saṃhitā*.

One of the earliest and the most worrisome signs of old age to appear on the body is the shrivelling and drying up of the surface skin resulting in wrinkles. Baldness and loss of hair are not far behind. According to Caraka, this condition is caused by the vitiated humor of fire which burns the scalp. Excess intake of salt may also contribute to this condition (Ca.vi. 1:18; sū. 26:42[3]). Grey hair makes its appearance almost simultaneously. With advancing age, chronic cough is a familiar complaint. During winter its bouts become particularly acute. In addition to being very discomforting, it is incurable and only a proper diet and regime can keep it in check. Wasting of the body in old age (*jarāśoṣa*) begins to leave its signs when the body becomes very old. Its symptoms include extreme thinness, depletion of semen, lethargy of sense organs and intellect, tremors, loss of taste and appetite (Ca.ci. 18:29.30).

The voice grows thin and faint like beats on a broken drum. Various discharges ooze out of the person's nose, ears, eyes and mouth. Finally, the reflexes slow down, decreasing free movement and mobility (Su.sū. 35:29). Such inevitable changes and losses are endemic to the human experience of growing older. One's ability to come to terms with these inevitable losses due to old age is a critical test of human maturity. Both the medical and moral texts which are aware of this dimension make use of a number of stock images from the religious perspective to make these losses bearable.

In the manner of the *Corpus Hippocraticum* ascribed to Hippocrates, Caraka implies that there are some diseases which are characteristic of old age, others such as the chronic cough, occur more or less frequently, and still others run quite a different course in old age. Both diseases and old age result when the balance among the three humors is disturbed. When the humors get excited, they bring about pathogenic changes in the body (Ca.sū. 20:7, 8). Old age is a product of the morbid interaction between the predisposing causes, humors and the body elements, which are deranged by the humors.

### *Semiotics of Aging*

While semantics principally deals with meaning in process (such as aging, see introduction), semiotics, as the study of signs, is concerned with the interpretation of the more enduring results or consequences of the processes. The semiotics of old age (to be discussed in the projected sequel to this study), therefore, is naturally relevant to gerontology and geriatrics. There is a clear recognition and awareness of this fact in Āyurveda, which recognizes that the physician's stock in trade is interpretation through signs of approaching death (*ariṣṭa*).

Application of semiotic principles to medical practice, accordingly, is well established in Indian medicine. All the three important medical texts consulted for this study discuss and establish various signs (*ariṣṭa*), first, to identify and recognize the observable signs of impending illness, old age and death, and second, to use them as adaptive strategies appropriate to particular semiotic environments. In fact, in Caraka's work the section on the signs of death ("Indriya Sthāna") precedes that on internal medicine "Cikitsā Sthāna".[44] Recent works in semiotics—particularly dealing with the question whether there exists any relationship between the human being and the function of signs—tend to support this long established hypothesis of Āyurveda (and of Augustine; e.g. *De Magistro*) that there happens to be a close relation between biological processes such as aging and semiosis.

Semiosis, in fact, is a pervasive fact of both nature and culture. Semiotics not only perdures through youth and adulthood, it is an essential feature of senescence. Old age, is, in fact, a system of signification, to which Peirce's and Augustine's notions of semiosis are eminently applicable (Sebeok 1977, 181). Repetitiousness in old people, for instance, which is regularly mistaken by others, not old, for an unwitting symptom of old age is really an index of old age. The slowing down of the bodily processes in aging is one of the most dominant signs associated with aging.

In the classical medical terminology of India, influenced by Buddhism, both the symptom and the sign of disease (including aging) are referred to through one term, *lakṣaṇa*.[45] Slowing down is the principal sign (*lakṣaṇa*) and frequently figures as a metaphor to illumine in more human terms the experience of aging.

Our texts assert that time has the dimension of depth as well as duration (see Helārāja's commentary on VP 3:9.28), which are often seen as an either/or situation. It is only with the realization that the duration aspect of time is not endless that one begins to recognize and appreciate the equally dominant role of the aspect of depth in the process of aging.

Another key sign (*lakṣaṇa*) employed to interpret the consequences of the process of aging, which is also most readily and clearly visible on the aging human body, is the unrelenting alteration of smooth surfaces and straight lines and contours of the body. The skin on different organs begins to wrinkle and roughen with age, bodily posture becomes curved, the memory is restructured and begins to lapse. The structurally essential parts of the body lose their suppleness and become firm and rigid.

The factors which are responsible for growth followed by decline in the aging body (Ca.śā. 1:102; 6:12) include:

1. Force of time (*kālayoga*).
2. Inherent tendency (*svabhāvasaṃsiddhiḥ*) Cakrapāṇi glosses it as the unseen force (*adṛṣṭa*).
3. Imprudence (*avidyatāḥ*).
4. Volitional transgressions (*prajñāparādha*).

This list effectively summarizes the principal Indian views regarding the aging of the body and the various signs it leaves on the body and mind in its wake.

By skillfully employing specific literary modes such as the simile and metaphor, many of our texts seek to capture this physical though elusive meaning of aging in response to the question of where aging and old age fit in the meaning system of the ideal life cycle. Since such modes describe in analog as opposed to digital fashion, they present an image of aging rather than a bare list or inventory of its predicates. In keeping with the analog mode of explication, similes and metaphors whether original or recycled, count as appropriate or inappropriate rather than as true or false. They are pressed into service as valuable instruments for making statements beyond purely logical verification.

Numerous metaphors in the "Jarājugupsā" section of the *Yogavāsiṣṭha* (ca. 800 CE), for instance, seem to have just such a function with a particular reference to aging. The basic subject matter pertains to the cultivation of disgust about the body by emphasizing the losses and insults heaped on it by the aging process. A typical metaphor operates as follows:

> Old age, which preys on the flesh of the human body, takes as much delight in devouring its youthful bloom, as a cat does in feeding upon a mouse.[46]

The gloss on this verse attempts to elucidate the metaphor by explaining that just as the cat devours a mouse in the hole after forcing it out from its hiding place, so does covetous old age excavate youth hiding in the body, and devours it with extreme pleasure. The Buddhistic tendencies of the *Yogavāsiṣṭha* in its evaluation of aging are obvious in this metaphor, which may be schematized as follows:

| old age | youth | cat | mouse |
|---|---|---|---|
| a | b | c | d |

Here youth (b) is to old age (a) as mouse (d) is to cat (c). From these four substantives the metaphor is created when the text expresses this relationship by the deletion-substitution method: old age/cat (*jarā/mārjārikā*): youth/mouse (*yauvana/akhu*). But metaphor is not merely a matter of naming old age as 'cat.' It is also bringing together in a lively, poignant way, the thoughts and impressions associated with two different things. Thus, in the present example, *both* old age and cat feast on a helpless being.[47] The imagery brings out succinctly the ideas of forlorn helplessness and utter futility associated with old age. In contradistinction to the Vedic poet who seemed unable to analyze emotions surrounding old age explicitly, authors of a text such as the *Yogavāsiṣṭha* do appear to have in their armory varying ways of recording psychological phenomena as perceived by them in the fact of aging. Through these age-related similes they manage to portray all the intensity of feeling worthy of any sophisticated writer. A relentless realism dominates in these gerontophobic (*jarājugupsā*) writings with didactic intentions. They also betray an uncanny ability to detect and express universal attitudes toward aging.

Through an elaborate metaphor of the wheel of life (*saṃsāracakra*) in the "Strī Parva" of the *Mahābhārata* (11:6 ff) the old sage Vidura seeks to console his cousin—the blind King Dhṛtarāṣṭra who is grieving over the loss of his hundred sons: A human life is akin to a woodland infested by an elephant (year/time). The person is in a constant danger of falling into a well covered over by a creeper (hope eternal), which is infested by bees (desires), rats (days and nights), a snake (death), wild animals (diseases), and a fierce woman (old age).

Thus by a profuse use of similes and metaphors, both Hindu and Buddhist texts such as the *Yogavāsiṣṭha* and *Buddhacarita* struggle to infuse meaning and direction in the human world that is full of contradictions and paradoxes, perhaps the greatest paradox being the predicament of aging and its *alter ego* death. Similes and metaphors, because they can be interpreted differently, permit our texts to evoke various images of old age (*jarā*): as an old and crooked hag, brigand and robber, hungry tigress, laughing hyena, shrieking owl, heinous she-heron, scheming feline and so on. They feature numerous circular, redundant statements showing by their repetitions that old age is unavoidable, sinister, macabre. This betrays a certain cultural anxiety in Indian tradition about aging and old age that begins to manifest itself with the rise of Buddhism and reaches its crescendo in the medieval texts such as the *Yogavāsiṣṭha*. By creating levels of persuasion through verbal images and myths they seek to pull us up onto the metaphysical level of interpretations. That constitutes the subject matter of chapter five.

# 3

# *Between Life and Death*

Given the fact that aging takes place within the confines of the body and is circumscribed by two structurally opposite life events of birth and death, it is essential to trace the traditional Indian ideas on the notion of time and change, since these largely underscore the dynamic and physical aspects of aging.

## *Time and Aging*

For a proper understanding of the discussion taken up in this section, it is crucial to bear in mind the important conceptual distinction between time as an abstract notion and as a temporality. While the former is used in the sense of a reified, absolute category with independent ontological status and influencing the mode of beings, the latter is understood as an expression of change which characterizes entities as their mode. In terms of its role in the aging process, time thus brings two important perspectives to bear.

One perspective posits a mechanistic temporal model where events and sequences are unilinear and progressive. Time is compared to the passage of an arrow through space. It is conceived to be an objective phenomenon existing without reference to human perception or social order. Time is ontologically prior to the consciousness of it. Temporality is really a series of atomic moments, a series of 'nows,' which exist literally for one moment—for the now—then perish to yield to yet another now (see below). History and all change in individual as well as in social life are powered by time and run in a forward irreversible direction like an arrow.

The other perspective takes a relativist view of time and opines that time is a phenomenon based on subjective perception. Time is that which in passing characterizes consciousness and being. Augustine, for instance, places the reality of time in inner experience. Both past and future must exist in the present if they are to be at all. Further, it is the self which permits past and future to be. Past events do not in themselves exist, only the images of them in the memory. Similarly, when we predict the future, it is not tomorrow we see but the foreshadowing of it in the present of the mind (Pilkington 1927, 284–301). Following Augustine, then, one may argue that in the consciousness of the aging individual there is a present memory of past events, a present attention to present events, and a present anticipation of future events.

*Vedic Vision*

In Indian tradition, too, similar perspectives on time are posited and consequently have important bearings on the envisaged role of time with relation to the aging process (see below).[1] The term *kāla* (time) does not occur in the *Ṛgveda* (perhaps with the exception of 10:42.9) nor is the nature of time elaborated. For the Vedic people, time is a moment in process as well as discontinuous instants collectively expressed as "year" (*saṃvatsara*) and identified with Prajāpati who is conceived as that articulation of the seasons effected by rituals.[2] Yet the Vedic poets earnestly pray to divinities to allow them to "live a hundred years", to live "forever". The Vedic person is certainly conscious of the temporal nature of existence, that life is ever fleeting and always too short. One is therefore encouraged to live according to the rhythm of nature: day and night, the seasons, the year. Yet one does not detect an attitude of escapism from time into timelessness, which begins to preoccupy the Upaniṣadic thinkers and the Buddhists. For the Vedic individual all the three worlds are temporal.

The Upaniṣads attempt to understand and transcend time, which is seen metaphorically as a brimful vessel (*pūrṇakumbha*). The *Maitrī Upaniṣad* (6:14–16) speculates on the form, manifestation and infinity of time. The sage Śākāyanya in response to the question of King Bṛhadratha argues that time, death and life (*prāṇa*) are identical. Time ripens and dissolves all beings in the great self, but he who knows into what time itself is dissolved is the knower of the Veda.[3] The next verse (6:15) posits two forms of the ultimate reality (*brahman*) in temporal terms: time and timeless.

That which is prior to the sun is the timeless and without parts. That which begins with the sun is concurrent with time that is divisible in parts such as a year (*saṃvatsara*). From the year creatures are produced, through the year they grow, and in the year they disappear. It is time that 'cooks' all created beings in the vast cauldron of his great self. One may detect in such an interpretation of time initial attempts to conceptualize the aging process in biophysical terms. This awareness of aging in relation to temporal change—which remains submerged under the more spectacular Upaniṣadic discovery of the non-temporal—is elliptically acknowledged by Patañjali:

> For here [in the world] nobody indeed remains firm in his self even for a moment; he either grows as long as he can or her meets destruction (*Mahābhāṣya* on Pāṇini 4:1.3).[4]

The theme is later picked up by Bhartṛhari:

> Nothing remains firm in its own self [without undergoing any change] due to its connection with masculinity or with femininity (VP 3:9.114).[5]

### *Buddhist Challenge*

Early Buddhism, on its part, controverts these views and instead argues that the real does not have a mode of being other than the mode of becoming. That which 'becomes' (ages) involves changes in its totality. There is no residuum or constancy of a self-identical substance. The radical intent of this metaphysical perspective caters to the scrutiny of what is empirical and as such is open to reflective verification. This stance of the Buddha is clearly recorded in the "Anatta Lakkhaṇa Sutta" of the *Saṃyutta Nikāya:*

> That which is embodied is not the self—*rūpa* (form) is not the self . . . whatever form there is—past, future or present . . . all that form is not mine (SN 3:1–188).

But it is in the Ābhidhārmika literature (particularly the *Mahāvibhāṣā*, a kind of thesaurus of early Buddhist dogmas) that one finds the first attempt to understand temporality as a process. As Sinha (1983, 85) points out the *Mahāvibhāṣā* on *Jñānaprasthāna* (the basic canon of the Sarvāstivāda school) declares that everything is real. But in asserting that, it does not posit the reality of past, present or future as three points in time; rather, it is the reality of things (*dharmas*) as past, present and future that is admitted. This reality is perceived in terms of the four aspects of the moment (*kṣaṇa*): the static (*sthiti*); the nascent (*jāti*); the decaying (*jarā*) and the cessant (*nāśa*). Śāntarakṣita (680–740 CE, according to Nakamura 1983, 265) argued that all existence is momentary and that things are instantaneous. A thing (*vastu*) is merely an efficient entity (*arthakriyākarī*) and its essence (*pratītyasamutpāda*) is momentary (*kṣaṇika*). Causation, the interdependence of moments following one another, produces the illusion of stability and uninterrupted continuity. A moment is that form of the thing which ceases as soon as it originates. The nature of a thing, thus, is not different from the thing itself.

The term *kṣaṇika,* therefore, is applied to the thing that does not continue to exist after its coming into existence which is identical with a moment, a point instant (*Tattva Saṃgraha* of Śāntarakṣita 288, 390, quoted in Joshi 1967, 248–250). A jar (like a body) is described as an efficient and variable product of labor, having an origin and existent. This truth is borne out by the declaration in the *Nyāyabindu* (3:12, 13, 15) that whatever is real is changing (Joshi 1967, 249).

Kamalaśīla, disciple of Śāntarakṣita (ca. 800 CE), further attacked the brahminical theory of intellectual time (*buddhimān kāla*) which, following the "Kāla Sūkta" of the *Atharva Veda* (19:53), visualized time as the conscious principle sensitizing the world. In his opinion, the idea of an all pervasive, eternal, durable matter (*vastu*) is a figment of the imagination. On the other hand, the doctrine of impermanence of things is the high water mark of Buddhist philosophy, which argues that human existence is twofold: universal and particular. While the former is cognized through understanding or reason, the latter is perceived through sense perception. This latter variety of existence consists of momentary, discrete entities which are in a perpetual flux or change, which usually is referred to by the technical term *viparinama*.

Buddhists make a clear distinction between change understood as objective fact and change as subjective evaluation. The source of suffering lies in evaluating change in terms of what is desirable and undesirable. For instance, change characterizing the transition from infancy to adulthood is positively understood as 'growth'. But the same process of change which brings about the old age and death is described as 'decay'. The liberated sage, on the other hand, neither grows nor decays.[6] He simply changes (or ages). In the Buddhist scheme of things one may conclude that there is no ager who ages, only the condition (*pratyaya*) of aging. Life is a continuity of instances involving change, arbitrarily divided into phases and stages and labeled as so many substantives. But substantives occur only in the construed (*saṃskṛta*) world of grammar. In reality, there are only verbs (indicating ceaseless activity and change), no substantives (Karunaratna 1979, 117).

### *Hindu Response*

Most Hindu philosophers subscribe to a modified view of time which differs from both the Vedic and Buddhist perspectives. The temporal process, it is argued, involves only a particular aspect of reality. The real is not exhausted thereby in its completeness. There is a certain aspect of the real which remains constant and self-identical over all temporal change. In Sāṃkhya-Yoga philosophy, this enduring substantiality is called *dharmin* (see below). The *Amarakośa* admits time as a distinct category and accords to it a separate semantic domain spread over sixty verses. It lists various measuring units of elapsed time from moment (*kṣaṇa*) to eons (*manvantara*).[7] Hindu philosophical and medical texts utilize a series of determinative compounds (*tatpuruṣa*) created with *kāla* as the base in order to convey the meanings and significance of time in relation to change (for example, *kālavipāka*, cooked in or by time).[8] Drawing on the philosophy of Nyāya-Vaiśeṣika, Āyurveda recognizes time as one of the nine substances (*dravyas*), an autonomous and self-subsistent principle, which is the matrix of all temporality (Ca.sū. 25:25). It is perceived to be the root cause of everything including the health and death of humans.[9] The entire universe is at the mercy of time and owes its existence and welfare to it. It is in the nature of time to cause changes in the matter (*pariṇāma*) and thereby disrupt the equilibrium and balance established in the matter (Ca.śā. 1:115). The human being is born through the agency of time and completes its assigned, predetermined term of life in due time. Time, in this context, has two faces:

1. As ever-flowing (*nityaga*) and modifying (*pariṇāma*), time is objective and the linear flow of moments causing the seasons (*ṛtu*) to happen (Ca.vi. 1:21[6]).
2. As modality (*avasthā*), time impels the mutable material nature (*prakṛti*) to development and growth (*vikāra*) (Zimmermann 1980).[10]

Cakrapāṇi's gloss on Ca.vi. 1:21[6] explains this dual nature of time lucidly:

> Subjectively perceived, time is measured in terms of various phases in life (*avasthā*); as objective framework, time is measured in terms of seasonal cycles (see also Zimmermann 1980).

Caraka buttresses this observation in the "Vimāna Sthāna" (8:128) and lays down the crucial therapeutical principle of treatment which must take into account and correspond to these two modes of time.[11] The expert physician (*vaidya*), therefore, must be able to appropriate both these modes of time as part of his geriatric therapy. The modal aspect of time is utilized to demarcate various phases of the lifespan, rites of passage and stages of evolving life. Along with the principles of three humors, the concept of the subjective and objective dimensions of time forms the theoretical framework on which Āyurvedic therapy rests. Time as modality deals with a particular phase of life and time that flows has reference to becoming appropriate (*sātmya*) to the seasons. Time, accordingly, is both the universal flow and the power of change (*pariṇāma*) as well as the progression of seasons (*saṃvatsara kālakrama* Ca.vi. 8:125 ).[12]

As a modifier time is the objective flow that influences the proportion of the three humors (Ca.sū. 11:42). It is, therefore, the task of the physician to take into account these movements of time in devising his therapy for the benefit of his patients, including the aged.

According to Caraka (śā. 1:47, 49, 50, 51), every substance having the characteristic of 'becoming' (*bhāvopapatti dharmī padārtha*) undergoes modification every moment. The primary cause of change, transformation (and aging), thus, lies in the production of beings (*bhāvotpatti*). The transformation by itself cannot be the motor cause of change, which lies in the self-nature of beings themselves (*svabhāva*). All visible or discernible change is coeval with the disappearance and destruction of the being (*bhāva*). Transformation (*pariṇāma*), therefore, is an inherent tendecy (*svabhāvaja*) of beings. Imbalance of the body elements (*dhātuvaiṣamya*) facilitates and collaborates in the creation of the future phase (*uttarāvasthā*).

Similarly, the concept of reformulation (*saṃskāra*) developed by Caraka (vi. 1:21[2]) may be taken to be analogous to the substantial modification (*dharmapariṇāma*) as expounded in the *Yoga Sūtra* (see below). Reformulation, explains Caraka, is the positing of a quality in a thing as conditioned and determined by a number of factors among which are included water, fire, place and time. All changes of the qualitative or the quantitative order (*guṇāntara*) as they occur in the process of aging, for instance, are brought about through the agency of reformulation.[13]

The human body as the composite expression (*bhāva*) of the cardinal elements possesses certain ontological characteristics and, therefore, undergoes modifications every moment. Over a determinate period of time one phase of the body disappears making way for the manifestation of the succeeding one by reason of transformation (*pariṇāma*) (Ca.śā. 1:57). Each future phase resides in the time-frame not yet come in the unmanifest mode (*avyakta*). It only becomes manifest (*vyakta*) by the power of time, as explained above. After remaining manifest as a certain phase (*kālasthiti*) over a period of time (*kriyākāla*), it ceases to be manifest (Ca.śā. 1:110–112).

This explanation of the role of time in the creation and destruction of the human body (and accompanied by its phases such as aging) is analogous to the physics and philosophy of modification (*pariṇāma*) as expounded in the *Yoga Sūtra* (3:9–15) of Patañjali and commented upon in the *Yoga Sūtra Bhāṣya* of Vyāsa and further elaborated by Vācasapti in answer to the searching question as to how change is possible at all.[14] This literature thus is relevant to our inquiry because it looks at temporality as a characteristic built into the structure of life and things. Reification of time as an abstract category independent of life is alien to the Yoga philosophy.

As Sinha (1983, xi) remarks, temporality in Sāṃkhya-Yoga is conceived not in terms of time as a transcendent condition of our being and cognition; rather it is seen in terms of the becomingness (which may be understood as aging) of phenomena as such, and its relationship to the cognizing consciousness (see Prasad 1984). In these texts dealing with *yoga,* change is often explained metaphorically with reference to the unique features of the process of aging as it occurs in inanimate (for instance, rice grains) and animate (cattle and humans) entities. For our purpose, then, this explanation will have to be reversed in order to highlight the explanatory account of the aging process buttressed by observations on change.

The explanatory accounts of the change in matter in Sāṃkhya-Yoga (and to some extent the Vedānta) are two of the more thoroughly worked out views on change through time in classical Indian philosophies.[15] The universe in their reckoning has a true beginning, and the temporal dimensions of process and change are real (not illusory) and good (not imperfect manifestations of some unchanging ideal supreme absolute). The time component of the symbolic reality, accordingly, provides an important clue to the structural patterns of the meaning of change.

The *Yoga Sūtra* account of change is especially useful because of its fully-fledged and rigorous causal explanation of change (*pariṇāma*) and sequence (*krama*) in terms of the threefold transformation (*pariṇāmavāda,* see below) taking place in the domain of the material nature (*prakṛti*). It also concentrates more fully on the actual moment-to-moment (*kṣaṇika*) processes involved in the change in matter, invoking for the purpose perceptive agricultural and pastoral models and metaphors. In fact, the *Yoga Sūtra* and the *Bhāṣya* of Vyāsa on it explicitly liken human growth and aging to various stages in rice farming (*Bhāṣya* on YS 4:3).

## *Change (Pariṇāma) and Aging*

The term *pariṇāma* (from *pari* + the verb *nam,* 'to bend') first occurs in the *Śvetāśvatara* (5:5) and the *Maitrī Upaniṣad* (6:10,3:3). Patañjali, the author of the *Mahābhāṣya* (not the redactor of the *Yoga Sūtra*) also uses it (1:3.1.11) in explaining the different phases occurring in an entity, which is said to: be born (*jāyate*); to exist (*asti*); to change (*vipariṇamate*); to grow (*vardhate*); to wane (*apakṣīyate*); and to perish (*vinaśyati*).[16] Already Yāska (ca. 800 BCE), in his lexicon called *Nirukta,* had discussed the doctrine of the six modifications of becoming (*ṣaḍbhāva vikārāḥ*) ascribed to a certain Vārṣāyaṇi. In this connection he defines *pariṇāma* as the modification of something not divorced or separated from its essence (1:1.3).[17] From the moment of one's birth up to death, the lifespan of the person is subjected to a number of modifications often compared to those undergone by the verb, which has becoming as its fundamental meaning.[18]

*Pariṇāma* in the sense of ripening occurs in the Pali Canon also, and the later Sautrāntika and Vijñānavādin Buddhist thinkers avail themselves of this technical term to analyze change as they understand it (see above). The *Amarakośa* recognizes a clear relationship between time and change in the concept of *pariṇāma* and lists it under the miscellaneous category (3:2.15).[19]

### *Aging as Triple Modification*

According to Patañjali, change or modification (*pariṇāma*),[20] though unique (YS 4:14), may be subdivided in three types:

1. Substantial modification (*dharmapariṇāma*). It takes place in the external and visible aspects, qualities and characteristics (*dharmas*) of a substance (*dharmin*).
2. Phasic modification (*lakṣaṇapariṇāma*) attributable to the chronological sequence (future-present-past).
3. Modal modification (*avasthāpariṇāma*), which pertains to the overall sequence of conditions or states in which the substance perdures itself over a definite period of time.

These three types of modification are universal and apply to the psychic apparatus as well as to the human bodies and all material objects in the universe. To elucidate this difficult aphorism of Patañjali, Vyāsa's commentary introduces the following concrete example: The substance clay (*dharmin*) may also appear as a moist lump or a water jar. These latter are its visible attributes or aspects (*dharma*). An attribute is the inherent capability of the substance (*dharmin*) particularized by its function. The manifestation (*vyakti*) of the attribute in a substance is dependent on space, time, shape and cause. Yet the transition into a lump or a jar does in no way alter the substance clay itself. But the lump and the jar do not merely have a spatial or qualitative existence; they are also modified by the conditions of time. Thus the jar may be said to be the *present* time-variation (*lakṣaṇapariṇāma*) of the substance clay. Its *past* time-variation was the moist lump. Its *future* time-variation, presumably, will be dust. Again, throughout this transformation conditioned by time, the substance, clay, remains unaffected. How do these phases through time occur? The question is answered with reference to the third type of modification (*avasthāpariṇāma*). It is said to be coeval with time which is posited as the succession of fleeting moments.[21]

Substitute the human body for the clay in Vyāsa's example, and we have a good explanation of the process of aging. Old age, for instance, does not manifest itself in a child at once, but gradually. That is how we understand and speak of the difference between objects, or between individuals who are young, old etc.

Aging is an external aspect or characteristic (*dharma*) of the body (*dharmin*). When a young person ages, manifest signs and symptoms of old age gradually become visible on the body. The predominance of the humor of water (*kaphadoṣa*) gradually ceases and paves the way for that of the humor of wind (*vātadoṣa*). This is substantial transformation (*dharmapariṇāma*).[22] The signs of old age were not visible when the body was young, since they were in the future timeframe. In the process of manifesting themselves on the aging body, they left their future timeframe and entered the present timeframe. Then, upon death of the aged person, they will relapse into the past timeframe. This temporal passage of the signs of old age, in our example, from the future through present to the past, is an instance of phasic modification (*lakṣaṇapariṇāma*).

The three temporal phases are characterized by modes (*avasthā*). With reference to our example these modes may be explained as follows: Everyone is able to keep the consequences of substantial and phasic modifications from manifesting upon the body for a certain duration. During that period of time the person is perceived to be young. The persistance of this mode of appearing young (technically, at least for two moments) in a sequence, is modal modification (*avasthāpariṇāma*). Thus any enduring mode such as youth or old age is really a succession of instants of similar pulsations, somehow maintained in a dynamic equilibrium despite the ongoing substantial and phasic modifications.

In a remarkable concluding aphorism of the *Yoga Sūtra* (4:33) Patañjali describes in a nutshell the relation between the ultimate unit of time (*kṣaṇa*) and the ultimate unit of the continuous process of change and transformation occurring in the universe, the sequence (*krama*), as one of correlation. The gerontological significance of this aphorism may be explained as follows.

Patañjali understands the moment as the minimal limit of time, just as the atom is the minimal limit of matter.[23] It is the time taken by an atom in motion in order to leave one point and reach the next point. A continuous flow of these moments becomes sequence (*krama*, see *Amarakośa* 3:3.147). But the moments and sequences cannot be combined into a perpetually real thing (*vastu*). This characteristic of time suggests that time does not correspond to anything (perpetually) real but is rather a structure constructed by a mental process and follows as a result of perceptions of words. Woods (1914, 288), elucidating this position of the *Yoga Sūtra*, comments that a moment belongs to the real objects, but there is no time outside the sequence of moments (Vyāsa on YS 3:52).

Two moments cannot occur simultaneously, because two things cannot occur simultaneously. When a later moment succeeds an earlier one without interruption, temporal sequence is established. The present, accordingly, is characterized by the presence of a single moment, there being no earlier or later moments in it. But those moments which are past and future are to be explained as inherent in the transformations (*pariṇāmas*). Vyāsa, in his gloss on YS 3:15, explains that sequence is recognized as such only at the final limit of the series of changes. The order of the sequence is thus a positive correlate of the order of transformations.

Vācaspati points out that this explains why rice grains, though carefully preserved in a granary, after a number of years are reduced to powder. Such a condition and consequence would not arise suddenly (*akasmāt*) in the case of newly stocked rice grain. Therefore, in the sequence of successive moments (*kṣaṇakrama*), this fact that the grains are reduced to powder is seen to characterize those grains which have entered into the sequence of very large, large, small and minute particles (*Tattvavaiśāradī* on YS 3:15).

The appearance of the signs of old age from their potential state in the ever-changing and aging body represents this sequential temporal transition from the unmanifest to its present state. The disappearance of the signs of youth, on the other hand, represents a sequential temporal transition from the present state to the past.

The sequence, thus, can only be perceived or established if there are clear qualitative and modal differences between the substance and its characteristics. A new piece of cloth does not become or appear old unless it has passed through sequence of moments. For the same reason even a new garment, although kept with care, after a time grows old (Vācaspati's gloss on YS 4:33). One may further infer, argues Vācaspati, that before the point or stage of visible or perceptible age is reached, it is preceded by the successive stages of relative but ever increasing age. In the beginning this (eventual) condition of age is only the slightest (in terms of its visibility), then slight, noticeable, more noticeable, most noticeable, and so forth.

These grades of age preexist potentially in all substances. The detection of sequence or the passage of time in a series of transformations is then, as it were, *post facto*. This may also explain the fact that though aging continues to take place from the moment of birth (see introduction), it is detected only after a certain period of time has elapsed.

Here the question may be raised: How can the self, which does not undergo change, nevertheless appropriate the experience of a sequence and, therefore, of aging? In other words, how can the self which in reality does not age still be referred to in terms of various age-specific phases such as childhood, youth and old age? The classical Indian tradition answers this question by explaining that persons in bondage (*saṃsāra*), not realizing that they are caught in the web of the modifying and manifesting world of nature (*prakṛti*), attribute the aging of the body also to the self. In the case of those liberated from the trammels of transmigration (*saṃsāra*), aging is *wrongly* predicated on them (*vikalpa*) by others.[24]

Whenever one aspect of a substance is immediately contiguous to another, the two are said to be in sequence. Sequence (*krama*) with respect to substantial modification (*dharmapariṇāma*) is established when old age becomes manifest upon the disappearance of youth. There is also a similar sequence established with respect to the phasic modification (*lakṣaṇapariṇāma*). By reason of there being a future timeframe of the signs of old age, there is a sequence to it in the present timeframe. Similarly, by reason of there being a present timeframe of a youthful body, there is a sequence to it in the past timeframe of a body in childhood. While youth is present or actual, old age is in future as potential, in that it will manifest itself when youth has become unmanifest and relapsed into the past.

The sequence with respect to the modal modification (*avasthāpariṇāma*) is also discernible from the fact that the age of a brand new water-jar, for instance, becomes evident first on its rim (*prānte*, because in the making of the pot, the rim is fashioned first), successively manifesting itself in a sequence in conformity to the succession of moments (Vyāsa on YS 3:15). This sequence is empirically discernible with respect to the age of the body also. Caraka, for instance, has carefully documented the sequential order in which various organs of the body come under the sway of the aging process.

The three timeframes (past, present and future) do not belong to the substance but to its attributes (*dharmas*). Thus, the process of aging is limited to the sphere of the body only. It does not touch the self. Further, changes brought about in terms of external attributes (*dharmas*) belong to the mode (*avasthā*) of the substance, not to the substance (body) itself. Thus, the same stroke is termed one when in the unit place, but ten in the ten's place and a hundred when in the hundred's place. Similarly, explains Vyāsa, in due course of time, the same girl becomes a young woman and a mother (YB on YS 3:13).

The foregoing explains how, with respect to the aging body, time is a positive correlate of the modes (*avasthā*) and phases (*lakṣaṇa*) of the body. The same self (which, unlike the body, does not age) is styled child, youth and the elderly being as a consequence of the phasic modification.[25] Karambelkar (1985, 358ff.) argues that modifications of the secondary signs or symptoms of a substance may be attributed to this phasic modification. Thus, in our example, the turning of the color of the hair with age is the prime instance of this type of modification.

Vācaspati explaining *Yoga Sūtra* 3:13, argues that any substantial modification with reference to the phasic modification exists really in all three timeframes (*adhvānah*). The past, though characterized by a unique timeframe, is not thereby completely severed from the corresponding future or present timeframes. Similarly the future, though having the specific future timeframe, is not, for that matter, completely severed from the present or the past timeframes. Yet, the past or the future does not, like the present, exist as a material thing, in that it has been changed into a particularized phenomenal form. While one frame of time is present, the two other timeframes are inherent in the substance (Vyāsa on YS 4:12, compare also to Augustine). Vācaspati further adds that if past and future are to be supposed as non-existent simply because they are not in the present, then the present also would be non-existent, because it is not in the past and the future (Woods 1914, 317).

It is not possible, however, for the timeframes to belong *simultaneously* to one and the same individual phenomenalized timeframe. What is possible is the presentation (*bhāva*) in successive times of its phenomenal form (see YS 1:11). Our conscious experience temporarily isolates successive phenomenal aspects of permanent (but modifying) substances. All phenomena are latent or implicit in the substance itself and become explicit or manifest under certain determined conditions (see also Vācaspati on YS 1:11).[26] This inference may be utilized to argue that it is conscious self-awareness that detects and isolates successive phases of the body as childhood, youth, middle age and old age.[27]

The foregoing suggests that by extrapolating insights revealed in the *Yoga Sūtra* in its discussion of how change occurs in matter, it is possible to explain 1) the physical and empirical nature of the aging process in humans, and 2) why chronological age is not the best or most reliable indicator for evaluating and feeling one's age. If we expect to understand our experienced and retained past as well as the future, then investigation into the structure of memorial consciousness in old age should proceed along the model of change in relation to time as suggested in the *Yoga Sūtra*.

Following Patañjali's theory of transformation, one may understand aging to be a relative process. Individuals of identical chronological age, for the same reason, are variously labeled 'aged', 'elderly' or 'old' suggesting why old age is a culturally constructed phenomenon. It might also explain how and why subjective time wears qualitatively distinct faces (or hats) in different social contexts as reflected in the classical Indian art and literature. A passage in the authoritative classical Hindu text on poetics (ca. 600 CE) the *Viṣṇudharmottara Purāṇa* (2:3.42ff), for instance, deals with conventions to be followed by sculptors and artists in depicting persons of various types. Sages, hermits, wandering mendicants, ministers, civic leaders, chamberlains and door-keepers should have (depending upon their profession) matted locks of grey or black hair. Widows should not be depicted looking beautiful. They are to be shown as white haired women wearing a white dress and devoid of any kinds of ornamentation.[28]

Reference to black, grey or white color with a view to indentify/label a person belonging to a distinct age group is a familiar device in art and literature of all cultures. After Obeyesekere, the meaning and signficance of the changing color of the hair and the relevant hairstyle for that age may be said to repose in two interrelated domains—its personal meaning for the aging individual in question and the socio-cultural meaning it communicates to the aging person's community and family. The greying matted hair of a hermit, for instance, is at once a fusion of symptom and symbol. This transformation of symptom (that is, somatic manifestation of changing coloration signalled by growing age) into symbol (of a hermit or a wanderer) is realized through the cultural patterning of consciousness converting at the same time eros into agape (Obeyesekere 1981, 34–35).

The matted grey hair and the shaved head act as markers setting aside their bearer as a special and redoubtable being distinguished by old age. Both act as public symbols whereby the complex personal experiences of the aging individual are crystallized into a public symbol. They come to mean total detachment from sexual passion because the behavior implied in a particular hairstyle and sexual behavior are consciously associated from the start. Thus, in several Jātaka stories, the king or other noble men are shown as renouncing family life and contemplating retirement in the forest upon noticing grey hair on the head.

The dynamics of change with time as it is explained in the *Yoga Sūtra* and *Yoga Bhāṣya* may also help relate the quality of human life and aging—how and why people in different stages of life are advised to follow age-specific norms in order to create their temporal milieu. Appropriate cultural symbols are designed to act as a means to interlock the diverse and uneven rates of the three time dimensions within the individual who is almost unconsciously trained to adjust the three time scales to his/her temporal world.

This may also help one to understand how people construct their past biographies and anticipate their future selves by considering their present situation. Time has meaning only insofar as it comes into our consciousness through the 'now' of our awareness of a stream of experience. People do not have a past, but rather an awareness of past, and not a future, but an awareness of a future. Thus, past and future can never be fixed entities for a person, but represent instead the relationship to them at any given now.

The body, too, is central to the experience of the self. The individual is not in the body or attached to it as an object but rather *is* the body. The body is the unique instrument through which individuals experience their insertion of self into the world and know the past and expect a future (Breystpraak 1984). The message of the Dharma Śāstras (see chapter one) is that the future must also be studied as it is *lived* and not as the future of the clock. The future is that which comes to meet the now. The past and future are intertwined into the now. The present constantly influences and alters the past, while the past and future give direction and form to the present. There is, thus, an intermingling of temporal frames and the experiences within each individual, which are continually open to reform and reconstruction (see YB on YS 3:13 and Augustine chapter 20, for which see Pilkington 1927).

Articulation of the triple transformation, which produces and shapes lived experience as well as the phenomenon of old age, involves both a contact and dialectic between an inner and outer reality correlated as temporal sequence. It is on the basis of such a sequence only that the individual is able to reconstruct in his/her life the changing modalities of being as envisaged in the model of the stages of life and duties. Temporality is a category of life and is inherent in the change itself.

This awareness is also reflected, as noted above, in the Āyurvedic definition of life as the continuous uninterrupted flow of lived reality (*anubandha*). The entire life cycle (*saṃsāracakra*) of human reality seems to serve as potential material for transformation. The idea of transformation (*pariṇāma*) thus includes its own concrete lived relation as part of its world.[29] It is not a mere abstract idea of the mind as a *res cogitans* but the human's total existence in its lived relations, which ought to provide the starting point for a genuine analysis of the human life cycle and existence.

Following Patañjali (and informed by Augustine), one may, then, conclude that a given moment in life can be a genuine human lived experience only if it is understood as comprised of all three modalities of human time (past, present and future). Such a model of human temporality based on the theory of transformation can suggest a positive interpretation of aging. It can avoid overemphasizing only the present (as is done in early Buddhism) or only the future (as happens in the Vedāntic view of liberation).

With the writers of the Dharma Śāstra texts, then, one must refute the obstinate clinging to the present or future alone. The existential acceptance of the future as the equally true temporal mode of existence is a necessary prerequisite for developing a successful strategy for coping with old age. One's present existence, accordingly, must be seen in terms of its future possibilities. Only such an authentic mode of understanding of human life and being across the three temporal frames will afford that true insight into freedom (*mokṣa*) as conceived in the Dharma Śāstras. The true mode of existence is 'being with time,' that is, a mode of being that changes with time.

As a measure of accommodation with the Buddhist understanding of personhood, the writers of the Smṛti works reformulated the orthodox views of personhood as not an innate or immutable self-substance. The passage of time and, with it, aging progressively reveals new and increasingly more authentic modes of being in the person. The primordial mode of human spirit and existence, therefore, is anticipatory of the future potential as well as exertive of here and now. But the revelation of the new modes of being with age, it is argued, is also conditioned by certain metaphysical factors—deeds (*karma*) and desires (*kāma*, see chapter five).

## *Aging and Death*

The way elderly people and others handle the prospect of death varies from culture to culture, depending on the society's world view, religious orientation, metaphysical conceptions regarding this and the next world, and the extent to which the society acquiesces to the event of death as the final reality. The precise nature of the relation between aging and death, therefore, is problematic, which has moved Robert Kohn (1971) to argue that aging in the sense of a name of a thing or process or entity is a naming-fallacy. Death cannot be attributed to aging, because aging is not a thing, or the sort of thing which can be a cause. One cannot die of old age but only of disease and so forth. 'Aging' in the expression 'to die of old age' is merely an elliptical term implying any number of factors. But it is not yet clear what these factors are.

The subject of aging in relation to death, therefore, seems to generate a distinct rhetoric and semantic ingenuity. In the graphic words of one modern writer:

> Death is that elusive narrative moment. With all words and no action, it is always lettered than lived. Verbally and iconically textualized, death is driven out of hiding into a visible condition of all textuality (Stewart 1984, 3–4).

Death, writes Stewart, seals the lips of ordinary rhetoric leaving room only for clinical report. It arrives not as a mirror of life but as a window on the void (Stewart 1984, 107). Similarly, in his preface to *Bend Sinister* (1947), Nabokov is moved to describe death as "but a question of style, a mere literary device, a musical resolution" (cited in Stewart 1984, 345).

In the Indian tradition, too, the task of making some sense out of the end product of the aging process that is death has resulted in a rich and varied profusion of religious and cultural responses. They may, however, be reduced to two: one response is content to see death as a termination of life, while the other sees death as some sort of transition from one mode of life to another. In other words, the phenomenon of death may be explained in terms of 1) termination or 2) transition theory. Both these explanations have found ardent supporters.

Old age is usually seen as a period of preparation for death and as such a propitious time for planning, reflecting, reviewing and summing up. Although death may occur at any stage in the life cycle, there is a natural tendency, in the post-Vedic world, to associate old age with death and dying. If old age is the final act of the human drama, then surely death is the final curtain. The Hindu and the Buddhist currents of thought have provided contrasting views on death and its relation to aging. Both nevertheless understand death as a form of erosion whereby life and the body are gradually worn away, and death is the inevitable end product of the aging process.

To a certain extent the threats of erosion posed by time, illness and accidents may be circumvented with proper nutrition and lifestyle. Still, the end to human existence may only be delayed, never absolutely avoided altogether. And just as the proto-Indo-European verb *ger* straddles the meanings 'to age' as well as 'to fall apart,' so also the verb *mer* combines the senses, 'to die' (Sanskrit *marate* and *mriyate*) and 'to reduce to pieces' (Sanskrit *mṛṇāti*, crush, grind).

It is interesting to note that in the *Amarakośa*, the category of death is assigned to the semantic domain called "Kṣatriya Varga". This suggests that at least in the early classical period, when this particular lexicon was compiled, death had acquired a certain halo of heroic and valorous meaning around it. This comes across clearly in the list of various synonyms for death.[30] It is preceded by a longer list of some thirty synonyms for killing (*vadha*), that is, death involving at least some degree of violence (2:8.112–115). Other words that topically and perhaps logically precede the entry on death deal with such typically warrior/ruler-related ideas and events as battles, armies, and strategic formations of fighting troops. This suggests that semantically death is linked, in some way, to violence (*hiṃsā*) as the logical outcome of the passionate temperament (*rajoguṇa*), which is said to predominate in all those who belong to the warrior class.

The violent aspect of death also comes out in the illustrative definition of the verb *jṛ* found in a compilation of the Sanskrit verbs based on Pāṇinian grammar (*Dhātupāṭha*) as "destruction on account of age (*jṛṣvayohānau*)."[31] Such semantics have strong implications for the understanding of the usual notions of death in Indian tradition, which views death as the reduction of the gross body to its constituent elements after the bodily conglomerate has survived over the designated period of time as measured by the aging process.

*Vedic Vision*

The Vedic hymns (Saṃhitās) envision the final dissolution of the body (i.e., death) in terms of the metaphors of separation of the gross body, the subtle body (*liṅgaśarīra*) and the self (*puruṣa* or *ātmā*). The three fall apart in the manner of a ripe cucumber detaching itself from its stalk as the popular Vedic metaphor puts it. Other analyses delve further and speculate on the ways in which the body itself crumbles into pieces after death. The teaching on death by the sage Yājñavalkya to Ārtabhāga (BAU 3:2.13) bears this observation out, wherein it is shown how extensive correspondences between the individual members of the cosmic and the microcosmic bodies come apart at death:

> The voice of the dead man enters the fire,
> his breath enters the wind
> eye enters the sun
> mind enters the moon
> ear enters the cardinal directions
> flesh enters the earth
> self enters the ether (*ākāśa*)
> body hair enters the herbs
> head hair enters the trees
> semen enters the water.

To Ārtabhāga's question, "what, then, remains of this man?", Yājñavalkya's response is elusive. He takes Ārtabhāga away from the general assembly and allegedly broaches the doctrine of *karma*. Yājñavalkya, however, is unequivocal in his claim that at death, the body dissolves into its constituent parts only to rejoin their cosmic counterpart.[32] In the next birth these same elements are drawn out of the cosmos and recombined into a human, animal and vegetal organism. Never is there any birth for the first time: every birth is a *rebirth*. Death conversely is never final but repeated (*punarmṛtyu*).

Identified with a Vedic sacrifice, death is viewed as a recurring and ritual act (*punarmṛtyu*). Each death repeats the death of the primordial man (*puruṣa*), which was also the first sacrifice (RV 10:90). Cremation of a dead person is, therefore, seen as a form of sacrifice. It is the final sacrifice that a person can perform offering its own body to ensure the continued existence of the universe. The Vedic sacrifice was also designed to allay the fear of death while one was still alive. Through the performance of sacrifice, an individual hoped to remain alive. "Deliver me from death, not from life", enjoins the poet to Maruts in a Ṛgvedic hymn (7:59.12, see also AV 18:3.61–63).

But death, particularly sudden and unexpected death, still holds all of its sting in the *Ṛgveda.* One hopes only to escape premature death, to live out a full lifespan (usually considered as spreading to seventy or to hundred years). The Brāhmaṇa texts, by contrast, attempt to tame death by gradual degrees: first to enable the sacrificer to live out a full lifespan, then to allow him to live for a hundred or a thousand years, and finally to attain some sort of vaguely conceived immortality (O'Flaherty 1985, 20).

A passage from the *Śatapatha Brāhmaṇa* (2:3.3.15) features the image of old age as a ferryman carrying individuals to the other shore to death. The ferryman is not so much a person as a personification. He is old age incarnate, and it is old age that carries us to death. It is also interesting to note in this passage the use of the masculine imagery in the personification and the positive appreciation of the role of old age. In later classical texts, the personification and imagery of old age is almost invariably in a pejorative sense, and makes use of a feminine image and substantive.[33]

Two key compounds, *jarāmaryam* (or *jarāmūriyam*) and *mṛtyubandhu,* feature prominently in the Saṃhitā and the Brāhmaṇa texts in this context. Discerning the precise nature of the relationship posited between old age and death in these compounds, however, is problematic. Because depending upon the way the compound is resolved—as a coordinative or as an exocentric—a different meaning is implied. In the Brāhmaṇa texts, however, they are used in the latter sense meaning one having old age as the extreme limit of life.[34] In the *Atharva Veda,* the compound *jarāmṛtyu* acquires yet another significance where it does not mean 1) death *and* old age (coordinative compound) or 2) death *as* old age (descriptive determinative compound). Rather, it is construed as an exocentric compound meaning one dying in old age or dying due to old age.[35] This reflects the generally positive appreciation of both old age and death in the Vedic society in that they are considered to be a very auspicious and desirable duo in the Vedic society. Repeatedly, the Vedic texts wish for death in old age rather than a death precipitated prematurely through accident, violence or disease in youth.[36]

The term *mṛtyubandhu,* which occurs in the *Ṛgveda* (8:18.22; 10:95.18) and particularly the Brāhmaṇa texts, is also relevant for the present discussion. Understood as a determinative compound, it signifies friend of death; but as an exocentric compound it may mean, 'one whose relation to the [unseen] is death.' In recognizing death as a comrade or the unseen companion of the human race, the sober realism of the Vedic world reveals a heroic, unperturbed attitude towards old age and death untainted by fantasy or the fear that would haunt young Naciketas or Siddhārtha (see below).

One Atharvan hymn (8:1) sees death in a novel perspective—as something that does not come only at the last moment of life. It permeates every human moment in life and act. In this sense this hymn invokes a blessing for the human journey which carries the individual from birth through old age to death. This is why it is recited at the initiation ceremony (*upanayana*) of the young twice-born boy. It begins with a startling salute to death, suggesting the intention of the hymn to lay emphasis in protecting the life of the boy when he has not yet fully lived it and assuring his parents. Thus long life (*dīrghāyus*) is a term used in the Veda to express the life lived until it has yielded all it had to give.

The Brāhmaṇa texts, which often catch the reader unaware, make surprising observations regarding death. The *Śatapatha Brāhmaṇa,* for instance, discounts the distinction between death and non-death and brazenly declares:

> *Death* does not die and thus within death itself there is immortality (ŚB 10:5.2.3–4).

Elsewhere, it proclaims:

> Death is not at the limit of life, but in the *middle* of it. In fact, one has to be born thrice in order to be immortal.[37]

One is first born from one's parents, second, by performing prescribed sacrifices, and third, after death. Here is something more colorful and provocative than the bland affirmation in the *Chāndogya Upaniṣad* (6:11) that life does not die.[38] Following Panikkar (1977, 534), then, it may be argued that in accord with the Vedic vision, death is not inevitable; it is only accidental. It is the snatching away of life before maturity is reached or the marriage is contracted and heirs are produced. Such a death is always an unnatural event, and it is always untimely (*akālamṛtyu*).

On the other hand, "the man of long life (*jaradaṣṭiḥ*)" as the Vedic hymns call the one who has fulfilled his lifespan, does not die; he does not experience a break, and thus, a trauma. The old person does not die. It is merely that the commerce with life (*vyāpāra*) is over after the three constitutive debts (*ṛṇa* and so forth, see chapter one) have been paid off. But not everyone, who is old in years, reaches long, fruitful life, maturity and immortality. It is not a question of mere length of days but of *growth* (a theme which is stressed in the Dharma Śāstra texts composed in the subsequent centuries) for which the lifespan stretching to one hundred autumns is certainly welcome but of which it is not the necessary condition. Time is more than its measurement by the passing of days and seasons; it is the qualitative coefficient of human growth itself (Panikkar 1977, 535).

By the time of the Upaniṣads, the meaning of the relation between old age and death undergoes radical change. Whereas death in old age (*jarāmṛtyu*) was seen as a fitting and proper end to a long and healthy life, the inspired sage of the *Muṇḍaka Upaniṣad* now casts old age and death as twin terrors and seeks to transcend them in the hope of the ultimate salvation:

> Truly, unsteady and leaking are those [ships] which take the form of sacrifice [The eighteen older sacred texts (3 × 4 Vedas + 6 Vedāṅgas)] in which the lesser [form of] knowledge is stated. Those fools who praise this doctrine as better [than that which is revealed here] truly go again to old age *and* death.[39]

In other Upaniṣads death is occasionally portrayed as, or associated with, a dancer. When Naciketas visits the world of death in order to obtain knowledge about dying, Death tempts him with many boons and finally offers him lovely women with musical instruments (*Kaṭha Upaniṣad* 1:23–25). But Naciketas ridicules them as objects that cause one's vitality to wear out with age (compare to the Ṛgvedic hymn to the lovely Uṣas, the goddess of dawn, who also robs people of their life). Reminding us of young Siddhārtha as depicted in the *Buddhacarita,* Naciketas spurns Death's gifts rebuking him in these words, "keep to yourself your chariots, dance and song". The association of the dance not only with aging but also with death persists in many later texts, wherein Indra is shown dispatching old age in the guise of dancing girls instead of death to destroy those practicing austerities with a view to become immortals (see *Padma Purāṇa,* 2:77).

In many Upaniṣads, then, old age begins to acquire a negative and pejorative connotation where *jarāmṛtyu* is construed as a coordinative compound to mean old age *and* death. Old age is thereby equated or elevated to the status of death and is equally feared. In summary, then, the Vedic world view steers a middle course between the two extremes: it avoids a tragic and almost obsessive attitude vis-à-vis old age and death, which will later become the hallmark of the teaching of the Buddha. It does not trivialize or ignore the place of old age and death in human life. Life is a great value; indeed, if properly understood, it is the highest value. It would appear to be the task of old age and death to help us realize the value of life and to treasure it (Panikkar 1977, 575).[40]

*Buddhist Repudiation*

The Buddha's pessimistic evaluation of life and death is to be found in his characterization of human life as a duration of unhappy and pointless moments, the final point of which is always an unexplainable and painful death preceded by old age and disease. This is evident from the fact that in Buddhist texts, following the practice already initiated in the Upaniṣads, the words such as *jarāmaraṇa/mṛtyu* or *jarāntakau* are construed as coordinative compounds, and they are usually understood to mean old age and death.[41] As a matter of fact, the practice of binding the concepts of old age and death into an exocentric compound to mean death in old age does not survive after the Saṃhitā period. Even the classical Hindu texts, deeply influenced as they are by the Buddhist questioning of the Vedic view of life, generally combine old age and death in a coordinative compound.

Not surprisingly, the negative evaluation of these two structured events in the human condition is particularly unremitting in its severity in the Buddhist tradition. To the Buddha, the human being is driven by the fear of death (and disease and decrepitude) rather than by the love of life. To conquer death, is to the Buddha, life's aim.[42] Responding to a question by a disciple named Rādha ("Rādha Saṃyutta", *Saṃyutta Nikāya* 3:188–201), the Buddha identified death with Māra, explaining that Māra, the principle of destruction, is found wherever the constituents of individuality are found.[43] In yet another discourse ("Mahāsatipaṭṭhāna Sutta", DN 2:290–315), he described death as the breaking up (*bheda*) of the five aggregations.

The Buddhist position with regard to the existence of humans and their life processes, then, is that it is subject to the law of dependent origination, which should be understood in the light of the vision of suffering (*duḥkhadṛṣṭi*) formulated as two fundamental principles: all is suffering (*sarvam duḥkham*) and everything is impermanent (*savvam anityam*). While the first principle is intuitively given, the latter emerges from the Buddha's analysis of the facts of life and its experiences. Since whatever is dependently originated is also sorrowful, existence *ipso facto* is suffering. Yet the *source of suffering* is distinct from the *experience* of suffering (see Varma 1973, 121–123, 137).

From the gerontological perspective, the Buddha seems to argue that old age is the source of suffering which is lived and experienced by all old people. Early Buddhist literature such as the Jātakas or the works of Aśvaghoṣa (*Buddhacarita* and *Saundarananda*) also blur this distinction, identifying old age itself with suffering and effectively constructing picturesque similes and metaphors to reinforce that identity. Consider these two elegant similes from Aśvaghoṣa's *Saundarananda*:

> Just as the sugarcane stalk is strewn on the ground to be dried for burning [as fuel] after extracting all the juice by squeezing it, so does the body, pressed in the mill of old age and with its vitality drained away, await the funeral pyre (SD 9:31).[44]

> Just as a saw, worked by two persons reduces a tall tree to logs, so does old age, ever closing in by the march of day and night, bring about the fall of vigorous inhabitants of this world (SD 9:32).

Thus, for early Buddhism old age, being dependently originated, is suffering and the elderly person and his/her lived experience also being so originated are suffering. *Duḥkha*, originally a word meaning a particular type of unpleasant experience, was extended to mean also an entity and a phenomenon (*vastu*). To that extent this line of interpretation resembles the Sāṃkhya thinking, which, too, believes that everything in the material domain (*prakṛti*) is characterized by happiness as well as by unhappiness and delusion. The result of this logic was that unless origination and embodiment come to an end, the pain of disease, old age and death cannot be eradicated. This would also require the arrest of the flow of moments. Since these moments are real, their arrest would involve a specific kind of disciplined effort, which is known as the eightfold path.

A human being is the only animal which is aware of the certainty of death, which is perceived as the ever-impending terminus. The fear of death and old age would, therefore, dissipate only if one were to reflect carefully on the nature of self and time. Life and the conscious experience of it occur only in the present. The present alone is that which exists and remains unmovable, like a rock which the unceasing flow of time flows around, but does not carry away (contrast with the relevant Vedic view expounded above).[45]

To surmount suffering, understood as disease, decrepitude and death, then, one should abandon the struggle for happiness and the elimination of unhappiness. Paradoxical though it may sound, one must, in the Buddhist scheme of life, embrace suffering as the true meaning of existence. Dying and death, thus, become the only real purpose of the birth and life process. In the moment of death all is achieved, for which the whole course of life was only the preparation and introduction. Disease, old age and death are the résumé of life.[46]

### *Hindu Response*

The views of early Buddhism on death and old age, as outlined above, are suitably modified by the Dharma Śāstras so as to harmonize them with the basic Vedic vision (see chapter one). Death as deliverance is understood to be that toward which one's inner resources and self-disciplined development should be directed, inasmuch as it is the consummation of life. Death is the *telos* of life. Though nature victimizes humans by giving them the capacity to foresee and fear old age and death, it is argued, it also provides a compensating antidote to the certainty of death, which the reflective reason can posit out of its own means.

In the epic literature and the Purāṇas, such explanatory accounts of old age and death are clothed in a distinctly mythic mode. To a certain extent, they are related to their counterparts in many Buddhist myths. Both share the same recurrent motifs and often propose the same solutions to the problems of old age and death, although they are posed differently. The inspiration for these myths may be traced to Yājñavalkya's explanation to Ārtabhāga's query (BAU 3:2.10) that death is an all-consuming fire of which the water (of knowledge) is the best antidote. When thus extinguished, this fire of death renders repeated death impossible.

Time happens to be the corrupting factor in many of the myths of the origin of old age leading to death. Whenever death is chased away from the earth, as it happens when a righteous king rules the earth (e.g. King Yayāti, see below) or when an extraordinary person undertakes severe austerities, the earth becomes overburdened and consequently people (particularly the elderly) must be killed. Two related verses of the *Mahābhārata* begin with just such an assumption of an amoral necessity for the raison d'être of death.

To the questions of Yudhiṣṭhira as to who is it that dies, whence comes death, and how does it stalk its prey, Bhīṣma responds that old age and death arose on account of the dangerous overcrowding brought about by an excess of people (perhaps old people) whose only flaw was that they did not die (or not soon enough). In another passage 'Death' declines to perform her prescribed duty (*svadharma*), which is to kill. Instead, she complains:

> How could you Brahmā create a woman such as I? How could I perform such a cruel task? . . . I will not kill sick children or old people (MB, Bombay Edition 12:250.9,25,41, quoted in O'Flaherty 1976, 229).

In these passages we find an interplay between an absolute and a relative morality in the attitude toward old age and death. In fact, moral judgments regarding not morality but old age and death are introduced (O'Flaherty 1976, 229. See also Dumézil 1971–74, 169).

As if taking its cue from such passages, the Hindu devotional (*bhakti*) literature progresses one step further by asserting that Śiva (or other major gods such as Viṣṇu, Devī or Kṛṣṇa) prevent old age and death from afflicting their respective devotees, although in one important myth Śiva declares his inability to manipulate the process of aging.[47] These ideas, too, may be traced back to the Brāhmaṇa texts, which state that certain enlightened beings are not subject to old age and death. The Upaniṣadic force of knowledge (*jñāna*) that challenges death is then replaced by the force of devotion (*bhakti*).

The epithet *kālāntaka*, which is one of the fourteen forms of death, was originally applied to the god Yama himself to indicate his role as the destroyer of the world. But in the Purāṇas it is transferred to Śiva. An episode from the *Bhāgavata Purāṇa* (O'Flaherty 1976, 232) is relevant to the present context:

> The sage Mārkaṇḍeya was fated to die at the age of sixteen. When his moment arrived, he was meditating and worshipping Śiva's symbol (*liṅga*). When the messengers of the god of death (Yama) came to take his life away, Śiva burst out of his *liṅga* and prevented the messengers from accomplishing their

> duties. Śiva then granted Mārkaṇḍeya the boon that he would remain sixteen forever and old age would never touch him (12:8–10).

But Purāṇic Hinduism also derives its attitude toward aging and death from the Saṃhitā and the Brāhmaṇa texts, often disregarding the Upaniṣadic worldview on life, which, in many instances is closer to Buddhism. Death is evil, and premature death is the sure sign of the gradual waning of righteousness (*dharma*) in each of the four ages (*yuga*), which also results in the steady and corresponding decreases of the human lifespan. Moralistic overtones in the explanation of old age and death, so frequent and familiar in the Purāṇas, are also to be found in passages of important Āyurvedic texts such as the *Caraka Saṃhitā* where it is specified which type of person ages and dies prematurely:

> As a result of leading a lifestyle which is not in accord with one's bodily strength; from eating beyond one's digestive capacity or eating the wrong kind of food; from allowing the body to deteriorate; from excessive intercourse; from relationship with evil persons; from restraining natural biological urges (Ca.vi. 3:38).

The early Buddhist view of life, which is diametrically opposed to the Vedic view, curiously comes alive again and receives endorsement from such unlikely quarters as the classical drama and poetry, which generally staunchly support the Vedic values. In *Raghuvaṃśa*, for instance, the sage Vasiṣṭha, who is the chief preceptor of the kings of the Raghu dynasty, in consoling King Aja who is mourning the death of his young and lovely wife Indumati, admonishes him in these terms:

> Wise persons know that death is the substratum of sentient beings and life is a mere deviation from that pristine condition. If a creature manages to be alive even for a moment, it is a gainer.
>
> The dull-witted lament the loss of a dear person as a dart shot through the heart, but the firm-minded regard the same as a dart removed, because such a loss opens the door to bliss.
>
> Since the [facts of the] relation and separation of our own body and soul are so well known, tell me, O king! why separation

> [on account of death] from other objects should at all distress a wise person? (*Raghuvaṃśa* 8:87–89).

Vasiṣṭha seems to argue that death, not life, is the norm of the human condition. Death is the substratum (*sthāyībhāva*) of which life and its phases, including old age are mere deviations (*vibhāvas*).[48] This view of life in relation to death is duly echoed also by Bhartṛhari in a charming simile:

> How can mortals find joy in life that resembles bubbles on the waves of sea? For a moment man is a boy, for a moment a youth tortured by love, for a moment a pauper, for another moment at the apex of prosperity. Then at the end of life's play with limbs tired in old age and with face marked by wrinkles he retires, like an actor, behind the curtain of death (*Vairāgyaśataka*, #49,50 in *Śatakatraya* of Bhartṛhari).

In the Hindu spiritual sphere often influenced by Vedānta (and perhaps by Buddhism), the disgust and meaninglessness of life as conveyed by the triune evil of disease, old age and death—including anxiety derived thereof—has been recognized as the instigator and the source of human striving for the release from the bondage of embodiment.

The basic subject matter of chapter twenty-two of the *Yogavāsiṣṭha*, a text heavily influenced by both Vedānta and Buddhism, is just that: cultivation of disgust for the vulnerable nature of the body by exaggerating the losses and insults heaped on it by the aging process. In dozens of clichéd similes fashioned for this purpose the main premise is succinctly stated at the beginning of the section and then additional details are added through resort to simile for emotional content and ornamentation. Paradoxically enough, the discourse on aging is presented by young Rāma to his aging father Daśaratha in the form of finely crafted and charming similes. Some of the poignant observations made by Rāma may be summarized below:

1. Old age wears out the body and strips the ego of its conceit. The aging body is compared to a creeper which, after flowering, fades, and turns grey (1:22.28).
2. Old age is a harbinger of deadly diseases. This process is compared to the chill blast of winter sweeping away the leaves of a tree (1:22.20).
3. Old age lays its icy hand on all mortals in due course. The de-

struction of the body through aging is compared to the destruction of lotuses by the falling snow, the freezing of the autumnal lilies by the wind or to the [river current] sweeping off a tree on its bank (1:22.20).
4. Old age leaves its calling card with ominous warnings. This is compared to the inauspicious cry of the she-jackal in the forest (1:22.26).

The similes descend in a torrent of rapid fire, one on top of another, virtually overwhelming the unsuspecting reader. One is caught out of breath, as it were, wondering how to relate old age meaningfully with a shrieking owl at one instant and with the laughing hyena at the next. The difficulty is compounded by the author's habit of rather nervously jumping from one simile to the next without developing the previous one. Nevertheless this barrage of similes on old age does succeed in lending a certain color and vividness to the depressing features of the aging process, emphasizing at the same time the most macabre facts of old age.

In contradistinction to the Vedic poet who was unable to analyze emotions surrounding old age explicitly, authors of a text such as the *Yogavāsiṣṭha* do seem to have in their armory varying ways of recording psychological phenomena as perceived by them in the fact of aging. Through these age-related similes they manage to portray all the intensity of feeling worthy of any sophisticated writer. A relentless realism dominates in these gerontophobic (*jarājugupsā*) writings with didactic intentions, betraying that uncanny ability to detect and express universal attitudes toward aging.

Through the profuse use of similes and metaphors, texts such as the *Yogavāsiṣṭha* struggle to infuse meaning and direction in the human world that is full of contradictions and paradoxes, perhaps the greatest paradox being the predicament of aging and its *alter ego* death. Freedom and reality understood as *nirvāṇa* or *mokṣa* begin where anxiety and fear of embodiment is overcome. Anxiety originating in the fear of disease, decrepitude and death must not be allowed to distort or prevent human vision and perception of that supreme reality, which can mediate and express itself only in the mode of tranquility (*śānti*) (Arapura 1973, 73). *Mokṣa* or *nirvāṇa* concerns this particular state of being and of abiding, which transcends the anxiety-laden world of becoming and aging and reposes in the sentiment of quietude (*śāntarasa*). This line of thinking really begins with certain Upaniṣadic seers and is endorsed by both Buddhismand Hinduism.

# 4

# *Coping with Stress*

The traditional Indian precepts and practices developed to cope with the stress and erosion caused by aging revolve around the concept of *vāja* (rejuvenatory and revitalizing force). Food is believed to be the chief source of *vāja* (often equated with *śukra* or *vīrya*). But in addition, the potential of *vāja* is also said to be affected negatively or positively by a number of factors such as psychological attitude or moral behavior. As pointed out in chapter two, the classical Hindu tradition restricts the sphere and the scope of the aging process to the gross body, which is deemed to be the product of five interacting cardinal elements. It also serves as the substratum to the conscious self (*ātman*).[1] The medical texts further state that the body, which serves as the substratum to the conscious self, is the product of the food eaten ( . . . *deho hyāhārasambhavaḥ*, Ca.sū. 28:41).

As such, the rate of aging, too, is thought to be subject to the quality and the quantity of food consumed. This line of interpretation, linking sustaining matter to the life process in a causal relationship, is based on Vedic revelation.

The spiritual significance attributed to the divine elixir (Soma) in *Ṛgveda* (9:18.3) or in *Śatapatha Brāhmaṇa* (3:9.4.22,23), appears to be the starting point in the Indian tradition for all the subsequent speculation about the mystery and the metaphysics of food; food is seen as imparting both physical and spiritual vigor to the embodied self. The *Bṛhadāraṇyaka Upaniṣad* (1:4.6), too, is moved to exclaim that this whole world, verily, is just food and the eater of food. In metaphysical terms, then, the nature of the sustaining matter (*anna*) and its significance to the body is intimately connected to the universal phenomenon of the need and hunger for food to stave off death by the body. This strange interlocking of hunger (*aśana*) and death (*mṛtyu*) arises from the inscrutable mystery of the mutual relation posited between nutrient matter (*anna*) and beings who consume it (*annāda*).

But whoever is the immediate or the ultimate 'eater' and whatever the nature of the 'eaten', the world itself has come into existence, according to the *Maitrī Upaniṣad* (6:12), because of the ceaseless desire for food on the part of the universe. Accordingly, it is now proposed that the ritual feeding of one's own body is to be substituted for the ritual feeding of the gods. Further, there is a manifold relationship between time and the universe (*kāla* and *brahman*), with food as the common denominator (MU 6:9–17). Having glorified food as the ultimate reality (*brahman*), it is then argued that time is the cause of food. The idea next passes over to celebrating time as the ultimate reality, and, finally, from this symbolic understanding of *brahman* as time, the idea reverts back to the timeless ultimate reality (*brahman*) as the mother cause of all causes.[2]

The above passages suggest how the classical Hindu views on the relation between the sustenance of the body and aging originated in the Vedic premises regarding the mythology of creation, healing practices, sacrificial rituals and nutritional theories.[3] The metaphysical explanation of food as one of the causal agents of the aging process, one may argue, originates in this generally held conviction that the material cosmos and the human body are at once complementary opposites, intimately interrelated and constantly interchangeable along homological lines. When the outer world is created, it is created out of the human being and its life process: whether in cosmogony, sacrifice or death.

Conversely, when the human being is created (anthropogony), his/her bodily nourishment and health-care is sustained with the stuff of the cosmos. The creation of the one implies proportionate decreation/decomposition of the other. The sum total of matter in the universe has existed and always will be the same. It merely alternates between cosmic and human, animal or vegetal forms. The human processes of birth, growth, aging and death are nothing other than moments of transition between the temporally determined macrocosmic and microcosmic transformations of matter. But such a hypothesis, admitting the interchange of forms between humans and the cosmos, has the effect of saddling each with the miseries of the other. The cosmic body becomes prey to the same physical and metaphysical ailments as humans—disease, decrepitude and death.

A myth from the *Śatapatha Brāhmaṇa* furnishes a similar cosmic signficance of food in relation to the restoration of the body:

> After he created the universe and the creatures, Lord Prajāpati relaxed and opened up. Food began to flow out of him. Gods then approached the fire god Agni and proposed that they would like to feed themselves on Prajāpati with Agni as their mouth (#4). When he acquiesced to their request, the gods heated up Prajāpati in Agni's fire and raised him upright as the world (#6) (that is, they nourished and sustained the universe, ŚB 7:1.2.1–7) (based on Eggeling's translation).[4]

The Buddhist view of the relationship between nutrition and human existence is equally intriguing. According to the myth of creation as recorded in the "Agañña Suttanta" of the Pali Canon:

> Once on earth there appeared an essence, which a greedy being tasted. Other beings followed suit and eventually they all came to rely on coarse food matter for their physical survival. They gradually lost the subtle component of the body, which consequently became heavier and substantial. Those who grew less addicted to material food, managed to retain their beautiful and ethereal form (see Paul 1979, xx-xxi).
>
> Consequently, time and temporality were integrated into the human condition. The beings, because they began to subsist on material food, gave rise to excrement and urine. The reliance on food for survival eventually gave rise to distinction

> between genders, sexual desire (*kāma*) and the notion of private property (see Wayman 1984, 275–76).

Paul (1979, xx-xxi) has speculated that this myth reveals the Buddhist understanding of the golden age in the remote past in which asexual, self-luminous, and noncorporeal beings lived blissfully without the need of gross, substantial food (*anna*). Although no cause for the loss of the golden age is offered, the emergence of sexuality and the gross body is attributed to the intake of gross food. The *Milindapañha* develops this theme further and identifies the five nourishing/rejuvenatory qualities or principles of food (*vāja*). It then hastens to add that *nirvāṇa,* too, possesses the same qualities but at the metaphysical level. Nāgasena summarizes the notion of *nirvāṇa* as food in the following statement to Milinda:

> As food, O king, is the support of all beings, so is Nirvāṇa, when it has been realized, the support of life, for it puts an end to old age and death (*Milindapañha,* dilemma 80).

## *Coping with Age-related Stress*

The preceding suggests how the concept of *vāja,* already broached in the *Atharva Veda,* would naturally become in Āyurveda an important tool through which religion, culture and gerontology are made to interact upon one another, generating a viable mechanism of coping with age. Food as the source of *vāja,* and, as such, of rejuvenation and revitalization, is freely eulogized in the Āyurvedic texts. Caraka, for instance, emphasizes that the genesis, development, and dissolution of not only the planet earth and its inhabitants but also of other worlds including heaven are dependent on food-matter (Ca.sū. 27:350).

Matter is said to flow between people, animals, plants and the universe in various ways. Food, as a specific complex of a highly important component of the universe, also figures prominently in this process. Matter is always in flux, though a dynamic equilibrium over a determinate period of time may prevail. In this cycle, as Lincoln (1986, 138–139) suggests, there is no fixed starting point and no termination. Propelled by the process of aging and natural death, matter moves back and forth between humans and the cosmos through the intermediary of plants and animals. This hypothesis that the world and the passage of creatures from state to state is 1) a transmission of energy from place to place through time and 2) a transformation of matter from one alloform to another (mutability, *pariṇāma*), is semantically incorporated in the pan-Indian concept of transmigration (*saṃsāra*).

Transformation and transmigration (*pariṇāma* and *saṃsāra*), thus, are connected doctrines which help us to define and understand the etiology of aging in that the concept of transmigration combines in itself the continuity of the afterlife with the concreteness of physical change. This is evident from the generally accepted meaning of the term *saṃsāra* as the act of going about, wandering through, coursing along, or passing through a series of conditions through successive states of birth, death and rebirth.

The rejuvenatory and revitalizing processes proposed in the concept of *vāja* and practiced in the medical texts with reference to aging, therefore, need to be understood in terms of the following metaphysical perspective implicit in the Indian ethos including Āyurveda:

1. There is a continual recreation or recuperation of the human organism from the food or drugs ingested.
2. The transformation of material substance into the human body involves the corresponding transformation of its alloform.
3. The nourishing process is a reversal of the creation account expounded, for instance, in *Ṛgveda* (10:90). Food was initially created from the body of the cosmic man (*puruṣa*) that was cut up (according to *Śatapatha Brāhmaṇa* 4:2.1–11, it was created from the body of horse, the principal sacrificed animal).

Conversely, eating food or ingesting a specially prepared prescription restores/rejuvenates to wholeness the body that would otherwise fall apart through malnutrition, disease, old age and ultimately death. Eating, thus, is conducive to the reappropriation of bodily parts from foodstuffs in the external universe where they reside in a different form.

The gerontological relevance and the rationale behind the Atharvan spells and charms and Āyurvedic prescriptions based on certain varieties of grasses and plants designed to grow hair on a bald pate or to turn grey hair into dark may, then, be understood in the light of the preceding. Hair and certain plants or herbs are seen as resembling each other in form. Individual hair is like a blade of grass since both tend to be long, slender and grow in clumps. Both are endowed with an inner dynamism for incessant growth. Again, hair grows on top of the head like the grass growing on topsoil. Thus, in many Purāṇic accounts of cosmic creation, trees are said to be the hair of the cosmic being (*puruṣa*). Finally, there is also the third level of linguistic/semantic homologies between hair and vegetal matter as indicated in the Sanskrit word *valśa*, which denotes both hair and sprout or shoot (Lincoln 1986, 88).

It is not difficult to understand, then, the homoeopathic nature of the cure for hair loss prescribed in the *Atharva Veda* and Āyurveda along the principles discussed above.[5] Chapter five entitled "Quantitative Dietetics (Mātrāśitīyam") of the "Sūtra Sthāna" of the *Caraka Saṃhitā*, is given to the quantitative and qualitative discussion of food (see also Ca.sū. chapters 6,25,26,27; Ca.śā. chapter 6). These chapters mention in detail the nutritive, curative, rejuvenatory and revitalizing actions of several hundred different edible and potable substances belonging to different classes. The body is nourished on these substances; the distinction between happiness and sorrow, disease, old age and health results from the choice of a wholesome or an unwholesome diet (Ca.sū. 5:63; 25:31,32).

Caraka admonishes that appropriate food should be consumed in rhythm with the twenty-four hour lunar cycle and the six-season solar cycle. Food eaten is put to proper use only if the individual has cultivated restraint over the palate and other sense organs. The act of eating is to be undertaken in the spirit that food is the ultimate reality (*brahman*) and eating is an act of sacrifice (*yajñakarma*) (sū.27:345–347).[6] Consumption of unwholesome food leads to suffering and old age. According to Caraka, food is deemed to be unwholesome when:

1. It is prepared from grains grown in the same soil year after year without alternating with other crops.
2. It is eaten without regard to the prevailing lunar or solar cycle.
3. It is eaten before food consumed earlier had been fully digested.

An important criterion of wholesome food is that it must be of the 'heavy' (*guru*) quality. Articles of food, which, in addition, are thick, unctuous, slippery, slow and stable in quality tend to generate the humor of water (*kaphadoṣa*) and augment its proportion in the body thereby providing a good potential source of resisting premature bodily decay and aging[7] (sū. 25:32–40, and Cakrapāṇi's gloss).

*Rejuvenation and Revitalization*

The rejuvenation (*rasāyana*) and revitalization (*vājīkaraṇa*) therapies of Āyurveda, based as they are on the intake of wholesome food, properly fall within the domain of preventive geriatrics in that they are proposed as a defense against the wear and tear of the body associated with the aging process.[8] In the Vedic texts, the term *rasa* is consistently used in the sense of water and its essence. The two are identified in the *Śatapatha Brāhmaṇa* (*raso vā'paḥ*, 3:3.3.18). The *Atharva Veda* frequently praises water (*rasa*) for its alleged properties of keeping old age away, resisting diseases and conferring immortality.[9] One particular myth (AV 11:6.23) refers to the legend of how Indra's charioteer Mātali obtained the immortalizing elixir (*amṛta*) by selling Indra's chariot, which Indra had thrown into water, thereby endowing it with immortalizing properties.

However, in later centuries, the term *rasa* underwent a gradual change and amplification in meaning and came to signify in Āyurveda a specific recipe conferring long, healthy life and warding off premature old age.[10] The principle idea underlying these two therapies is the presupposition that appropriate diet (*āhāra*), when supported by a prescribed and sane lifestyle in conformity with the prescribed code of moral behavior (*vihāra*), will activate the rejuvenatory force (*vāja*). It is said to combat bodily erosion caused by the aging process by replenishing bodily matter that would otherwise be lost with the passage of time. This fact—that the passage of time poses various threats to the human body—is already recognized in the semantics of the proto-Indo-European verb *ger* (Sanskrit *jṛ*) which combines the meanings of 'to grown old', 'to break up' and 'to wear down', thereby suggesting that the aging process is one of the gradual erosion and loss of some vital principle or matter.[11]

The intake of food or the ingestion of certain substances with recuperative potency helps ward off bodily loss due to old age. The incorporation of specific substances—such as plant or mineral extracts, for instance, are said to ward off the bodily attrition evident in the loss of hair in old age. Āyurveda has promoted rejuvenation and the revitalization therapies as two coping mechanisms of aging on the basis of the creation mythology already discernible in certain Vedic texts. For example, the *Atharva Veda* (5:5; 4:12.1) recounts how a specific healing plant (Rohaṇī) came into existence from the dismembered portion of the body of a primordial victim, and how the same plant can now be used to restore the material substance needed to mend injuries to that same bodily member in a human being.[12]

With reference to the existence of such homological building blocks, matter and energy may be said to be shifted back and forth between the macrocosm and the microcosm to counter the threats posed by the aging process. This constant and varied motion of matter from one entity to another easily occurs, because at the most fundamental level people, plants, animals as well as the universe originate in the same cosmic stuff. Their apparent differences are only superficial distinctions of form. Each entity in the universe is merely an *alloform*, an alternative shape, of all the others. The metaphysical underpinnings of this presupposition are to be found in the categories of generic concomitance (*sāmānya*) and variant factor (*viśeṣa*) in the *Caraka Saṃhitā* (Ca.sū. 1:44,45).

The medical texts view aging as initiated and sustained by time (*kālaja*) from the moment the five cardinal elements and the self (*ātmā*) come together to produce the fetus. The process of aging is also coeval with the flow of moments that follow each other in quick and continuous succession (see chapter three). Aging of the body, therefore, is an unstoppable, irreversible and inevitable process. No therapy can arrest aging or cure the diseases, disabilities and discomforts engendered by it. Potentially, any age-related therapy may only delay the onset of old age and/or help manage and cope with the stresses of aging.

Typical geriatric therapies of rejuvenation and revitalization are, therefore, construed only as coping mechanisms which may 1) delay aging, 2) prevent premature aging or impotence and, 3) provide energy to be able to accomplish the prescribed tasks in old age provided the therapy is undertaken as a prophylactic measure in one's younger years (Cakrapāṇi on Ca.śā. 1:114,115).[13] Under certain extenuating circumstances man may undergo them while he is a married householder and without a son but in any event they must be completed *before* he leaves that stage.

### *Rejuvenation Therapy*

This therapy is alleged to procure, for the individual undergoing it, various beneficial and positive changes in all the seven bodily elements (*dhātus*) beginning with the most fundamental of them, the nutrient fluid (*rasa*). The therapy is said to help prevent premature old age, minimize the negative and adverse consequences of old age that manifest themselves naturally in course of time, and help the individual to strive diligently for the prescribed ends in life (*puruṣārthas* or *eṣaṇās*).

In addition, the rejuvenation therapy is said to produce various miraculous results on the aging body and mind. According to Caraka, it promotes longevity and health, preserves youthful vigor, disperses stupor, torpor, fatigue, exhaustion, indolence and weakness. It tones up flabby muscles and sagging organs, stimulates digestion and maintains a wrinkle-free, lustrous skin (Ca.ci. chapter 1). According to Suśruta (sū. 29:12), the rejuvenation therapy, in addition to delaying the onset of old age, also guards the subject against approaching senility and physical deterioration.

On the basis of the role assigned to such natural phenomena as the sun and wind, rejuvenation therapy is divided into two major categories or methods: 1) treatment in the nursing home; and 2) nature-cure treatment.

*Treatment in the nursing home.* The mode of entering a nursing home for the treatment (the term employed by Caraka is *kuṭīprāveśika*) involves the isolation of the subject under treatment from all contact with nature for an extended period of time. It is prescribed in the case of those individuals who are reasonably healthy, strong willed, self-controlled and endowed with sufficient means to bear the expenses involved (Ca.ci. 1:4:27). Suśruta lays down additional conditions by ruling that this treatment is not available to those who are:

1. Unable to restrain their senses.
2. Idlers and lazy.
3. Incompetent sloths.
4. Addicted to various vices or habits.
5. Sinners.
6. Skeptics who would doubt the efficacy of the treatment (Su.ci. 30:4).

Those who are eligible for the treatment must, in addition, cultivate specific psychological traits and habits valued in Indian tradition. These include a commitment to speak only the truth, abstention from excessive consumption of wine, alcohol and tobacco, observance of celibacy over the duration of the treatment (which may run for ninety days or more) and restriction of food intake to milk and clarified butter (*ghee*) only. Compliance with these preliminary conditions is supported by a long passage in ci. 1:4.30–38, wherein Caraka states that no one who has not rid himself of the evil habits of the body and the mind can ever expect to come by the benefits resulting from rejuvenation treatment.

In fact, the passage also contains an optional rejuvenatory prescription solely based on the cultivation of certain ethical virtues and practices (*ācārarasāyana*). These include:

1. Repetition of holy chants and giving of alms.
2. Revering gods, cows, brahmins, teachers, seniors, and the village elders.
3. Commitment to nonviolence, compassion, and moderation through developing balanced habits.
4. Acquiring knowledge of meteorology and nosology (the science of compounding medical prescriptions.

Such an individual will reap all the benefits of the rejuvenation treatment without submitting to that therapy proper. Should he, in addition, undergo the regular rejuvenation therapy under the supervision of a qualified physician (*vaidya*), he will profit from *all* the good effects of the rejuvenation treatment promised in the medical texts.[14]

The medical component of the treatment is to be administered by a qualified physician in an isolated dwelling situated not far from a town where all the requisite medicaments, raw materials for concocting a special regimen and so forth, are readily available in plenty. The retreat itself should have a qualified physician, attendants and brahmins ready at hand (Ca.ci. 1:1.17–23). The doors and the windows of this retreat should be small and strategically located so as to prevent direct access to sunshine or the wind. Two smaller huts, one inside the other, should be constructed within this outer dwelling, so that in the innermost hut darkness will prevail even at noon. The idea is to recreate in the subject an ambience and mood similar to that experienced by the fetus in the womb.

The treatment begins on an auspicious day, time and place, that is, during the northern movement of the sun and in the bright half of the month when the day and the constellation are propitious (the magical (*daivavyapāśraya*) component of the therapy, see below). The subject should be both physically and mentally pure and serene. He should be firm in his resolution, purpose and faith, and single-minded in application (Ca.ci. 1:1.22,28). The treatment is to be preceded by certain bodily purifications resembling the familiar yogic purificatory practices. Caraka also adds that the subject must be in the first phase of life and one whose body has been purged of old blood.

The purification principally involves the purging of the pathogenic factors, that is, the three deranged humors, in the months of April–May (Caitra), July–August (Śrāvaṇa) and November–December (Mārgaśīrṣa) respectively. The subject is then put on a rehabilitatory diet consisting of barley gruel mixed with *ghee* for a period ranging from three to seven days depending on his bodily constitution. This will purge his intestines of all fecal matter. Suśruta emphasizes the importance of this essential preliminary step with reference to a homely simile:

> The rejuvenation therapy is ineffective in a body that is not properly purged, just as a dirty cloth even though dyed fails to shine (Su.ci. 27:4).

At this stage Caraka (Ca.sū. 16:18,19) suddenly announces that after undergoing this purificatory treatment, the subject will hardly age at all and will live a long life free from all diseases (in all probability this tactic is introduced principally to discourage both the subject or his physician from skipping over this preliminary but essential step).

Only then can the physician (his epithet used in this context is *kālavit*, that is, knowledgeable of the role of time in the process of aging) successfully administer the rejuvenation therapy with a view to restoring the ideal proportion of the seven bodily elements, to reducing the subject's susceptibility to diseases, and to slowing down the pace of the aging process (Ca.sū. 7:48,49). Further details of the treatment vary depending upon the particular prescription used. The fruits, plants and herbs used for such preparations must be collected (often personally by the subject undergoing the therapy) from the Himalayan or other designated forests in their proper seasons and in a perfect and flawless state. Pure honey, milk, clarified butter, rock salt, and minerals also figure as rejuvenating agents in many of these prescriptions.

The method of rejuvenation therapy in a nursing home as outlined in the compilations of Caraka and Suśruta is a very lengthy, cumbersome, time-consuming, labor-intensive and expensive affair. Only the rich and the twice-born males, with material means to engage a fleet of attendants and caretakers (e.g., the brahmin, the nurse and the attendants) to wait upon them over a period of six months, could avail themselves of this method.

*The nature-cure treatment.* In this method the subject is fully exposed to the wind and sun as part of the therapy (the term used in the texts is *vātātapika,* meaning the sun and wind treatment). It was designed for the benefit of the average individual with limited means. It is argued that other distinct advantages the nature-cure method has over the nursing home method are that it can be started without undergoing the preliminary purifications (Ca.ci. 1:4.28–29). It is also less susceptible to toxic side effects than the hut residence treatment, which involves a larger number of drugs and doses. Further, this treatment may be interrupted or suspended in midcourse without harm (see *Aṣṭāṅgahṛdayam,* "Uttara Tantra" 39:144–145). It also does not envisage the constant supervision of the physician; the subject merely follows his instructions and takes the prescribed recipes.

*Revitalization Therapy*

A virile, youthful look with a stallion-like vigor and athletic body notwithstanding advancing age is a popular, ideal male image that has been cultivated in most cultures and traditions. Interest in and preoccupation with the pursuit of youth in old age has prompted numerous systems of medicine the world over to promote aphrodisiac potions claiming to generate an inexhaustible store of semen (the definite sign of virility) and great phallic strength. In Indian tradition, already in the *Atharva Veda,* several charms are listed promising increase in male virility (4:4). These charms make a specific reference to horse (*vājī*) as the standard of virile power. Occasionally the bull, elephant, goat or the ass also serve as the measure of comparison (Karambelkar 1961, 49).

In Āyurveda such practices and prescriptions are defined by Caraka as a process whereby a man may acquire vigor and be able to copulate frequently for long periods without fatigue (*vājīkaraṇa vidhi,* Ca.ci. 2.4:50,51). For Suśruta revitalization is a recipe that can rectify the depleted or scanty production of semen (*śukra*), a natural consequence of aging, as well as its deficient or poor quality resulting from the deranged humors (ci. chapter 26).

Cakrapāṇi explains the essential meaning of the concept of revitalization in a neat and clear gerontological context stating that *vājīvidhi* is intended to render the sexually weak and feeble individual (*avājī*) vigorous, virile and energetic (*vājī*). He equates the substantive *vājī* (which also means food as well as horse) with semen, and *vājīkaraṇa* as the remedy that increases the store of semen. *Vājī* also means, according to him, an improved capacity to ejaculate semen with force during intercourse.

Nonetheless, Caraka is quick to admonish that the revitalization therapy is valid only within the framework of the model of life stages (see chapter one). As such, it is recommended to males belonging to the first three classes only. Secondly, only the householder may resort to revitalization therapy for the expressed purpose of enabling him to procreate a son so that he may discharge one of his three debts (*ṛṇa*, see chapter one). The rationale behind this restriction is buttressed with two appropriate similes by Caraka:

> Fragrance manifests itself in the bud only when it is mature enough to blossom. Such is also the case for semen in man. A man desirous of long life must not, therefore, copulate with a woman while he is still a teenager [when the semen is not fully developed] or when he has grown old [when the quantity of semen has depleted].
>
> An adolescent boy copulating with a woman would dry up in no time like a pond containing only a little water. Similarly, an old man copulating with a woman will crumble at once like a dry, sapless, worm-eaten and decayed piece of wood at the mere touch (Ca.ci. 2:4.41,42).

Even the householder must cultivate certain ethical and cultural traits and norms in order to be eligible for the revitalization treatment. He must be aware of and respectful to the presence of self within (*ātmavān*) and must restrain his senses (*jitendriya*). He must live according to the prescribed codes of positive health and of moral behavior (*svasthavṛtta* and *sadvṛtta*, Ca.ci. 2:1.3–4). The purpose of the revitalization therapy is to enable such a householder to obtain a son in his old age because he was unable to procreate a son in his young age.

The most virile agent for such a man is his own wife (*vṛṣyatamā*) provided she is also good looking, young and cultivated (Ca.ci. 2:1.7,8). Caraka reiterates this observation in a charming simile (which incidently is also used by Aśvaghoṣa to draw just the opposite conclusion, see chapter three).

> Just as the juice circulates in the sugarcane . . . even so semen pervades man's body. Stimulated by the warmth of mutual erotic desires and acts [with his wife], semen will spontaneously rush out to unite with the ovum during copulation (Ca.ci. 2:4.46–49).

Sex with such a partner in moderation will make such a man long lived. He will age slowly, his body will retain its glow and vigor (Su.ci. chapter 24). As the medical texts envisage it, the revitalization therapy is designed to bolster the failing libido and the urge for sex attributed to impotency caused by abnormal physiological or psychological factors, as well as by old age. This is sought to be achieved by:

1. Increasing the production of the semen (*śukra*).
2. Improving the mechanism of its delivery during the sex act.
3. Improving the fertilizing quality of the sperm.

It is interesting to note that Caraka is also aware of the psychosocial dimension of sexuality. He recognizes the role and value of proper social interaction (*entregens*) in the sustenance of sexual vigor. He therefore counsels men and women to seek persons of their own age-groups and social circle in order to acquire and maintain virility (Ca.ci. 2:3.21–23).

## *Managing the Stress of Aging*

Āyurveda enjoins that a constant vigilance and a regular daily and seasonal routine (*dinacaryā* and *ṛtucaryā*), when kept according to the moral and social prescriptions compiled in various medical and moral texts, will check the depletion of *vāja*, which, in turn, will prevent premature aging and help retain sexual vigor despite advancing age. For that purpose Caraka suggests various measures that range from warm baths, gentle exercises and oil massage to the regular intake of selected wines and diet that includes meat.[15]

The use of prescribed eye-salve and eye-drops, for instance, is recommended to retain good eyesight even in old age. Smoking of pipes containing specific medicinal herbs is said to preserve mental alertness despite advancing age. Regularly lubricating the nostrils at prescribed times with medicated oils retards the onset of senility and maintains acuteness of sight, smell and hearing (Ca.sū. 5:57–

59). Daily massage of the scalp and hair with approved vegetable oils prevents insomnia, baldness, grey hairs and sagging facial muscles (Ca.sū. 5:81–83). Special measures are recommended for the maintenance of health in old age during seasonal changes. Three times a year, at prescribed seasons, the body should be cleansed of all accumulated waste matter by sudation, steam-baths, emesis, purgation and enemas (Ca.sū. 7:47).

The following dicta, from the *Brahmavaivarta Purāṇa* emphasize the moral component of personal hygiene:

> The sprinkling of water upon the eyes, application of oil to the soles of the feet, putting oil drops in the ears and anointing the head with oil—these are the methods to keep back decrepitude. Staying away from walks in the sun in autumn, consuming well cooked grains and rice served hot, also avert decrepitude. Walks in the spring season, warming the body moderately before the fire, and sex with a young girl keeps old age away (1.17.34–42).

On the other hand, engaging in practices forbidden in the texts such as the Dharma Śāstras or the Purāṇas, is said to be conducive to premature aging:

> Consuming parched meat, sex with an old woman, sitting in the morning sun, [consuming] yogurt which is not quite ready—all these accelerate the aging process (*Brahmavaivarta Purāṇa* 1:1.17.45).

The rejuvenation and revitalization therapies and prescriptions as expounded in the medical texts are based on the idea that certain substances, categorized as follows, are the source of *vāja* (rejuvenatory and revitalizing force):

1. Herbs and herbal products: Śatāvarī, Āmalaka.
2. Animal secretions: milk, honey.
3. Fruits: grapes, mangoes, dates.
4. Grains: *śāli* variety of rice, wheat barley, sesame, lentil.
5. Animal flesh: goat, peacock, sparrow.
6. Minerals: gold, silver (Ca.ci. chapters 1,2).

The above products are said to increase the quantity of semen and to improve its quality. When ingested regularly in the manner and proportion prescribed by the physician, they are said to prevent premature ejaculation which is recognized as a sign and syndrome of premature aging. Occasionally, specific products such as Śilājatu (mineral pitch) exuded from certain varieties of rocks heated by the rays of the sun are also prized. Caraka, in fact, claims that there is no disease which Śilājatu cannot cure (ci. 1:3.48–65). For centuries it has also been known as the aphrodisiac par excellence, and even today one comes across itinerant 'doctors' peddling what they claim to be Śilājatu to young couples honeymooning in the hill resorts of India.

Caraka does not include preparations based on other minerals such as mercury or sulphur, which first came into vogue with the establishment of the Rasa and Siddha (alchemy) systems of medicine in South India toward the beginning of the common era. Ramacandra Rao (1985, 90,91) traces the beginnings of the Siddha system to a Taoist doctor from China who settled in the Pazhani hills of Tāmil Nāḍu. It allegedly sought to bring about, first, transmutation of certain base metals such as mercury or copper into gold or silver and, second, to bestow perennial youth and virile power (*kāyasādhanā* or *dehasiddhi*) on those ingesting such preparations (*vaidyamappu*).

By 700 CE, prescriptions based on this system had already begun to appear in certain Āyurvedic texts also (Cakrapāṇi, for instance, refers frequently to the mercury-based preparations). Proponents of these schools claimed that their mercury-based preparations were superior to the herbal preparations of the classical Āyurveda. Their potency, it was argued, was liable to deteriorate rapidly since it was a function of a number of uncontrollable variables—the season, habitat, age, sex and the bodily constitution of the patient.

Further, Āyurvedic preparations had to be concocted out of a large quantity of raw materials, many of which were not readily available or were very expensive. The process of formulating, compounding and dispensing these preparations generally was tedious, cumbersome, time consuming and labor intensive. The period of treatment was also long, often stretching into months. The doses were large and numerous and required expensive food adjuncts such as milk or honey.

In brief, Āyurvedic rejuvenatory or revitalizing remedies were deemed to be (justly so, one may add) beyond the means of the average individual. As against this, the mercury-based potions were, it was claimed, more potent, longer lasting and provided quicker relief or cure. Whereas the potency of the Āyurvedic preparations disappeared within one year of their compounding, the potency of the mercury-based potions *increased* with age (see *Śārṅgadhara Saṃhitā* 1:1.50–53). The doses of the mercury or mineral-based rejuvenating prescriptions were, it was claimed, quick acting, better tasting and required only a fraction in quantity as compared to the doses prescribed in the Āyurvedic system.[16] The compounding and dispensing of the doses was rational and standardized so that just one dose applied to all regardless of the age, sex, and bodily constitution of the subject (*Rasacaṇḍānśu*, "Pūrva Khaṇḍa" 8:9, quoted in Sharma 1975, 469). It was further claimed that some of these preparations had the capacity to render the subject ageless (*ajara*) and immortal (*amara*).[17]

Sharma has argued that the Rasa school of medicine which arose in Śaivite circles in South India was developed and made popular by Buddhist monks and physicians. According to the Rasa school, mercury is the seed of Śiva (Harabīja) and mica that of his consort Śakti. When Śiva and Śakti come together, that is, when mercury and mica are combined, the resultant compound acquires the power of vanquishing death. Mercury, therefore, is the best means of spiritual liberation, because it endows the body with the necessary immutability (*piṇḍasthairya*) which is an essential prerequisite for spiritual realization.

Geriatrics developed as a separate medical and clinical branch only in the present century. But traditionally, the treatment and prevention of diseases and disabilities in the aged has been an integral part of general medicine in major ancient civilizations. The culture-bound character of geriatrics as it has evolved in Āyurveda is discernible from the fact that selection and employment of drugs, diet and the overall life style to be adopted by the elderly—though rationally determined (*yuktivyapāśraya*)—is also skillfully blended with appeals to divine and magical interventions (*daivavyapāśraya*) with a view to assure successful treatment.[18]

These latter include the chanting of the sacred formulae (*mantra*), fasting (*upavāsa*), wearing of consecrated beads or magical stones (*maṇi*), sacrifices (*homa*), observances of vows (*vrata* and *niyama*), the collection, cleaning, compounding and dispensing of medicines accompanied by rituals and so forth. Active participation of the elderly in these treatments is deemed to be a necessary conditon particularly at the psychological level (*sattvāvajaya*), which may include such yogic practices as concentration and meditation. This is intended to promote the therapeutic efficacy of the food or drug administered to the elderly patient (Ca.sū. 11:54).

The threefold basis of geriatrics or even general medicine in Āyurveda reveals its close affinity with ancient medicine as propounded in the *Atharva Veda* (particularly *daivavyapāśraya*), on the one hand, and classical *yoga* as expounded by Patañjali (*sattvāvajaya*), on the other (see Nespor and Singh 1986). Caraka's admonition that the success or failure of the treatment is a function of the sum of the deeds committed by the individual in his present and past lives undergirds the eclectic and practical approach of the medical school. The *Caraka Saṃhitā* (śā. 1:53.116, 117), for instance, states that the influence of actions done in past lives determines pathogenesis in the present or the future life. But this fatalistic stance is immediately balanced by a rational declaration that "bearing in mind past symptoms, prophylactic measures taken today will avert disaster/disorder tomorrow" (Ca.sū. 11:58–63). It is supported by an appropriate simile:

> Just as a dam is raised so that the floods may not destroy the crops as they did in the past, so the treatment given today will prevent a possible disaster tomorrow (Ca.śā. 1:90,91; ni. 6:12–15).[19]

This suggests that some of the typical Hindu precepts and practices promoted in the classical medical texts to cope with the stress of aging are perceptive enough to warrant further scrutiny in the light of modern findings in gerontology and geriatrics. Rules about the dietetics pertaining to old age are also of equal importance. Despite certain alterations (necessitated by the introduction of modern medicine), they are largely respected by the majority of Indian men and women even today. More recently one gerontologist has argued in a similar vein, claiming that there is no one single factor that plays such a significant role in contributing to the ultimate health status, general well-being, and quality of life of the elderly woman (or man) as does nutrition (Mitchell 1985).

The Āyurvedic understanding of aging is nonetheless conceptually puzzling because aging is also viewed as disease. Since aging is a disease, it seems to argue, the aged should not be abandoned as useless but be treated with due respect so that they can resume and maintain their roles as useful members of society. To speak of aging as disease also entails some notion of it being improper.[20] The sense of impropriety, however, cannot be based on aging being unusual or unnatural; since everybody grows old. Only 'premature' aging, therefore, may be judged diseased or unusual when it becomes manifest in people earlier than usual. Calling aging disease, then, may be a way of identifying a condition which is controllable and manageable with proper preventive therapies, such as rejuvenation and revitalization. The material of geriatric relevance from Āyurvedic texts, accordingly, is likely to be found helpful to the development of an indigenous policy and program for elderly health care and welfare in modern India.

# 5

# Interpretations

In the introduction it was pointed out that traditionally, in the formulation of Indian texts, thought and meaning become enmeshed in the web of semantics, physics and metaphysics in order to confer specific significance upon various life processes. With reference to aging, for instance, persons quickly notice its distinct signs on any adult body, but one may have to be convinced by others of the same fact with respect to one's own aging body. But these perceptions, even if organized, have no clear meaning unless mediated by religious or cultural symbols. Aging, thus, is one situation in life where the problems of meaning and interpretation become especially acute when a sharp and uneasy awareness of old age in the form of indelible and clear signs on the body and mind dawns on the individual. Old age also precipitates a profoundly disjunctive experience in the inner life of individuals by confronting them with the psychologically traumatic event of the approaching end. It further aggravates the matters by daily diminishing vitality that threatens personal integrity and identity. It would seem strange if these experiences, which occur and recur in the life of the human species, had not been given various interpretations.

Relevant religious and cultural ideas on aging, accordingly, are not only shared but also manipulated by persons and groups to resolve particular problems of meaning by mediation through certain metaphysical concepts. Such an expression and investment of meaning and interpretation in terms of metaphysics is ubiquitous in Indian and perhaps in any tradition—from the definitions of the physical world and the social reality to the conceptions of otherworldly realms and even the existential domain—so that human pain and suffering are endowed with precise metaphysical significance.

Naturally, ancient Indians could not rest content with the fact that people inevitably grow old and die. They had to reflect on this phenomenon and verbalize it in order to provide a satisfying meaning and interpretation, whether in positive or negative terms. But they soon discovered that it is not very meaningful to posit that aging is merely an accident or a chance event as some early schools of Indian philosophy such as the Ājīvikas did. On the contrary, when it was suggested that aging is due to bad *karma* in this or past lives, or to the movement of planets, or to the drying up of vital energy (*vīrya*), the personal and public experience of aging was suddenly invested with a tangible meaning.

It is, therefore, not surprising to find that in their attempts to inscribe the meanings of aging and death in the life process, certain passages in our texts imperceptibly dovetail into metaphysics. To cite just one example, the basic Āyurvedic doctrine that the body and mind are intimately connected invariably draws medicine to the frontiers of philosophy and metaphysics.[1] This tendency is already discernible in the Vedic texts (e.g. Saṃhitā and Brāhmaṇa) with respect to such age-sensitive concepts as rejuvenation (see chapter four) and immortality. It is argued therein that the subtle body, mind and self are sustained and carried over time by a variety of metaphysical causes. The chief among these causal agents are deeds (*karma*) and desire (*kāma*), which are said to underlie the merely physical and biological explanations of human beings who age and die and yet continue to go through the rounds of transmigration (*saṃsāra*).

A very relevant example of how a new meaning of old age is created through the promotion of a myth is to be found in the story (see chapter one) of young Siddhārtha when he confronts old age for the first time in his youth. The episode, which is retold in manifold versions in various Buddhist sacred texts in different languages, tells us also much about the shifting spectrum of the Buddhist understanding of old age. Briefly, the story, as told in cantos three and four of the *Buddhacarita,* runs as follows:

> Young Siddhārtha once drove out of the city and happened to see an old man with a white head, bent on a staff . . . On his next outing he happened to see a sick man . . . and then a dead man. On his fourth and final visit he happened to see a renouncer.

The myth next lets us understand that no one else but the young Siddhārtha 'saw' these very common events in the human life, that is, he alone was able to discover the hidden meaning behind these mundane phenomena—that old age, disease and death are suffering, and that by renouncing worldly life one can eradicate these sufferings. Myth, simile and metaphor, therefore, are crucial to understanding the meaning of human life and its various processes (including aging) in Indian tradition. Myths are stories told to manifest a particular aspect of the cosmic order and thereby provide a given community in which they are alive with ways of stretching past experience in the present. Created to inform people about their self-identity and the framework of significance in which they operate, a myth incorporates in itself different religious and cultural symbols in a complex narrative. It thereby seeks to recommend a way of life and endorses a set of moral principles and guidelines to those who believe in it. This is so because the telos of Hindu and Buddhist metaphysics, as Organ (1970, 146) aptly explains, is to cope with the suffering inherent in the human condition. It accordingly prescribes techniques for the alleviation of suffering.

A physician of the soul who merely identifies the malady is not a true physician. In true Hindu and Buddhist tradition, therefore, myth is made to serve another important function—to put the aspirant on the way to spiritual liberation, which in our present context may be interpreted as the recovery of true insight into the nature of human life and its processes including aging (as the myth recounted above amply indicates).

## *Metacauses of Aging*

The Vedic seers were not overly preoccupied with establishing the etiology of aging and death, since it was believed that, by performing the prescribed sacrificial rituals or spells, the gods could be contacted and influenced to assure a long, healthy life here on earth and an immortal and joyous life in the hereafter. This promise and hope of the eternal life tended to reduce the fear and significance of aging and suffering here in this world.

In their attempts to answer the questions about the universe and the nature of human life in it, the Upaniṣadic seers tended to reject the simplistic Vedic ideas and the means of manipulating the universe and the human body through divine intervention. Their solution instead lay in reinterpreting the concept of the self in relation to the universe, on the one hand, and to the body on the other. For this purpose, the Upaniṣads introduced the concept of *karma* to account for the meaning of life whereby the process of aging ceases to be a threat to the self which is perceived to be ageless and eternal. The self gets embodied, it is now argued, because of desire (*kāma*), which, in turn, creates willing capacity (*kratu*) in the individual. As one wills so one will become and accumulate the store of good or evil acts (*karma*) (see BAU 4:4.2–6).

Buddhism and classical Hinduism posited additional causal elements, all related in one way or the other to the central concept of *karma*, to serve as a metaphysical explanation of the aging process. Śaṅkara, for instance, argued that empirical reality as well as embodied existence are nothing but a complex of the organs of action (*kāryakaraṇasaṃghāta*) intended to produce the experience of human suffering (which includes aging, see *Brahma Sūtra Śāṅkara Bhāṣya* 2:2.19; 3:4.7,8). The following are other causal factors with *karma* as the common thread running through all of them:

1. Determinate human action.
2. Divine intervention.
3. Hereditary traits.
4. Extenuating circumstances.
5. Potent action of extraordinary personages such as seers, magicians, and soothsayers.
6. Potent action of certain substances such as plant extracts and minerals.[2]

Illustrative accounts depicting the positive or negative implications of these factors for the aging process in terms of acceleration or deceleration are to be found in the Nikāyas, Jātaka stories, Epics, Purāṇas, and the Āyurvedic texts. But the origin of aging—the crux of the problem—is often awkwardly glossed over in such accounts. The "Manuṣyaka Sutta", for instance, merely declares that various stages in the life of the sentient being are nothing but names (Chaudhuri 1976, 228). Aging, thus, is denied, but without adequately explaining why.

### *Kāma and Aging*

The Ṛgveda suggests that for the Vedic Indians death was but the crossing from one level of existence to another. That the unborn self of the departed one (*aja*), after due rites of purification by fire, retires to a land of joy and sunshine is also asserted in the *Atharva Veda*. According to Miller (1974, 132), two trends of thought are perceptible in these verses. First, there is the desire for a long life here on earth with its corollary avoidance of premature death and secondly, the wish for immortality and the equal avoidance of death. Continued physical life and immortality, however, are not held to be equivalent. For this reason, it is not always clear whether the desire expressed is for immortality in spirit or in the body.[3]

*Ṛgveda* (10:121.2) is probably the earliest instance where the shift from the physical to the metaphysical aspect of immortality is attempted.[4] It is stressed in this hymn that the sun (the golden germ),[5] conceived as the son of Prajāpati, is an image of immortality whose shadow is death itself. The phrase is based on a pun (*śleṣa*) on the substantive *chāyā*, which means both shadow and likeness or reflection. This is a striking enigmatic statement of the paradox of time which brings death, but which is also an image of immortality.[6]

The deeper meaning inscribed in the pun is that the one and the same god (Prajāpati/Hiraṇyagarbha), paradoxically, is *both* the creator and the destroyer of human life and its acts. For this purpose, the outward or surface meaning is carried in the imagery of the physical and the visible sun, on whose passage is predicated the measured and elapsed time (see Johnson 1980, 65). The third meaning of *Chāyā* connotes the shade or refuge from the heat and destruction caused by the sun or elliptically by time, as suggested in two Ṛgvedic hymns to Agni and Rudra respectively (6:16.38 and 2:33.6). When mortals die, it is not a literal death but a symbolic death that renounces attachment to mortal reality. In another Ṛgvedic hymn (7:59.12) to Śiva (Tryambaka), the poet enjoins the god to deliver him from death but not from immortality, by which is implied, once again, not a literal immortality but rather a full life span, reckoned to be one hundred years.[7]

With the emergence of the Brāhmaṇa texts new rituals are introduced to assure longevity, progeny and heaven after death. But at the same time they also begin to move away from a merely physical understanding of life and death. It is now held that only *mortals* can aspire to be immortal. Immortality is not sheer deathlessness, the mere continuation of a given earthly and temporal condition. It is, rather, the overcoming of death, the penetrating and passing through it (ŚB 2:3.3.7).

"Death is bathed in light", claims the *Śatapatha Brāhmaṇa;* "death covers itself in splendor" (ŚB 10:5.2.4).[8] Elsewhere it is declared that, "He who performs the *rājasūya* sacrifice transcends all kinds of death, and old age alone is his death (*jaraiva mṛtyurbhavati,* ŚB 5:4.1.1.). This hope is also expressed in the prayer offered on behalf of a child by its parents "Let father heaven and mother earth give you death in old age."[9] The *Kauṣītaki Upaniṣad* (2:10) also provides a meaning of immortality which is, as Deussen (1980, 1:41) notes, along a horizontal plane. Immortality is something handed over by a dying father to his son. By his birth and by the birth of his son, the father has contracted a debt (*ṛṇa*) with life. In a moving ritual performed at the moment of death and the transmission of immortality (*saṃpradāna*), the dying father repays his debt by passing on to his son all that he has, the prayers, the sacrifice and the portion of the world which he is. Thereby the immortality (as a hereditary trait) of the father is assured and the continuity between generations is maintained.[10]

In the Purāṇic mythology, immortality is attained by activating the potency inherent in austerities (*tapas*). In the Vedic hymns, the practice of austerities is said to produce fertility, but in the Upaniṣads it is undertaken to attain release. As O'Flaherty (1973, 76–77) points out, release and progeny are forms of immortality, both promising continuation of the self without the body. It may be argued that with the emergence of Buddhism as a competing soteriology the followers of orthodoxy were forced to make an existential choice between the spiritual life underscored by renunciation and the desire for the 'immortal' life in the body.

This dilemma is somewhat awkwardly posed in the following episode from the *Śatapatha Brāhmaṇa* (10:4.3.1–9).[11] The setting is a sacrificial session undertaken to gain immortality. Death feels threatened by the prospect of humanity obtaining immortality through such sacrifices and addresses the gods:

> Death: If this is so, then, surely all persons will become immortal. What will be my fate?
> Gods: From now on no one will become immortal with the body. After you have appropriated the [gross] body as your share, then only shall whoever deserves immortality [either by wisdom or works] attain it (translation is based on Eggeling 1963).

Grmek (1958, 29) has observed that the roots of cultural gerontology as the art and science of aging began as an inquiry into the characteristics or the qualities of long-lived people. By nature, the human being is, as Horace put it, *laudator temporis acti,* and apt to believe that predecessors lived a happier and longer life. Over the centuries, much speculation and many myths have been created to explain why certain individuals were favored with long life. Thus, the themes of immortality or, more realistically, longevity and rejuvenation, go together. Who would want to be eternally alive as a decrepit, old man/woman? Indeed, most would prefer a short life that is full of youthful vigor. A Greek myth graphically portrays the plight of Tethonos whose lover, Eos (comparable to Ṛgvedic Uṣas), asked Zeus that Tethonos may be deathless and live forever but forgot to ask for agelessness and its specific corollary, eternal youth. He therefore continued to age with growing years and eventually lived only to curse his immortality devoid of youthful vitality (see King 1986).

Not surprisingly, people have always struggled to find a panacea for an eternal youthful life. Most societies value life and seek to prolong it, and the main cultural practices are dedicated to survival and the maintenance of human life, provided that it could be lived in relative comfort. The quest for longevity and youthfulness predates all organized religions and cultures and is as universal as people's consciousness of the inevitability of their own death and the roots of that quest stretch back to the dawn of time.

Health and youth are, some have claimed, contagious like disease. Since senescence is loss of vital energy, it was believed that by remaining in close contact with young maidens lost youth and vigor may be regained. King David, accordingly, took the young virgin Abishag to bed, presumably to inhale her breath and thus restore something of his lost youth. Curiously, though, one does not come across any legend of a similarly motivated old woman taking young, virgin males into her bed. Rabelais (1893, 348–351) does conjure up such scenes from his imagination, but documented instances of such a practice are difficult to find.

Grmek (1958) has pointed out that faith in *shunamitism* (opotherapy), perhaps the oldest method of rejuvenation, and certainly widely held, is based on the belief that human physical and psychological properties are closely related to certain bodily organs in humans and animals/plants. If these organs are eaten, it is believed, aging organs may be reinvigorated. This principle is endorsed in Āyurveda and a number of prescriptions based on it are in circulation as popular rejuvenating remedies even today in India (see chapter four).

In the Indian tradition discussions concerning longevity and rejuvenation are also presented in the mythical mode and structured in terms of three basic themes or ideas. First, the idea that people lived much longer in the ancient past but lost that privilege because of some moral flaw is prevalent in many Vedic, Buddhist and Hindu texts.[12] Bosch (1960, 63), quoting Ronnow, argues that originally in the Vedic texts the divine nectar (*amṛta*) is nothing but the elixir of life of folklore and myth. It was a magical means of sustaining actual life and providing protection against ill-health, old age and death. Since this very triune evil was also defeated by the Buddha (see below), he came to be regarded as the bestower of immortality (*amṛta*) upon humankind.

Another favorite theme refers to the land and people of Uttarakuru, a mythical and fortunate race, that once lived in the far northern regions of India and enjoyed a marvelous longevity. In that land grew the magic *jambu* tree, whose fruit had the property of conferring immunity from illness and old age and lengthening life to a thousand years.[13]

A desirous and lustful old man seeking rejuvenation is yet another popular motif in Indian tradition. Usually it revolves around an old sage who, through the help of the twin divine physicians (Aśvins) or the fire god (Agni) obtains a young wife.[14] The favorite simile employed in the Vedic texts refers to the refurbishing of an old chariot at the hands of a skilled carpenter. But the Buddhists, in keeping with their wont, satirically make use of the same metaphor to come to the opposite conclusion that the body, subject to death, ages and eventually breaks down like an old chariot.

The more popular and better known among these legends concerns the old and decrepit sage and ascetic Cyavana, abandoned by his sons and others, to whom the twin divine physicians (Aśvins) restore youth and strength, with the result that his marriage to a young princess named Sukanyā survived.[15] It also figures in the subsequent *Jaimini* and *Śatapatha Brāhmaṇas,* the *Mahabhārata* and the *Devī Bhāgavata.* This legend may be viewed as the Indian attempt to resolve the tension between, carnal love and physical finitude (Eros and Thanatos). While the desire is personified by the fatally beautiful but faithful princess Sukanyā; the finitude of the mortal body is represented by old Cyavana.

In the *Ṛgveda* (1:106.6) Cyavana is rescued by the Aśvins from a pit where he was restrained and separated from his young wife. In the Brāhmaṇas (JB 3:120.120–129), he is depicted as an old husband with a failing libido scheming with his young wife to trick the Aśvins into rejuvenating him. As amplified in the *Śatapatha Brāhmaṇa,* Cyavana assumes a shrivelled form and lies in a pit as if abandoned. The sons of King Śaryāti find him and pelt him with clods. The incensed Cyavana sows discord between the king and his sons. He is appeased only after he has received in marriage the young daughter of Śaryāti (ŚB 4:1.5.3–7). In the *Mahābhārata,* the core legend is retouched in that old Cyavana is lustful and capable of satisfying his wife even before his rejuvenation.[16] In the *Devī Bhāgavata,* the premise regarding the sexual prowess of old Cyavana is reversed and he is depicted as an unsatisfactory old man eagerly seizing the opportunity morally to coerce King Śaryāti into offering him in marriage the young princess Sukanyā.[17]

The legend of Cyavana, as it comes across in Indian art and literature, from the *Ṛgveda* onward, is the prototype of the enduring motif of eros and the failing libido through aging—an apparently senile and [as a result?] inadequate husband and his young, faithful wife. It reinforces the assumption that age brings with it changes in physical appearance, a more negative evaluation of the body, and the assumption that with age sexual vigor disappears. The caricature of Cyavana also reveals another implicit assumption that an older person's interest in sex is, at best, inappropriate and, at worst, unnatural and disgusting. Yet, aging men are not as burdened by cultural norms regarding their sexual functioning as aging women are. The rejuvenation of the old ascetic for sexual purposes, though a popular motif, goes against the prescriptions in the legal digests (see chapter four). The medical texts, however, prescribe specific rejuvenation treatment for genuine hermits so as to enable them to attain liberation (Ca.ci. 1:1.78–80).

### *Sex Drive and Premature Aging*

In the Indian tradition, thus, men as well as women are subject to constraints of cultural and religious assumptions about the expression of their sexuality and their age. Sex is not reproduction, even though occasionally the two have been equated by reifing sex as a concept and associating it with both the finer and baser qualities of the body (see Frayser 1985, 237, 418). In the texts studied here, however, the connection between procreation and aging and the implication that immoderate sexual activity is the principle cause of the acceleration of the aging process recurs in many Hindu and Buddhist myths.

Woman as the symbol and source of fecundity becomes not only the abstract or metaphysical cause of aging and old age, she is also used as the specific instrument of the gods physically and morally to corrupt men and, in particular, sages and seers. This is reflected in the misogynist stream that begins to flow in the Indian intellectual tradition after the Saṃhitā period (see chapter one) when first the Upaniṣadic doctrine of the chain of rebirth, and then the Buddhist doctrine of dependent origination, promoted the view that reproduction ensnares beings in the painful cycle of existence.

As a corollary of this development, abstract Vedic goddesses or female ogresses, such as Uṣas of Ālakṣmī respectively, are branded with increasing frequency as the transempirical cause of aging and death. Decrepitude, disease and death—originally visualized as male gods—now begin to appear as malefic or wicked goddesses. Already in the *Ṛgveda,* Uṣas, the goddess of dawn, is described as a beautiful dancing girl appearing in the east and luring men with her beguiling charm. But the same hymn also reveals another side of Uṣas that is less alluring.[18]

Uṣas is said to be born daily, causing mortals to age with every passing day, wearing away their lifespan and shrinking human generations in the manner of the hunter woman cutting short the life of the moving birds by clipping their wings (RV 1:92.10). Here the central metaphor evidently refers to Uṣas as a measure of time, appearing day by day to mark the steady approach of old age and death. The secondary metaphor is that of a courtesan who wears men out and destroys them by aging them. It is also implied that this siphoning off of the vital forces of men, though disastrous and harmful to succeeding human generations, keeps Uṣas herself forever young, thanks to the vitality she has stolen like a cunning gambler (RV 1:124.4).

In early Buddhism, too, the mythical mode of discourse is constantly employed to associate the origin of old age with the appearance of sexual drive and hunger. In the "Māra Saṃyutta" of the *Saṃyutta Nikāya,* a collection of twenty-five Suttas (SN 1:103–127), lust and death combine with old age in the image of Māra, the devil. Pāpmā Mṛtyu (death), who as evil is already present in the Brāhmaṇa texts, furnishes the prototype for the later Buddhist imagery of evil Māra. His three daughters—Tāṇhā, Ratī and Aratī—come to disturb Siddhārtha when he has become the Buddha and is enjoying the bliss of spiritual awakening. The daughters of Māra first flirt with the Buddha in the guise of young virgins but without effect on him. Then they also appear as middle aged and elderly women. Yet they utterly fail to distract or corrupt the Buddha. When the Buddha eventually vanquishes Māra (that is, lust and desire), he effectively vanquishes disease, decrepitude and death. This Saṃyutta, therefore, is just one of the many tracts from the Pali Canon which abound in enigmatic statements designed to invoke the condition of agitation (*saṃvega*) by pointing out the evanescent nature of worldly objects, desires and joys.

The impermanent nature of desires is also metaphorically depicted in the *Yuvañjana Jātaka,* which almost recreates young Siddhārtha's departure from home (see chapter one):

> Prince Yuvañjana visiting his pleasure garden sees morning dew drops strung like pearls. His charioteer, when asked to explain what they were, identifies them as dew drops which fall in the cold season. But Yuvañjana fails to find dew drops later in the day. It is explained to him, then, that the heat of the mid-day sun destroyed them all (Fausböll 1962, 5:120, #460).

In this story the dew is cleverly turned into an enigma to demonstrate how the worldly pleasures, though joyous and beautiful, are as transient as the morning dew. When his query is answered, the prince grows extremely agitated and observes:

> Like the dew drops on the tips of reeds indeed are the life experiences of living beings. I will no longer be afflicted by sickness, old age and death (Fausböll 1962, 5:120, #460).

Following Johnson (1980, xxv–xxvi), it may be argued that the dew image clarifies the hidden or deeper meaning of life: the experiences of living beings are created and destroyed by time, one's own deeds and desires are, like the dew, evaporated by the sun's heat.[19] This insight into human contingency is central to the age-sensitive philosophy of Buddhism. In facing and accepting the evanescent character of the aging body, Buddhism seeks to lead the aging individual to see his/her body and the world as they really are (*svalakṣaṇa*) by producing anxiety (*saṃvega*) for heuristic purposes. The quest for spiritual awareness (*nirvāṇa*) is created, continued and brought to fruition in the face of the truth of the triune evil of decrepitude-disease-death.

In the Purāṇas, this Buddhist theme of the triune evil is clothed in the metaphor of family. Old age is popularly described as the daughter of time. Diseases are her brothers and the family wanders around the world (looking for victims).[20] As conceived in the *Viṣṇu Purāṇa* (1:7.33–34), the family, with evil (*adharma*) as the head, is composed of feeling (*vedanā*) and delusion (*māyā*) and their children—disease (*vyādhi*), old age (*jarā*), grief (*śoka*) and thirst/desire (*tṛṣṇā*). In the *Bhāgavata Purāṇa,* old age as the daughter of time goes around the three worlds in search of a groom.[21]

The theory of the progressive contraction of four ages (*yugarhāsa*), endorsed in both Hinduism and Buddhism, implies not merely a diminishing length for each age but also a corresponding diminution in longevity, strength and stamina for those who live in them. Usually this sorry state of affairs is traced to lax morals with regard to sex. But a long lifespan is assured to those who lead a virtuous life. In the "Cakkavatti Sīhanāda Suttanta" of the *Dīgha Nikāya* the Buddha explains how a decadent lifestyle in ancient times eventually reduced the lifespan of man to a mere ten years:

> There will come a time, brethren, when the descendants of those [immoral] humans will have a life span of ten years. Among humans of this life span, maidens of five years will be of a marriageable age. Among such humans of reduced life span, it will occur . . . let us now abstain from taking life.
>
> They will then increase again both as to their span of life and as to their comeliness . . . now it will occur to them to do

> still more good . . . so they will practice religious piety . . . thereby eventually their progeny will come to live eighty thousand years. Their maidens will be marriageable at five hundred years of age (DN 3:58–79).

The classical Hindu texts trace a similar moral and physical decline at both the cosmic and individual level to three factors:

1. Indiscriminate employment of sense organs to gratify worldly desires (*asātmyendriyārtha*).
2. Incorrect adjustment of daily and seasonal activities (*dinacaryā* and *ṛtucaryā*) in terms of diet (*āhāra*) and daily routine activities (*vihāra*).
3. Errors in judgment (*prajñāparādha*) with respect to moral conduct and intellectual thinking (*ācāra* and *vicāra*).

It is argued that premature old age, disease and death as well as shortening lifespan are the direct consequences of these moral lapses at the individual level (Ca.sū. 11.43).[22] At the collective or social level, a general qualitative deterioration of the habitat, time, and water resources of that community is attributed to the higher incidence of immorality (*adharma*) and wrong deeds committed in previous lives resulting from the collective defective application of intellect (*prajñāparādha*).

Several Purāṇic myths describing and explaining the raison d'être of the Kali Yuga are relevant to our discussion of sexual desire as a metaphysical causal factor of aging. The composite legend of Yayāti as told in the first book of the *Mahābhārata* and several Purāṇas is analyzed below by way of illustration.

### *The Legend of Yayāti*

The reversal and exchange of old age for youth for the purpose of satisfying sexual appetite, a variant in the theme of rejuvenation, underscores a series of myths created around the core legend of King Yayāti, who first appears in the *Ṛgveda* (1:31.17) as a patriarch and sacrificer. In the later texts he is described as blinded by polluting desire.[23] The main story, as told in the *Padma Purāṇa* (1:1.66.62–83), may be summarized as follows:

> There once ruled a virtuous king by the name of Yayāti. He had created heaven on earth by 1) performing austerities,

> 2) scrupulously following the prescribed duties, and 3) by instituting the cult of Viṣṇu-Kṛṣṇa in his kingdom. As a result, his subjects became free from the claws of decrepitude, disease and death, and lived for a long time. Everybody appeared to be under twenty-five forever.
>
> Then Yama (god of death) approached Indra complaining that earthlings became immortal and free of old age, etc.. Indra—wishing to get rid of the parallel heaven on earth—summoned the celestial beings (*gandharvas*), the god of love and desire (Kāma) and the nymphs (*apsaras*) and asked them to bring Yayāti to heaven by any ruse.
>
> Disguising themselves as actors they came to earth and entertained Yayāti in his court. Old age, who had taken the form of a beautiful woman, deluded Yayāti by her charm and sweet songs; he consequently neglected to adhere to the ritually sanctioned practices, and as a result old age was able to seize him and age him.

The now aged Yayāti once went hunting and found a beautiful girl Aśrubindumati with a maidservant Viśālā, on a lakeshore, who revealed the girl's identity to Yayāti in a story:

> When Śiva burned Kāma, his wife Ratī wept at this lake. From her tears were born sorrow, old age, separation, misery and grief. From the tears shed from the left eye this beautiful girl was born.

Yayāti is seized by passion for the young girl. In order to enjoy her thoroughly and for a long period, he exchanges his old age for the youth of one of his sons. But after he had enjoyed the girl for twenty years, she began coaxing Yayāti to accompany her to heaven. Yayāti first hesitates but eventually yields, reasoning:

> Each person's fate is determined by its own good or evil *karma*. Those actors who came to me in disguise caused old age to enter my body. I will, therefore, go to heaven, abandoning my people even though they then will be a prey of Yama, the god of death.

He then took back his old age from his son and prepared to go to heaven, but his subjects did not want to live without him and accompanied him to the world of Indra.

The sinister aspect of womanhood as the harbinger of old age also surfaces in another version in the *Padma Purāṇa* (1:2.76.18–30; 1:2.77.1–4). It is related how, instructed by Indra, old age (*jarā*) took the form of a beautiful girl to dance before King Yayāti, who had attained eternal youth by his just and righteous rule. Assisted by the god of lust (Kāma), as stage manager, and by his wife Ratī (the goddess of sexual pleasures), old age deludes the king and enters him. By succumbing to the demonic charms of dance, song and emotion, King Yayāti loses his powers of self-control and visions of righteousness (*dharma*) which made him immortal. Here the dancers are death's minions: old age and desire. When the dance is over, old age is exposed as the hag she really is.[24]

As it is featured in the *Mahābhārata* ("Ādi Parvan" chapters 70ff.), Kāvya Uṣanas, the chief preceptor of the demons (Daityas) and the father of Devayānī, who is married to Yayāti, is infuriated by some impudence of Yayāti and, therefore, curses him so that Yayāti is at once stricken with decrepit old age. But he relents when supplicated and mitigates the curse so that Yayāti may be able to exchange his old age for youth, if he were to find a willing person.

Yayāti's four sons refuse to volunteer for the exchange, citing various reasons. Yadu, the eldest son, begs off without hesitation pointing out that old age brings with it many inconveniences as to drinking and eating. Turvasu is no less pre-emptory: old age prohibits pleasures, destroys beauty, memory and life itself. Druhyu's objection is that an old man cannot enjoy women, chariots and horses. Finally, according to Anu, old people eat like children and soil themselves constantly.[25]

But the youngest son Puru is moved by pity for his father, whereupon the exchange is effected. Yayāti then rules justly and enjoys the pleasures of life for a thousand years. He then transfers the mantle to Puru and enters the forest as a hermit. The *Liṅga Purāṇa* reproduces a summary of the legend of Yayāti in essential details but adds the following reflection on the insatiable nature of desire despite age. As he takes back old age from his youngest son, Yayāti observes:

> With age one's hair, teeth, eyes, ears do age . . . But greed for life and wealth remains ageless (1:1.67.22,23).

Myths incorporating the theme of the magical manipulation of age are unusual in Indian tradition. The only other reference to this motif is to be found in the story of the devout old sage Saubhari

(*Bhāgavata Purāṇa* 9:6.39–55). He was once bathing in the river Yamunā when he happened to meet the king of fishes making love to his wife. Smitten with passion, Saubhari approached King Māndhātṛ and demanded one of his fifty daughters in marriage. Afraid to displease the old ascetic and yet unwilling to marry his daughter to a decrepit suitor, the king vacillated. Finally he agreed that if any one of his daughters should consent to marry Saubhari, the king would approve of the marriage. But on his way to meet the girls, Saubhari transformed himself into a handsome youth and eventually married all the fifty girls. Soon, however, he discovered that his passion for them continued unabated. He therefore retired to the forest and spent the rest of his days worshipping Viṣṇu.

The legends of Yayāti and Saubhari are the Indian variant of what Dumézil (1971–74, 94–95,194) has called the Indo-Iranian myth of the magical manipulation of the aging process.[26] But the Indian version is further embroidered with moralistic overtones. The characters of Yayāti or Saubhari are probably modeled after a lusty and virile king or a devout old sage struggling to indulge in the joys of sex into ripe old age. Yayāti is seized by remorse in his final days and commits suicide. His example is followed by some of his subjects out of a sense of strong loyalty to him. Yayāti's sex impulse symbolizes how the blind drive of sexual hunger goads and impels the embodied self to irrational actions. Yet, the body as a vehicle for satisfying the sex urge cannot, in the very nature of things, escape the clutches of old age and death.[27] It also suggests that the fear of old age rests not so much on the burden of advancing years as on its increasing infirmities, in part attributable to one's deeds and desire. Aiyangar (1983, 297) finds the clue to the legend of Yayāti in the etymology of the name Yayāti, which he traces to the substantive *yātāyāta*, meaning the vortex of birth and death (*saṃsāra*).

Following Defourny (1978, 154) the principal theme of the myths of Yayāti and Saubhari may be schematized as follows:

*dharma* = absence of carnal desire = youth
*adharma* = carnal desire (*kāma*) = old age

The direct relationship between excessive or immoral and unlawful sex with women and premature aging is also posited in the *Brahmavaivarta Purāṇa* (1:16.47–52), where Viṣṇu in the guise of a young brahmin boy gives a discourse on pious living to an assembly, which includes a young woman whose husband has died recently as the result of a curse. In his discourse Viṣṇu preaches that sex with a woman in her menses, a prostitute, a childless widow, a procuress, a wife of the sacrificer for the servile (Śūdra) class or a woman in her menopause or eating food from such women is tantamount to killing a brahmin. Accompanied by this sin, decrepitude visits such an individual.[28] There is a constant amity also, the boy narrates, between sin and disease. In fact, sin definitely engenders old age, diseases and other adversities.[29] But it flies away at the sight of a religious and pious person who worships Hari (Viṣṇu). Decrepitude and diseases cannot subdue a worshipper (*bhakta*) of Viṣṇu.

Similarly, in the *Bhāgavata Purāṇa* (4:25) the sage Nārada recounts to King Prācinabarhiṣaṭ the allegorical story of King Purañjana with a view to point out the evil consequences of immoral sex on aging. Purañjana, one reads, was captivated by the charms of his wife and enjoyed her for a long time without realizing that the passage of days and nights was reducing his lifespan. The consciousness of Purañjana was polluted by lust, passion and desire, which resulted in his siring of eleven hundred sons, though in the process he lost half of his life (4:27.5,6). Nārada concludes that attached to both deeds and desire and *karma* (*kāma*), Purañjana arrived at that disagreeable stage in life (that is, old age), not welcomed by those who are attached to worldly objects and pleasures.[30]

### *Karma and Aging*

*Karma* as the determinate causal factor controlling the human lifespan and death is first tentatively broached in the *Bṛhadāraṇyaka Upaniṣad*. Early Buddhism, too, endorses the idea that *karma* acts like a clockwork which, while running down, always winds itself up. This life is a product of the *karma* accumulated in the course of preceding lives. But at the same time, acts done in the present life produce new *karma* which will ripen (*vipāka*) in the future, determining the destiny and state of being of the individual in his/her following existence, which may be in a higher or lower species. To put it in traditional terminology, a person's present life is conditioned by his/her *prārabdha karma*, that is, by *karma* which has started bearing its fruits. *Saṃcita karma* is the reservoir of *karma* that is awaiting fructification and *saṃcīyamāna karma* is that which is being accumulated as a result of actions carried out in this existence (see *Matsya Purāṇa* 181:10,17,18; 182:20,21).

The fatalistic (i.e., *karma*-determined) nature of the aging process is apparent in the preaching of the elder Nārada to King Muṇḍa, who is grieving over the death of his wife. It is incorporated in the *Aṅguttara Nikāya* in the following maxim:

> There are five objects which cannot be changed: avoidance of old age, disease, death, decay and transiency (Gonda 1975b, 4:43).

But the concept of *karma* as the fatal cause of life and death rises to preeminence in classical Hinduism. Since it is now believed that the self is compelled to encounter the effects of the previous deeds, the question arises as to why the self comes under the sway of corporeality, that is, why it is embodied at all in the first place? The problem of what aging is thus also depends upon what is understood by the notion of human beings and their embodiment. It must also be determined just what it is that ages. Do both the self and the body age or is it just the body that ages and dies? In that event is the self eternal and ageless?

The typical classical Hindu explanation of this initial embodiment of the person is sustained by a cosmology composed of ideas drawn from both the Vedānta and Sāṃkhya systems, a practice commonly followed in many segments of the medical texts such as the *Caraka Saṃhitā*, the *Mahābhārata* and the Purāṇas. According to these sources, Brahmā Prajāpati (grandfather of all creatures) first created a body for himself. He then created the material universe or the womb of the universe (*pradhāna* or *yoni*). Following him, every subsequent embodied creature has this dual nature: the invisible, nonmaterial, spiritual essence of the self (*puruṣa*) and its material vehicle—the visible, corporeal abode or the body. Prajāpati then ordained a temporal boundary to this composite structure as well as transmigration (*parivṛtti*) and a returning (*punarāvṛtti*) of the portion of that complex.

A number of Purāṇic passages provide the metaphysical underpinnings of the processes of death and birth in great detail, in typical Indian fashion. That is, they begin (following the pattern set in the myth of the primordial man (*puruṣa*) in the *Ṛgveda*) with death and then proceed to birth. The sadness of death and the unwillingness to accept it as final are clearly reflected in several discussions on dying.[31]

The embodied self (*jīva*) is the carrier of the karmic deposits (*karmāśaya*) and is identical with the subtle body, which is swifter than the wind (*liṅgaśarīra* or *ātivāhika*).[32] Several Purāṇas posit yet another range of development and another body to experience it (e.g., *Matsya Purāṇa* 141:67ff). The "Uttara Khaṇḍa" of the *Garuḍa Purāṇa* is a voluminous but disorganized collection of ideas dealing with death, the dead and the beyond. Chapter 35 of this text, called "Preta Kalpa", deals with the nature of these suspended souls, the very embodiment of karmic ambivalence, literally hanging between life and death. The widely prevalent classical Hindu view of the rebirth mechanism, evident in this chapter, is strongly biological in tone. The aging person comes to the point of death in its aged body, the phenomenal self (*ahaṃkāra*) and the organ of intellect (*buddhi*).

After severing its connection with the gross body (*śarīra*), the self dwells for twelve days in a transitory ghostly form (*preta*). When freed from this limbo through ritual offerings (*śrāddha*) by the son of the deceased, the ghostly form travels upward to the realm of the father (*pitṛloka*) to remain there for an indeterminate period. Eventually, it is brought back to earth with the rain, enters the food chain through absorption by a plant, and finally becomes associated with the seed of a male who has eaten the fruit/seed of that plant (Deussen 1972, 357–58). The act of intercourse 'introduces' this self into the womb where its new body will grow (*Yājñavalkya Smṛti* 3:3.71–72). The force of *karma* operates at this stage in determining which potential father will eat which plant, thus generating in the self a set of circumstances appropriate to its prior experiences (Jaini 1980).

A verse from the *Subhāṣita Ratnabhāṇḍāgāra* (3:555) also records that the following five things concerning the embodied self are determined in the fetal stage itself: lifespan, *karma*, knowledge, wealth and death.[33] Another verse from the *Mahābhārata* (12:233.8) admonishes that while *karma* binds the dying person's self to the gross body composed of sixteen elements, knowledge releases it (the self), which then remains forever unmanifest and without organs (that is, without body).[34] In the nonmedical texts, such as the *Yājñavalkya Smṛti*, key passages champion the idea that multiple combinations of the factors including *karma* determine the production and rate of aging. Not infrequently, divine action or intervention and time are seen as conspiring to determine, control and guide aging.[35]

The chief hermeneutic tool employed for the purpose of positing the concept of *karma* in relation to aging is the creation of two important determinative compounds: storehouse of deeds (*karmāśaya*) and maturation of deeds (*karmavipāka*). Viewed thus, *karma* is of two kinds:

1. Acts done by an individual through his/her own free will (*puruṣakāra*).
2. Acts done unconsciously or done under the complete control of some dominant organ or agency (*adṛṣṭaphala*).

All individuals have a natural tendency to act, and their present actions are to some extent modified by latencies of the actions committed in previous lives. The system of Vedānta goes even further, claiming that the whole empirical reality is nothing but the requital of *karma* by its actor. The purpose of the human life, body and its lifespan (*kāryakaraṇasaṃghāta*) is to produce that requital in the form of maturing *karma* and the incidental suffering (see Deussen 1972, 353). The latent force behind present or future actions originates in the reservoir or the storehouse of *karma* which ripens with time and determines individual existence in three fields:

1. Birth (*jāti*).
2. The span of life in the present body (*āyus*).
3. The quality of the experiences of the present life (*bhoga*).

The storehouse of *karma* is unigenital, that is, it is formed in the life immediately preceding this one and affects only this life. The lifespan determines the period of time during which the other two fruits of antecedent *karma* are experienced.

*Bad Karma and Aging*

Ideas on old age and death are further connected to deeds (*karma*) which are evil (*pāpa*) by the moral element (*dharma*) that is integral to the concept of *karma*. The gods inflict old age and death upon mortals, either because they recognize their necessity or because they are jealous or inadequate (see above, the legend of Yayāti). In many Vedic verses death is evil (*nirṛti*), which is often stated as a simple equation. Like other forms of evil, death has snares.[36] The opposite of evil (that is, death), therefore, is long life (AV 3:31).

In the Upaniṣads, too, death is sometimes called evil (Pāpmā Mṛtyu, BAU 1:3.11; 1:5.23) and is listed together with other forms of evil such as old age and sorrow (CU 8:4.1). But generally, the more typical view is that life, as the cycle of rebirth, is evil, and the highest goal is release from that evil (*mokṣa*), which a Ṛgvedic hero would have shunned as a form of eternal death (O'Flaherty 1976, 213–214).

By introducing the new angle of the divine intervention to the Upaniṣadic concept of *karma*, classical Hinduism posits that the human being is not necessarily responsible for the aging of its body. Nor is *karma* made to bear the brunt of the blame in this context. In some texts gods are shown as being capable of overcoming aging in themselves (*nirjarā devāḥ*) or in the human beings they favor. These views lead to several myth cycles in which God/Goddess creates the aging process as a positive action in the universe, acting either as a direct instigator of the aging process or himself/herself determining that there ought to be physical corruption of the human body.

This is clearly brought out in chapter 13 (Brahmakhaṇḍa) of the *Brahmavaivarta Purāṇa*, which broaches the story of young Upavarhaṇa, the son of an old king of the Gandharvas. On account of a certain youthful impudence, he was cursed by the god Brahmā and died. His wife Mālāvatī supplicated god Viṣṇu, who appeared before her in the guise of a brahmin boy. He consoles Mālāvatī and at her request produces before her the god of death (Yama), time, and death.

Death is described as a black woman, hideous in appearance with six arms and clad in red apparel. She stood on the left hand side of Kāla who has six faces, twenty-four eyes and six legs. He, too, is black and wears red garments. When queried by Mālāvatī with regard to the premature death of her husband, death replies that she merely executed an order of providence. When Kāla is asked by Mālāvatī to account for his role, he disclaims any direct responsibility and points the finger at Yama. He then reminds her that ultimately everything takes place at the wish of Lord Kṛṣṇa (1:15.21–44).

When Viṣṇu observes that Mālāvatī's questions have not been satisfactorily answered, he volunteers to instruct her on how to prevent diseases, decrepitude and death invading the human body. In the process he identifies diseases as the sons of death and old age as her daughter (1:16.34–42). The *Mārkaṇḍeya Purāṇa*, too, traces the genesis of aging to unrighteousness (*adharma*). Injury was his wife; and from the two, untruth (*anṛta*) and destruction (*nirṛti*) were produced. They married each other and produced fear, deceit, hell and suffering. These latter, in turn, gave rise to death and misery. From death were born disease, old age, grief and anger (50:29–32).

In the *Anugītā* (14:17.6–39), a philosophical text inserted in the "Aśvamedhika Parvan" of the *Mahābhārata*, Kṛṣṇa [Vāsudeva] relates the ancient dialogue that took place between Kaśyapa and a brahmin pertaining to the nature of human action and its consequences to human birth and death. In response to Kaśyapa's query "How does the body perish and how is another body constituted?", the brahmin, by way of answer quotes a perfect master (Siddha):

> The human mind becomes overwhelmed with fear, doubt, anger and despair when it is haunted by the fear of approaching death. Consequently, this person develops poor eating habits and begins to eat improper food at irregular hours. This leads to psychological infirmities disrupting the balance of the three humors. Finally, death is preceded by severe psychosomatic disabilities[37] (see also above P. 70).

As part of a wide ranging discourse to Yudhiṣṭhira on various ethico-religious topics the sage Mārkaṇḍeya elaborates on the twin doctrine of deeds and transmigration (*karma* and *saṃsāra*) (MB 3: 179–221; see particularly 181:11–21). During the primal era, all selves were ensconced in pure and auspicious bodies. Being free from physical weaknesses and moral ambiguity, all persons were observant of holy vows, truthful and godlike. They thereby lived a life of a thousand years. But in due course they were overwhelmed by the twin vices of desire and anger. Consequently, due to moral corruption, they were ordained (literally *cooked*) to premature aging, death and transmigrations. Ever since, human destiny is controlled by death.

Similarly, in the *Brahmavaivarta Purāṇa,* Viṣṇu in his manifestation as Nārāyaṇa, prophesies the social conditions that will prevail in the land of India after Gaṅgā (the sacred river in North India) returns to Viṣṇu in his world (Vaikuṇṭha), when the five thousand year term of the age of Kali comes to an end. Toward that period, men and women will be diseased and smallish in stature. Through the power of Kali, they will look aged even when only sixteen, appearing decrepit by the time they turn twenty. Women, too, will develop prematurely, with menses beginning at the age of eight (1:7.31–40).

A great many inquiries and observations regarding old age are often introduced in our texts at moments of extreme duress, when a certain unforeseen misfortune has disrupted normal life patterns. Such crises are attributed to a variety of untoward events—discouragement in the face of an onerous task (e.g., Nanda's monologue in *Saundarananda*), a humiliating defeat, killing or massacre in battle (e.g., Dhṛtarāṣṭra's observations on old age and death after he has lost one hundred sons in the battle), subjection to a terminal illness or curse (e.g., reflections on old age by the accursed King Yayāti, see above), or death (e.g., widowed Mālāvatī's questions to Death and Old age in *Brahmavaivarta Purāṇa*).

The juxtaposition of differing views on old age in the *Mahābhārata* and the other texts is a poignant commentary on classical Hindu speculation and experimentation regarding the relation between the doctrines of deeds, desire and aging. Both are subjected to a close scrutiny. But such a simple dichotomy of propositions is unusual. Usually the etiology, in this instance of aging, is further complicated by the introduction of other variables or factors such as nutrition, fate, chance or accident.

Often, through the medium of myths, balance is struck by the introduction of the conflicting Buddhist views amidst the older Vedic views. Thus, it is possible for an Indian myth (e.g., of Yayāti) to imply that the evil of old age in human life on earth is necessary, desirable and intended by god, that age in life is relative and yet to attribute at the same time a potential of growth and development to age. Evil in aging must be accepted, but much good in old age must also be pursued and accomplished. These views together provide a working solution to the problem of old age, a framework in which humankind as a whole, and each individual, may function in the face of an ultimately insoluble and inevitable problem (see O'Flaherty 1976, 379).

By the judicious use of the mythical mode of inscribing meaning, the authors of our texts securely locate the meaning and significance of aging and old age where it belongs—in the human body and mind as circumscribed by the lifespan and in the heart of the lived experience, which somehow also transcends the purely physical dimension. The mythical and metaphysical expressions of aging in our texts are not a random collection, but rather are structured in terms of an identifiable model that is implicit in the mythos of the Indian tradition. They also suggest that aging is not just an amorphous or porous feeling, but rather, that it has an elaborate cognitive structure. The similes, metaphors and myths of aging are not mere flights of fancy. They are contrived to furnish a number of nuances and shades of meaning as to what aging is about.

The Purāṇas, too, address a number of provocative issues pertaining to the relation of deeds and desire to aging, and propose a variety of coping mechanisms supported by metaphysical reflections on these ideas. But at the same time the opportunity for probing conceptually challenging propositions is not seized. The legend of Yayāti, for instance, provides an ideal setting for lively or provocative discussions between father and sons in which refusal or acceptance of old age would each time be justified by a series of well-balanced arguments. The myth of the genesis of the model of the life stages (*āśrama*) involving Arundhatī in the *Śiva Purāṇa* ("Rudrasaṃhitā" 6:42–44) is yet another instance. The Purāṇas examine the same episode from various angles reflecting a measure of diversity as well as incongruity of ideas. At the same time parallel motifs reappear constantly (see the stories of Yayāti or Cyavana). This suggests that the Purāṇas draw upon a common store of general notions on life (first broached in the Vedic texts) and its processes such as aging. But at the same time they reserve the right and freedom to recombine and modify these ideas with reference to important Buddhist insights on aging. These storytellers and mythographers appeal, therefore, to a multivalent range of ideas on aging at the same time recognizing a number of causal factors at work.

## *Etiology of Aging*

The medical texts concur with the Dharma Śāstras and the Purāṇas in positing that *karma*, among other factors, is the womb to which the etiology of aging may be traced. The assembly of sages which discussed the etiology of diseases (and reported in the *Caraka Saṃhitā*) suggests that it could not agree on a single principle of causation of diseases. From this one may extrapolate that they would also fail to agree on a single factor or theory of the etiology of aging. Or to put the matter affirmatively as Weiss (1980) does with respect to the etiology of illness, like their Vedic forebears, the medical texts, too, were prepared to embrace (or at least tolerate) a diverse array of doctrines in the conviction that while the result of the aging process is oblivion, it is caused by a variety of factors.[38]

Consequently, in medical and moral texts, contradictions and inconsistencies appear in the elucidation of the etiology of aging at the metaphysical level. The tension is built from the beginning, because of the potential of conflict between 1) the desire to prevent, postpone or delay death, but thereby assuring old age and, 2) the desire to live a long life without aging. Unsuccessful resolution of this conflict leads Caraka and Suśruta to propose contradictory hypotheses on aging in the context of the rejuvenation and revitalization therapies.

It is consequently posited that aging is a disease and disorder originating in exogenous (*āgantu*) factors such as *karma* and as such not treatable by purely rational application of medical theory (*yukti*).

It must be supplemented or supplanted by other paramedical means such as fasting, repetition of sacred formulae (*mantra*), gifts to brahmins, observance of vows (*vrata*), pilgrimage, practice of *yoga* and so forth (this component of the therapy is known as *daivavyapāśraya*, see chapter four). The *Caraka Saṃhitā* (sū: 20.3ff), accordingly, divides all diseases into two categories: endogenous (*nija*), attributable to the imbalance of the three humors, and exogenous (*āgantu*), caused by demons, poison, wind, fire and battle injuries. But exogenous conditions may be reduced to bad judgment (*prajñāparādha*), which violates good sense (Ca.śā. 1:98, 116–117, see Weiss 1987).

In that context, the concept of *karma* is harnessed in two major ways: to bind and control the metaphysical dimension of the etiology of aging and its consequences to the human body and mind. Not only is it made to answer for the biology of the aging process based on the dynamic equilibrium of the three humors *per se*, but also the factors responsible for the quickening or the slowing down of the aging process are attributed to deeds (*karmaja*). Similarly, the predictability of the life expectancy and experience of an infant on the basis of the examination of various signs on the body—quality of hair on the head, texture of the skin, size of the head, earlobes, eyes, and so forth—is also said to be determined by the infant's *karma*.

Other features indicating subsequent pathology of the body include the quality of the aging process and its developing rate. This is attributed to the fate (*daiva*) of the person and as such to his/her *karma*. In other words, the embodied being is the product of the fruit of actions performed through delusion, desire and aversion (Ca.śā. 1:53).[39] The *Caraka Saṃhitā* (śā. 4:36) also elaborates and specifies an additional component—the three constituent properties (*sattva*, *rājas* and *tāmas*) which are also understood as the three humors (*kapha*, *pitta* and *vāta*). The quality and rate of aging are determined by the relative proportion of these constituents in the body.[40]

Āyurvedic texts, thus, wrestle to cope with the typically Indian penchant for compromise and accommodation. For that purpose the concept of *karma* is redefined in its relation to aging by introducing yet another moral category—bad judgment (*prajñāparādha*). Ātreya, for instance, affirms to his principal disciple Agniveśa:

> In this Age of Kali the life span is one hundred years. It may be fully lived out by harmonizing it with one's own con-

> stitution, by performing good deeds and by attending to good health and hygienic practices (Ca.śā. 6:29,30. See also Cakrapāṇi's gloss).

Bad judgment (*prajñāparādha*) emphasizes the importance of abandoning wrong habits and cultivating correct ones. Thus, after discoursing on the increasing immorality and the corresponding decreasing lifespan over the course of four Ages (*yugas*) leading to the present age of Kali, Ātreya is questioned by one of his disciples Agniveśa, who is troubled by the determinative weight allotted to *karma*—is the lifespan always fixed or is it not?

Ātreya's answer is that the individual lifespan is a function of both fate and human effort (*daiva* and *puruṣakāra*, Ca.vi. 3:29–35). Fate is created through actions committed in previous lives, but human effort is what is done in this life. When both happen to be noble, life is long and happy; when both are bad, it is otherwise. Evil acts of great enormity would definitely reduce it. But the bad effects of moderately unjust actions can be neutralized by moral behavior (*sadvṛtta*), wholesome diet and physical activities (*svasthavṛtta*, see Dasgupta 1968, 2:403).[41]

In the light of the foregoing, it may be concluded that in the Āyurveda and Dharma Śāstras, the law of *karma* acquires a metaphysical dimension, though its empirical content and consequences are acknowledged and retained. The idea is to employ it as an escape clause and a safety valve against insufficient or no clinical or empirical evidence (see Weiss 1980). The fatalistic and immutable elements of the doctrine of *karma* are reconciled with a more practical empirical attitude toward human life by harmonizing it 1) with the physical theory of aging based on Patañjali's treatment of change (*pariṇāma*) in relation to time (see chapter three) and 2) the social theory of the stages of life proposed in the Dharma Śāstras (see chapter one). Thus, by instituting a significant cognitive shift, the doctrine of *karma* is accommodated for its psychological and emotional utility with reference to the process of aging.

# *Conclusion*

The present study was undertaken with the assumption that in India's religious and literary heritage there is a wide range of attitudes and images of aging which, if critically examined in the light of modern gerontology, could substantially contribute toward the development of a culturally nuanced contemporary Indian gerontology. As a first step toward this future enterprise, the survey of the history of the dialectic on the meaning of aging from the Vedic through the classical period was undertaken in chapter one.

It revealed a variety of responses to aging which are historically and empirically conditioned—that is, in large measure, they were related to, and determined by, changing structures of sociopolitical power and the patterns of religious thought and culture of India. In Vedic texts penetrating reflections and analysis based on the empirical experience of the meaning of aging and growing old were found to be absent since the lifespan of the Vedic Indians was so short.

But from about 500 BCE, prodded by Buddhism, Indian society gradually moved away from a naive acceptance of aging as continued growth to a more sophisticated understanding of old age as a distinct stage of life characterized by decline and decrepitude. Old age, along with illness and death, became the source of the most fundamental conflict between the brahmin and Buddhist thinkers regarding the meaning and purpose of life.

Subsequent intellectual and religious thought in Indian tradition, it may be argued, is colored by this creative tension arising out of the differing interpretations of the human condition and the meaning of aging in life. Early Buddhism saw the aging life, culminating in death, as an unremitting agony and monotony. The solution to this human predicament was conceived epistemologically in terms of the four noble truths. Ascetic renunciation of worldly life in family and community figured as an integral component of this solution, which was designed to vanquish the triune evil of old age, disease and death.

The Hindu Smṛti works, on the other hand, located the meaning of aging in the process of life itself, rather than in an ascetic spirituality opposed to or transcending it. Human life is the dynamic flux that surrounds and moves through the aging individual. It is to be realized *within* the context of the broader familial and social model of the stages of life. The crystallization of the idea that old age is a distinct stage of life with its own unique meaning and purpose was a complex, dialectical process which began in the age in which the Buddha lived (ca. 500 BCE) and continued for several centuries.

The contribution of Buddhism to this development lay in sensitizing the prereflective Vedic mind to the fact that aging is an irreversible and inevitable process leading to disease and death. When this awareness spread rapidly into the mainstream of the society, old age came to be associated with a major social problem inviting the brahmins to respond in their role as the custodians of social organization, welfare and control. The result was the development of the ideal model of the stages of life (*āśramas*), and the institutionalization of old age as the final stage in life in which to strive for spiritual liberation.

This articulation of the stages of life model and its formal and ritual incorporation in the Dharma Śāstra texts was designed to counter possible social disorganization which, it was feared, might otherwise ensue from societal neglect of the elderly as a particular age group in the wake of the Buddhist appeal to young men and women to renounce the world. The propagation of the ideal of a well-integrated family life and social organization based on popular Hindu cosmology combined with the progress in medicine and health-care created a relatively favorable environment for the elderly during the classical period. In brief, the chief contribution of the Dharma Śāstras lay in steering a middle course between the naive gerontophilia of the Vedic Indians and the neurotic gerontophobia of the early Buddhists. The tradition of the care and culture of aging and the aged, thus, is a post-Vedic phenomenon initiated and fostered by the writers of the Dharma Śāstras.

Our study also reveals that in their attempts to 1) locate and map out the field of activity with respect to the aging body, and 2) to trace the etiology of aging in metaphysical terms, these texts consistently resort to similes, metaphors and myths. The notion of aging, consequently, emerges as so many iconic images of the upward and downward, as well as forward, march of life through time and space:

1. *Aging as a marker of life's journey:* This sense is suggested in a number of Dharma Śāstra texts by the institution of age-specific rites of passage phrased in the optative mood, which effectively set off one period of life from another by reason of privilege or duty.
2. *Aging as growth and maturity:* The individual's growth and development with age are conceptualized positively in physical, material, psychological or spiritual terms.
3. *Aging as decline and loss:* The later phases of life and the associated meanings are evaluated negatively as violence, loss and finitude.
4. *Aging as an accomplice of death:* The meaning of aging as a handmaiden of or a minion to death is proposed in striking similes and metaphors in many of our texts.

The above images serve to assert, on the one hand, that 1) aging is pain and suffering, 2) the gross body, which is its locus and field of operation is impermanent and impure, and 3) true liberation can be achieved only when the process of aging is stopped, sacralized or sublimated. On the other hand, it is just as emphatically insisted that the liberation by the self is possible only in the embodied state which is under the sway of the aging process. Aging, thus, is posited as the necessary vehicle or energy that unfolds the path of liberation before the embodied self. The suffering and losses associated with aging are the key to the liberation experience. This suffering is what alerts us to the insubstantiality of the world (*saṃsāra*). The pain of aging is, therefore, a useful shock mechanism to awaken people from the mirage of this-worldly existence (*saṃsāra*).

But, in order for this to happen, one must develop a proper awareness of the body, its lifespan and its meaning. The traditional Indian views on these topics were examined in chapters two and three with reference to change (*pariṇāma*) in relation to time as past, present and future. Our findings indicate how close the relationship is between religion, culture and gerontology. The analysis of the concept of *pariṇāma* shows the extent to which it underscores the Indian understanding of 1) the process of aging, 2) the model of the stages of life, 3) the concept of *karma,* which is pivotal to all Indian religions, and 4) the rejuvenation and revitalization therapies of Āyurveda designed to cope with the stress and other adverse consequences of aging.

This relationship between culture and gerontology as mediated by the concepts of *pariṇāma* and *karma* is the crux of the Hindu, and to a certain extent, Buddhist soteriological endeavor: One must experientially cultivate the awareness of the evanescent and aging character of embodiment and then actualize and guide it toward liberation.[1] Regardless of the particular method or dogma selected for this purpose, all approaches focus on developing the metaphysical understanding of the modes of aging as rooted in time (*kāla*), deeds (*karma*) and desire (*kāma*).

Our texts hasten to point out that from the mundane perspective, the metaphysical understanding of aging does not prevent or eliminate the suffering of aging but, rather, allows us to find meaning in it and thereby lessen its shock. Knowledge is seen as an essential ingredient of any defense mechanism alleviating the pain of aging. From this standpoint, the wise and liberated individual is the one who has lived in harmony with life's true meaning and purpose. It is significant that in suggesting answers to these questions from the worldly standpoint, the Dharma Śāstras and Āyurveda take a career-oriented stance, notwithstanding the disruptive powers of the aging process. None of them preach retirement (e.g., enforced leisure, absence of a meaningful role, or the empty-nest syndrome) in the modern sense of the term, even in the face of extreme old age. To that extent it is an important corrective to the modern evaluation of old age as a time for formal retirement and rest.

To be sure, our texts talk of disengagement and retreat. But this disengagement from the active householder's norms is for the sake of reengagement to the tasks of self-realization in old age. For this reason, these texts do not advocate a 'sick rôle' for the aged, because they do not reduce aging to disease (with the exception of certain passages in the *Caraka Saṃhitā*) or old age to illness. As such, they seem to provide meaningful ways of 1) coping with the stress of old age, 2) maintaining high morale and life satisfaction in aging, and 3) avoiding boredom. That these enduring ideas have filtered down to the lowest strata of Indian society to this day is evident in George's (1981) study of the elderly in Madras city, which concludes that, "the vast majority of the elderly remain active and carry out their routine tasks without help or assistance."

The large number of myths that the Hindu and Buddhist texts reveal about the subject of aging indicates how deeply troubled as well as interested Indian tradition has been concerning aging, and how difficult it is to interpret the aging process meaningfully. This hypothesis was critically tested in chapter five. The intricate intertwining as well as discrepancies discernible in these myths (e.g., Cyavana, Yayāti) reveal the complexity of the Hindu and Buddhist mythology on aging. Though both the viewpoints endorse the belief that aging leads to human suffering, they disagree as to its relation to suffering. This is one of the more fascinating features of Indian tradition. A variety of possible causes of and responses to aging are proposed somewhere, so that our texts furnish a wide range of meanings. The strength of the composite Indian view of aging, therefore, may lie in the possibility that some of the concepts may be found to be compatible with the theories of modern gerontology.

One such concept which needs to be further investigated is *vārdhaka* ('old-agedness'), which may be heuristically resolved into two components—aging (*pariṇāma*) and old age (*jarā*), for the purpose of analyzing age-determined relationships. While aging seems to refer to the inevitable biological and psychological processes, old age is conceived as the psychosocial and cultural experience and meaning of the perceived aging activity. In the traditional Indian understanding, old age includes secondary personal and social responses to a primary malfunctioning in the individual's physical and/or psychological status. It involves responding cognitively and valuatively to both the benign and malign manifestations of the aging process in the body and mind.

Viewed from this perspective, the traditional Hindu moral and medical works provide typical patterns of shaping the aging experience into the predictable behavior and experience of old age along class-based social and cultural norms and roles. Such a construction of the phenomenon of old age from the aging process appears to be an important function of these texts. That is, old age is depicted as responses to aging in an attempt to provide it with a meaningful form and explanation as well as control.

Paradoxical as it may sound, old age as a culturally constructed phenomenon is part of the mechanism of learning to cope with aging and all that it entails. Gerontologists today recognize that the key to a relatively healthy old age without stress lies in

1) Planning for an active late life as a career, and 2) Learning the appropriate mechanisms of coping with old age from early in life. The present study indicates that the profession of gerontology in modern India should further undertake:

1. A critical evaluation of the potential relevance and utility of the model of the stages of life to contemporary needs, since it is based on the hypothesis that successful adaptation and adjustment to life in old age depends on the experience of relative isolation and deprivation (in terms of physical comforts) in one's formative years as a student.
2. The reorientation of geriatric practice in the light of Āyurveda since it advocates the incorporation of appropriate dietary habits and personal hygiene in one's early life to assure a healthy late life.

It is true that in the past, social welfare and medical treatment for the elderly were mainly devised for the benefit of the male members of the landed, ruling and priestly classes. It is also true that the efficacy of the Āyurvedic treatment is subject to numerous variables. Such conceptual or practical weaknesses of the Dharma Śāstras or Āyurveda must not, however, deter social scientists; with imagination and sympathy, these former may be turned into positive features in the development of a truly indigenous Indian gerontology.

# Notes

## Introduction

1. More recently, Thapar's *Ancient Indian Social History: Some Interpretations* (1978), based on textual sources, also followed a similar approach with encouraging results.

2. This line of interpretation was suggested, in part, by Lincoln (1986, 4–5).

3. Chaitanya (1975, 52) refers to the belief that every Vedic hymn is the condensed expression of a triple meaning—an overt prayer for material prosperity, a homage to the gods, and a veiled allegorical notation of a profound philosophical intuition (the source of this informatiion, however, is not identified).

4. Needless to say, they are indebted to the earlier endeavors by established scholars; and are duly included in the bibliography.

## Chapter 1

1. The prayer is repeated in AV 19:24.4.

2. *Jarāyai tvā pari dadāmi jarāyai ni dhuvāmi tvā. Jarā tvā bhadrā neṣṭa vyanye yantu mṛtyavo yānāhuritarān chatam.*

3. Keith (1922, 90) has argued that so much stress is laid on longevity as a great boon that it must have been rare. Gonda (1975a, 300) observes that Atharvan charms aim at the regretably large numbers of deaths and

Ghurye (1979, 283) notes that although the "Marriage Hymn" of the *Ṛgveda* (10:85) prays for a household composed of three generations living together under one roof, that ideal might not have been universally achieved. Finally, Zysk (1985, 8) has argued that the Vedic Indian considered himself to be healthy if his life-time was long, i.e. if he could repeatedly witness the rising sun. Bhargava (1971, 206), on the other hand, has vainly sought to demonstrate that the Aryans of the Vedic age were a long-lived people by referring to RV 1:164 and 7:6,16.

4. Recently Young (forthcoming) has suggested that the brahmin's self-interest lay in propagating the fear of death in the minds of the gullible Vedic Indians.

5. Sarao (1987) has argued that urbanization made its feeble beginnings around the seventh century BCE. The whole of early Buddhist literature presupposes the existence of urbanization, though urbanization saw its real glory under Buddhism itself.

6. The Śramaṇas were strivers who put primary emphasis on personal training in a method or program of salvation available to anyone (men or women, high or low) willing to learn it. They stressed personal effort (*śrama*) and practice, not sacrifices (as propounded in the orthodox Brāhmaṇa texts) or metaphysical speculation (as engaged in by the Upaniṣadic thinkers). Their doctrines or explanations centered on the personal experience of teachers like the Buddha or Mahāvīra who served as exemplars to others (Hopkins 1971, 53).

7. The poet pleads with the gods not to cut short his life before its due term. In yet another hymn, the wish is expressed that Nirṛti, the goddess of death and dissolution, would take away (literally swallow) old age (RV 5:41.15,17).

8. In later Upaniṣads these events are sacralized by identifying them with the symbolic sequence of sacrifices (*yajñas*) based on the fire god (Agni). The performance of *brahmayajña* is prescribed in the first quarter, *karmayajña* in the second, *tapoyajña* in the third and the *jñānayajña* in the final phase of life. See Śaṅkara's gloss (bhāsya) on *Brahma Sūtra* (3:4.47–50).

9. The Buddhist elder Nāgasena describes the method (whereby the Buddhists brought this about) by narrating a simile to King Milinda:

> Just as the carpenter, discarding the soft parts of the wood, takes (only) the hard parts, just so the Bhikshu . . . forsaking the path of the discussion of useless theses to wit: the everlasting life theory, the let-us-eat-and-drink-for-tomorrow-we-die theory, the theory that the soul and the body are one and the same, that the soul is one thing, the body another . . . (RhysDavids 1969, 2:361–362).

10. Gośāla is said to have conceptualized the ideal human lifespan in terms of eight developmental stages (*aṭṭhapurisa bhūmiyo*) in order to reach perfection (*jina*) (Barua 1970, 314).

11. Grmek (1958, 29) has observed that by studying the inscriptions of ancient Roman tombstones, scholars have determined that the average duration of life at that time was between twenty to thirty years. Though corresponding figures are not available for the Vedic period, they must not have been far removed from those for the ancient Greek or Roman periods.

12. Patañjali's *Mahābhāṣya* (5:1.59, see Limaye 1974, 343) suggests that he considered the average lifespan in his time (ca. 300 BCE) to be between sixty and seventy (*ṣaṣṭirjīvitaparimāṇamasya ṣāṣṭikaḥ. Sāptatikaḥ*).

13. In the legend of Yayāti told in the *Padma Purāna* (1:2.76.23), the aged patriarch and the founder of the lineage is compared to the giant Banyan tree spreading its roots and branches in all directions. In like manner, the sons, grandsons and great-grandsons are described as spreading and sinking their roots.

14. *Vayadhammā saṅkhārā, appamādena sampādethā'ti.*

15. There is no doubt that classical Hindu texts such as the epics and the Purāṇas, influenced by the Buddhist ideas, do identify old age with suffering. In the *Mahābhārata*, for instance, a mysterious bird Pūjanī elucidates to the brahmin Brahmadatta that suffering is old age, suffering is contact with the undesired and suffering is deprivation of a desired thing:

> *duḥkham jarā Brahmadatta duḥkhamarthaviparyayaḥ duḥkham cāniṣṭa-saṃvāso duḥkhamiṣṭaviyogajam* (MB 12:137.59).

16. Consider the observations of Christopher Lasch (1978, 210), who identifies the irrational terror of old age and death with the emergence of the narcissistic personality which takes no interest in the future. Such individuals are dissatisfied with the traditional consolations of old age, the most important among which is the belief that future generations will in some sense carry on his/her work or life [compare to the Brāhmana-inspired notion of horizontal immortality discussed in chapter four]. They reject as naive the faith or conviction that one lives on vicariously in one's children (or more broadly, in future generations) which thought reconciles one to the inevitable superseding—the central sorrow of old age, more harrowing even than loneliness.

17. Thapar (1982), citing Warder (1956), has suggested that the growth of renunciatory tendencies at this time have been attributed, in part, to the disorientation which followed on the breakup of clan based society with the emergence of urban centres and the authority of state systems.

18. Gombrich (1985) notes that Buddhists do not even have the term *svadharma*—behaving in the manner appropriate to one's station. Their values are universalistic: what is right for one must be right for all.

19. Consider the secular ethics of familism taught to young Sigāla by the Buddha in the "Sigālovādasutta" (DN 3:180–193).

20. In the opinion of Olivelle (1978), the brahmins had never felt comfortable with the element of choice introduced by writers such as Gautama; this prompted the Smṛtikāras to revise the Dharma Sūtra model of the stages of life. In the redefined, classical model, choice is eliminated and the stages are related to definite periods of a man's life. In this scheme one has as much freedom in choosing a stage as one has in growing old.

21. In an interesting note to Dilemma 71 (1969, 127–128) RhysDavids points out that it is always taken for granted that the Buddhists were reformers, as opposed to the brahmins who wanted to run still in the ancient grooves. But there is another side of the question that has been entirely overlooked. Brāhmaṇas and Upaniṣads may be seen as reform following reform. Buddhists are to brahmins much more like socialists (New Democrats in the Canadian context) to liberals, than like Liberals to Conservatives. But rather than working out a totally new system the brahmins grafted new reforms on the old roots surviving underground.

22. This is evident from the controversy raised by different commentators around the relevant passage from the *Raghuvaṃśa* of Kālidāsa regarding whether or not the ruling classes (Kṣatriyas), as members of the broader twice-born (*dvija*) class, had a right to go through the third stage of life, that is, the forest hermit.

23. Thaper (1982) has argued that, seen from a diachronic perspective, the stages of life (*āśrama*) theory was generated from an interaction of social needs, historical process and ideological concerns.

24. *Śatāyurvai puruṣo vibhajya kālam anyonya anubandhyam parasparasya anupadyatakam trivargam seveta* (KS 1:2.1–4).

25. These very ideas appear as premise to be refuted (*pūrvapakṣa*) in the *Buddhacarita* of Aśvaghoṣa. King Śreṇya of Magadha is disturbed by young Siddhārtha's resolve to abandon the world. He, therefore, tries to persuade Siddhārtha by reiterating this traditional Vedic teaching.

26. . . . *gārhasthyātsthānādāsŕamādūrdhvam gantumicchan . . . sambandhasya vicchedam karavāṇi.*

27. *Gautama Dharma Sūtra,* perhaps the oldest law-book, has barely a page on the rules of the ideal-type it calls *bhikṣu.* As against this, the rules

of behavior for the Buddhist monk as compiled in the Pali Canon and dating from roughly the same period, fill three volumes in translation.

28. The description and duties of the four stages are succinctly presented in the *Mahābhārata* in a discourse by the sage Parāśara to King Janaka:

> *adhītya vedānstapasā brahmacārī*
> *yajñāṅśaktyā sanisṛjyeha pañca*
> *vanam gachhetpuruṣo dharmakāmah*
> *śreyaścitvā sthāpayitvā svavaṃśam* (MB 12:286.30).

29. In like manner, the *Viṣṇu Smṛti* (96:27) admonishes the wandering ascetic (*saṃnyāsin/yati*) to reflect upon the destruction of beauty by old age.

30. Coomaraswamy has traced the stereotype of the wandering ascetic to the enigma of the sun as presented in the legend of King Hariścandra and his son Rohita in *Aitareya Brāhmaṇa* (7:13–18) where it is stated:

> Kali [Age] his lot who lieth down, Dvāpara [Age] his who would feign cast off, Tretā [Age] his who standeth up, Kṛta [Age] he reacheth who marcheth—keep on going, keep on going . . . (quoted in Johnson 1980, 98–99).

Johnson also adds that in the age of the Brāhmaṇas wandering was an innovative spiritual path. Wandering strivers (Śramaṇas), first mentioned in the *Śatapatha Brāhamaṇa*, produced the Upaniṣads, early Buddhism and Jainism.

31. Etymologically *āśrama* is derived from a̱ + the verb *śram* (strive). Its cognate substantives include *śrama* (striving) and *śramaṇa* (striver and by extension ascetic). *Aśrama* would, therefore, mean place where one strives. With this etymology in mind, Young (1981) surmises that in the compound *gṛhasthāśrama* the original etymological meaning of *āśrama* is dispensed with to protect the fundamental human and Vedic institution of marriage as inscribed in the substantive *gṛhastha*.

32. One cannot say that elderly women fared any better in the Buddhist lay society or the religious order (*saṃgha*). As can be inferred from the monastic code for the monks and nuns (Vinaya), the nuns had only limited scope as preachers. They occupied, according to the letter of the Vinaya, the position of novices with respect to the monks, however senior they were in age to them. This endorses the generally held view that Buddhism acquiesced to the androcentric orientation of the larger Indian society and did not seriously challenge the prevailing social norms regarding women.

33. Bāṇa in his *Kādambarī*, identifies such persons as *gṛhamuni* or *bhavanatāpasa*. These were householders pursuing the norms of the hermits or the wandering mendicants. According to Agrawala (1969, 30), this was a

new ideal that first appeared in the Gupta age. Such persons were also known as Vaikhānasa and belonged to the Bhāgavata sect.

34. In the *Raghuvaṃśa*, when prince Aja is reduced to tears at the thought of his aging father, King Raghu, turning a hermit, the latter relents and consents to retire to a modest hut on the outskirts of the city (8:10–14).

35. The *Yājñavalkya Smṛti* (3:3.142) explicitly links, with the help of an appropriate metaphor, advancing old age with an increasing capacity for knowledge of *brahman:*

> Sweet juice already exists in an unripe cucumber. It is perceived only when the vegetable ripens. Similarly, the knowledge of *brahman,* which already exists in the unripe self, may manifest itself with advancing years.

36. This argument is based on Thapar's (1982) observation that each stage in life is characterized by three phases—initiation, liminality and reintegration.

37. Quoted in Herman 1976, 267.

38. Schopenhauer (1982) seems to have captured the Hindu view of life in a very homely metaphor. He compares life to a fabric or piece of embroidery, of which, during the first half of life, a person gets a sight of the right [correct] side, and during the second half, of the reverse [incorrect, wrong]. The wrong side is not so pretty as the right, but it is the more *instructive:* it shows the way in which the threads have been worked and sewed together.

39. Schopenhauer (1982) points out that the first forty years of life furnish the text, while the remaining thirty supply the commentary. Without it we are unable to understand aright the true sense and coherence of the text, together with the moral it contains, and all the subtle application of which it admits.

40. There are occasional statements in the Pali Canon that go against this claim. The "Mahāsāropama Sutta" of the *Majjhima Nikāya* records the following observation attributed to the Buddha:

> There are certain youths who outwardly being allured by the life of monks leave the household life. As monks they receive presents, esteem and repute. They become puffed up and disparage others. Thus they grow remiss and become prey to ills (MN 1:192–197).

41. Quoted in Herman 1976, 218. See also Varma 1973, 377–382.

42. In the *Buddhacarita* (1:48,51) we come across King Śuddhodana, who has recently become the father of Siddhārtha, day-dreaming that Siddhārtha will retire to forest in his old age, because [the condition of] old age, like austerities, helps develop equanimity and renders one nonchalant.

43. It need not be assumed that this compromise, worked out in theory, always achieved a practical expression in reality. In fact, the notion of gerontocracy in the social and political organization of India, which survives even today, may be said to be the true legacy of the Dharma Śāstras.

44. It is instructive to note what Maves (n.d.) has to say in this context. He hypothesizes that the nature of religious experience may be different at different stages of adult life. Implicit in what he perceives as the developmental roots of religious experience, expressions, and needs is the deeper perception of the developmental roots of aged individuals themselves. As the embodiment of progressive human nature, the aged individual represents to a unique degree, actualized and finalized humaneness.

## Chapter 2

1. The *Padma Purāṇa* (2:1.64.58) posits this relation charmingly—The self and the body both have a friendly persuasion (*ātmā kāyaśca dvau etau mātrārupau ubhāvapi*).

2. Nietzsche held in utmost contempt the cultivation of suffering and urged that one becomes a 'free spirit' through embracing the body in all its finitude. Physical frailty of the body, therefore, should be taken as one of the colors that human existence will have (Gadow 1986).

3. The idea is poetically expressed in the *Śvetāśvatara Upaniṣad* (4:3):

> The woman thou art, and the man,
> The maiden and the boy,
> And born thou growest everywhere,
> As old man on a staff.
> (Deussen 1972, 153)

4. The Irish-French writer and playright Samuel Beckett expresses the idea that persons are both "same, yet another; that no entity existing in time is *ever* the same from one moment to the next" in a similar vein. Act two of *Waiting for Godot*, for instance, features the following exchange:

> Vladimir: And you are Pozzo?
> Pozzo: Certainly I am Pozzo.
> Vladimir: The same as yesterday?
> Pozzo: Yesterday?
> Vladimir: We met yesterday. Do you remember?

Pozzo: I don't remember having met anyone
yesterday. But tomorrow I won't remember having
met anyone today
(quoted in Rabuzzi 1984).

5. With certain modifications, the wheel metaphor is also presented in the *Atharva Veda* (9:14[9].13–14).

6. See Sāyaṇa's gloss on RV 1:164.13.

7. A distant echo of this idea is found in Schopenhauer's imagery of the wheel of the ungrateful King Ixion who was punished by Zeus by having him fastened to a burning wheel which rotated continuously. Zeus also made him deathless so as to make his punishment never-ending. Well versed as he was in both the Greek and Indian myths, Schopenhauer longed for a universe where the wheel of Ixion stands still, the stone of Sisyphus is at rest, the sieve of Danaides is put aside and the agony of Tantalus is in abeyance (Knox 1980).

8. This account is based on Verdu 1979, 101. In Bāṇa's *Harṣacarita,* we come across a similar discourse by the erudite Buddhist monk Divākara to King Harṣa's sister Rājyaśrī, who is grieving over the treacherous murder of her husband. Juxtaposing the image of the body, conceived as machine (*gātrayantra*), on the water-wheel, Divākara explains how the long ropes [of birth, old age, death and so forth] keep the water-wheel [of *saṃsāra*] turning round and round (Agrawala 1969, 236–237).

9. According to Sāyaṇa's gloss, the *devatās* are to be understood as the vital breaths (*prāṇa, apāna*), sense organs and so forth entering the human body in the manner of the cows entering their pens.

10. The hymn is addressed to Agni, the fire god, who is invoked to consume the mortal body of the person who has died. *Aja,* the unmanifest and unperishable component in the body, is characterized by Sāyaṇa as symbolizing the inner self (*antarapuruṣalakṣaṇa*), which is devoid of a material body and sense. Curiously though, Geldner (1951 3:148) discredits this sensible and convincing interpretation of Sāyaṇa and translates *aja* as goat (*Bock*).

11. Consider also the Atharvan hymn (18:3.71) to be recited by the priest to invoke Agni (the fire god) to consume and return to cosmos the components of the dead body (*śarīra*) of the priest's patron.

12. Sāyaṇa's gloss on AV 11:10(8).4 views the gross body (*śarīra*) as incorporating within itself the capacity for knowledge (*jñānaśakti*) which never leaves the self and the capacity for action (*kriyāśakti*) which, upon death, transmigrates with the subtle body (see below).

13. Sāyaṇa's gloss on AV (11:10(8).31) observes that at death only the gross body (*sthūlaśarīram*) is consumed by fire, not the seventeen-member subtle body including five organs of knowledge, five organs of action, five breaths and mind.

14. The *Praśna Upaniṣad* (1:4ff) features an exchange between the sage Pippalāda and a certain brahmin wherein the old myth of Prajāpati is invoked to explain how Prajāpati created the universe by bringing forth into existence two principles: moon/matter (*rayi*) and sun/life (*prāṇa*). *Prāṇa* thereby is endowed with an ontological rather than strictly physiological function.

15. See, for instance, the "Nābhanediṣṭha Hymn" in the *Aitereya Brāhmaṇa* 6:5.27.

16. *Śarīramiti kasmāt. Agnayo hyatra śrīyante jñānāgnir darśanāgniḥ koṣṭhāgniriti* (Kapani 1976).

17. The human lifespan is equated, in this Upaniṣadic passage, with the three libations (*stūtyādayas*) the householder is supposed to offer daily. His first twenty-four years constitute the morning libation because the sacred formula of the sun (Gāyatrī Mantra) on which it is based has twenty-four syllables in it. His next twenty-four constitute the mid-day libation because the Triṣṭubh hymn, which accompanies it, has twenty-four syllables. The final forty-eight years are his evening libation, because it is accompanied by the Jagatī hymn having forty-eight syllables (CU 4:16.1–5).

18. Compare this view to the *Yoga Sūtra* dictum that all is suffering for the one with discriminating intellect (*duḥkham eva sarva vivekinaḥ* YS 2:25).

19. Occasionally, such a realistic appraisal of aging is also evident in the Pali Canon. The following exchange between the Buddha and his chief disciple Ānanda, as recorded in the "Indriya Saṃyutta" of the *Saṃyutta Nikāya* bears this out:
[Once while massaging the old tired body of the Buddha, Ānanda happened to remark]:

> It is strange, the Blessed One's complexion is no longer pure and clear, and all the Blessed One's limbs are relaxed [become flaccid] and wrinkled, and the body is inclined forward, and there is seen a change in the faculties of sight, of hearing, of smell, of taste, of touch.
>
> This is indeed is so, Ānanda. In youth one is by nature subject to decay, in health by nature, subject to disease, in life (*jīvite*) by nature subject to death (SN 5:193–243, see also Jennings 1974, 356–358).

20. In the Pali Canon the terms "Sutta" and "Suttanta" are used interchangeably.

21. Cakrapāṇi's gloss on Ca.sū. 1:42 explains these two synonyms as:

1. Life is that which is [relatively] stable even though the body is momentary and transient (*nityam śarīrasya kṣaṇikatvena gacchatīti*).
2. Life is that which attaches itself to other bodies with form (*anubadhnātyāyuraparāparaśarīrādisaṃyogarūpatayā*). See also Ca.Vi. 8:91).

22. An imaginative simile from the *Bhāgavata Purāṇa* (5:61) brings this out clearly:

> Food cooked in the morning turns bad by the evening; one cannot, therefore, expect the body nourished by that food to be eternal.
>
> *Yat pratar saṃskṛtam cānnam sāyam tacca vinaśyati tadīya rasasaṃpuṣṭe kāye kā nāma nityatā.*

23. According to Cakrapāṇi's gloss (Ca.śā. 1:50,51), these verses are meant to prove the eternal existence of the immutable and ageless self tied to a body which is mutable and aging. Thus, the youthful body of a person named Devadatta is not identical with Devadatta in old age (compare Beckett's ideas on this topic, cited by Rabuzzi 1984).

24. *Visargodānavikṣepaiḥ somasūryānilā yathā dhārayanti jagȧddeham kaphapittānilāstatha* (Su.sū. 21:8).

25. This verse suggests that the medical tradition of India resembles other ancient medical traditions of China and Greece in formulating its medicine from generic physiological and cosmological concepts and in the organization of its practice. The arrangement and balance of elements in the human body are said to be microscopic versions of their arrangement in society at large and throughout the cosmos.

26. *Rasajam puruṣam Vidyādrasam rakṣet prayatnataḥ* (Su.sū. 14:12).

27. Caraka (Ca.sū. 6:3–6) makes it clear that the sun, the wind and the moon, governed by time as well as their special nature and orbits, constitute the causative factors of the manifestations of the seasons, humors and bodily strength. Thus, the seasonal and dietary regimen practiced by a person who knows the seasonal homologation with regard to behavior and diet, promote his/her vigor and complexion. The method of rejuvenation, called Vātātapika, is based on this premise (see chapter four).

28. *Puruṣa* is an important concept in Indian philosophy and is defined variously in different schools of thought. Pāṇini (*Uṇādi Sūtra* 4:74) defines it as that which moves forward (*puraḥ kuṣan*). The *Amarakośa* defines it as that which has body as the locus (*puri dehe sīdati tiṣṭhatīti,* 1:4.29; 1:6.1) and lists its two synonyms— *ātmā* and *kṣetrajña* (knower of field). He identifies *kṣetra* with *śarīra* (body) observing that body is that which perishes (*kṣīyata iti kṣetram śarīram*).

29. The entire chapter five called "Individual as the Epitome of the Universe" (Ca.śā.) deals with this homology.

30. Cakrapāni's comments (on Ca.śā. 3:8) point out that the compound *antarātman* is used here to distinguish the empirical self as a causative factor of the embryo as distinct from the physical body composed of the six elements (*dhātus*).

31. This assertion is consistent with the basic Sāṃkhya doctrine that it is only the properties of the substance that undergo change. Patañjali's *Mahābhāṣya* (1:1.5) makes a similar point in stating that gold [as a substance] unites with a particular form [and property] and appears as a lump.

32. Cakrapāṇi insists that this description of the embryo as composed of six elements is not in contradiction to the assertion made in Ca.śā. 1:17 that the human being is composed of twenty-four elements. He, however, does not satisfactorily demonstrate how.

33. See also the chapter on "Kāyajugupsā" in the *Śiva Purāṇa* ("Umā Saṃhitā", #23).

34. The lexicon of Amara (*Amarakośa*) similarly dissects the male and female life cycle into three phases and labels each with clear and precise terms (2:6.7ff).

35. *Vayastaśceti kālapramāṇaviśeṣāpekṣiṇī hi śarīrāvasthā vayo'bhidhīyate* (Ca.vi:8:122).

36. Suśruta, on his part, regards middle age (*madhyāvasthā*) as stretching between the ages of sixteen and seventy and subdivides it into five phases: growth (*vṛddhi*), up to the age of twenty; youth (*yauvana*), up to the age of thirty; fullness (*sampurṇatā*), up to the age of forty; loss (*hāni*), between forty-five and seventy; and old age (*jīrṇāvasthā*), from seventy years and up (see Su.sū. 35:29).

37. Caraka acknowledges that there may be persons with a lifespan stretching beyond the average one hundred years, in which case it may be divided into the same three phases. The first phase would stretch to thirty-six years, the second to seventy years, and the remaining lifespan recognized as the third. On the other hand, those with a shorter lifespan will have the first phase reduced to twenty-five years, the second phase until age of fifty, with the remaining years being spent in the third phase.

38. In the "Āraṇyaka Parva" of the *Mahābhārata* (3:230), for instance, is to be found a discussion on the influence of the planets on the human body and its aging (See also Su, "Uttaratantra", chapter 37).

39. Wayman (1963, 360–361). In the same article he has also compared these phases to those proposed by Ptolemy.

40. *Iyam hi nidrā Nayanāvalambinī lalāṭdeśādupasarpatīva mām. Adṛśyarūpā capalā jaraiva yā mānuṣyasatvam paribhūyam vartate.*

41. *Kṛtāntasya dūtī jarā karṇamūle samāgatya vaktīti . . . .*

42. *Tam karṇamūlam āgatya rāme śrīrnyasyatāmiti kaikeyīśaṅkayevāha palitachadmanā jarā.*

43. At ci. 2:4.43 Caraka lists, along with old age, worries, diseases and *karma,* too little or too much sex with women, as the causes that deplete the semen of man thereby causing premature aging (see Cakrapāṇi's gloss).

44. Cakrapāṇi's gloss on Ca.ind. 1:1 justifies this strategy (developed in Ca.sū. 10:8) by explaining that a physician must first learn to determine the extent and severity of the patient's disease before taking up his case.

45. Sebeok (1986, 46) has observed that the term symptom usually appears in conjunction with sign. As a technical term, it occurs both in medicine and semiotics.

46. *Jarāmārjārikā bhuṅkte yauvanākhum tathoddhatā paramullāsamāyāti śarīrāmiṣagardhinī* (YV 1:22.25).

47. Consider Yeats' (1983) depiction of old age through similar metaphors:

> What shall I do with this absurdity—
> O heart, O troubled heart—this caricature,
> Decrepit age that has been tied to me
> As to a dog's tail?
> "The Tower"
>
> An aged man is but a paltry thing,
> A tattered coat upon a stick.
> "Sailing to Byzantium"

## *Chapter 3*

1. Bhartṛhari in his *Kālasamuddeśa* (VP 3:9.1–6) lists as many as ten different theories of time known to him.

2. *Taittirīya Āraṇyaka* (1:2) states that behind the year (*saṃvatsara*), which is the visible form of time, there lies the supreme essence of time (*ādhisattvakāla*) which is compared to a big river expanding in depth and space (see Deshpande 1985).

3. *Kālātsravanti bhūtani kālādvṛddhim prayānti ca kāle cāstam nigacchanti kalo mūrtiramūrtimān.*

4. *Na hīha kaścit svasminnātmani muhūrtamapyāvatiṣṭhate. Vardhate vā yāvadanena vardhitavyam. Apāyena vā yujyate* (see also Limaye 1974, 253).

5. *Yogādvā strītvapuṃstvābhyām na kiñcidavatiṣṭhate. Svasminnātmani tatrānyad bhūtam bhāvi ca kathyate.*

6. *Muni . . . santo na jāyati na jiyyati na kuppati nappiheti* (MN 3:246, cited in Karunaratna 1979, 119).

7. It defines time as that which measures (*kalyate saṃkhyāyate kālah,* 1:4.1). Compare also to Suśruta's definition— *sankalayati kālayati vā bhūtāniti kālaḥ* (sū. 6:3).

8. Other similar compounds include: *kāladharma* (characteristics of time), *kālasvabhāva* (the nature of time), *kālayoga* (by virtue of time), *kālasātmya* (congenial to time), *kālalīlā* (play or the deeds of time), *kālakrama* (sequence, order of time).

9. *Kālajastveva puruṣaḥ kālajāstasya cāmayāḥ jagat kālavaśam sarvam kālaḥ sarvatra kāraṇam* (Ca.sū. 25:25).

10. It is tempting to compare this Janus-faced characteristic of time with the ancient Greek understanding of time as reflected in the concepts of *chronos* and *kairos*. While *chronos* stands for the passing time of scientific quantification, *kairos* suggests that certain times are more significant than others. Paul Tillich's concept of "crisis", for instance, is based on it (see Beer 1979, 30).

11. *Āturāvasthāsvapi tu kāryākāryam prati kālākāla-saṃjñā . . . na hyatipatitakālamaprāptakālam va bheṣajamupayujyamānam yaugikam bhavati; kālo hi bhaiṣajyaprayogaparyāptimabhinirvartayati.*

12. *Kālo hi nityagaścāvasthikaśca tatrāvasthiko vikāramapekṣate, nityagastu ṛtusātmyāpekṣaḥ.*

Here *vikāra* signifies the given phase in life as determined by the relative balance of the three humors. These, in turn, are affected by the seasons, which are the creation of time as temporality (*nityaga*). Caraka provides a similar explanation elsewhere (. . . *kālaḥ punaḥ saṃvatsaraścāturāvasthā ca* Ca.vi. 8:125).

13. *Karaṇam punaḥ svābhāvikānām dravyāṇāmabhisaṃskāraḥ. Saṃskāro hi guṇāntarādhānamucyate . . .* (Ca.vi. 1:21.[2].

14. The term *pariṇāma* occurs a total of eleven times in the *Yoga Sūtra* (2:15; 3:9,11,12,13,15,16; 4:2,14,32,33). The cognate negative abstract noun *apariṇāmitva* (non-changed-ness) occurs once at 4:18.

15. These views are also endorsed by the Dharma Śāstras (*Manu Smṛti* 6:76–77 and *Viṣṇu Smṛti* 96:27,31,46–48) in that they provide a realistic interpretation of time, history and change with respect to the individual, thereby allowing a positive evaluation of the lifespan.

16. The corresponding terms given by Caraka (śā. 5:8) are: cause (*hetu*), birth (*utpatti*), growth (*vṛddhi*), decay (*upaplava*) and dissolution (*viyoga*).

17. *Vipariṇamata ityapracyavamānasya tattvādvikāram.*

18. As enumerated by grammarians, they are—genesis (*janma*), existence (*āstitvam*), transformation (*pariṇāmah*), growth (*vṛddhiḥ*), decline (*hānam*) and destruction (*vināśam*).

19. It is defined as *pariṇāmo vikāro dve same vikṛtivikrīye*. See also Pāṇini 3:3.18 and 8:4.14. Mallinātha, commenting on a verse from Bhāravi's *Kirātārjunīyam* (2:4), glosses *pariṇāma* as the time of fructification or the state of maturity (*pariṇāmaḥ phalakālaḥ paripākāvasthā*). Time as *pariṇāma*, and, as such, a cause of aging, is also suggested in a verse from the *Viṣṇudharmottara Purāṇa* (39:51):

> People are mostly void of proportion (*pramāṇahīnatā*) because of the power of time and condition.

20. In order to avoid repetition *pariṇāma* is variously rendered in the present study as change, transformation, modification and mutation.

21. This account is based on Feuerstein 1979, 102–103.

22. Karambelkar (1985, 358) explains *dharmapariṇāma* in terms of the transformation of a caterpillar into a butterfly.

23. The *Amarakośa* includes "moment" in the miscellaneous semantic category, defining it as *nirvyāpārasthitau kālaviśeṣotsavayaḥ* (3:3.47).

24. The *Vākyapadīyam* of Bhartṛhari provides a similar interpretation of the three timeframes. The three courses of time (*adhvānah*—past, future and present) are indeed established as devoid of sequence just like darkness and light. But the sequence results in them with regard to beings. Helārāja's gloss explains that the three times are like roads: just as travellers perform a continuous series of comings and going on roads, likewise, beings, experiencing transformations in the three courses of time engage in a continuous series of coming and going (disappearance and appearance). Thus, a being which exists in future course, the same one having fallen in the present course, falls again in the past course (VP 3:9.52, see also P. S. Sharma 1972, 76).

25. It is also defined as that by which particular time is demarcated (*lakṣyate aneneti lakṣaṇam kālabhedaḥ*).

26. Compare to Bhartṛhari's concept of the power of time (*kālaśakti*), and its two aspects—sequence (*krama*) and restriction (*jarā*). As *krama*, *kālaśakti* activates the developmental process. As *jarā*, it stunts development draining all energy and vitality from life and initiates decline:

> *Jarākhyā kālaśaktiryā śaktyāntaravirodhinī sā śaktim pratibadhnāti jāyante ca virodhinaḥ* (VP 3:9.24).

27. Consider in this context *Vākyapadīyam* 3:9.39, which states that beings transfer their form (perceived by the intellect) upon time and vanish.

28. *Vibhartṛkāḥ tu kartavyāḥ striyaḥ palitasaṃyutāḥ* (2:3.73.34).

29. It is tempting to compare this with the condition which is characterized as "being-in-the-world" by Heidegger (*In-der-Welt-Sein*).

30. Some of the synonyms are—*pañcatā* (fiveness, that is, the five cardinal elements to which the gross body is reduced at death), *kāladharma* (the property or the characteristic of time, *diṣṭānta* (end of fate), *pralaya* (dissolution) and *nāśa* (destruction) (see *Amarakośa* 2:8.116).

31. It is significant that the substantive *hāni* (loss) itself is derived from the root *han* to kill. Similarly, Sāyaṇa in his gloss on AV 11:10(8).19 defines old age as the end state causing destruction on account of age (*jarā vayohānikarī caramāvasthā*).

32. "I cause you", says the Atharvan priest (AV 12:3.22), "who are earth, to enter the earth; this body of yours, which was well integrated (*samānī*) is [now] disintegrated (*vikṛtā*)" (see Lincoln 1986, 127). This notion of decomposition or disintegration is also present in the concept of *nirṛti* in the *Ṛgveda*, which Renou (1955, 11–15) explains as a derivative in *ti* (thus bearing *a priori* a dynamic value) from the root *ar* with *ṛ* indicating a certain fixed order or cosmos. Because of the prefix *nis*, *nirṛti* inversely signifies disorder or entropy.

33. Lincoln (1980) speculates that in the Centum linguistic grouping of Indo-European languages, the ferryman of the dead is the personification of old age carrying souls off to death. But in the *śatam* grouping, the ferryman is the personification of a religious ideal/savior carrying souls to death. It may be argued that the Vedic religion, which resembled the Centum grouping, tended to be non-soteriological in nature. It was much more concerned with questions of winning a good life in the here and now than with the questions of salvation in the hereafter.

34. See ŚB 12:4.1.1. Eggeling (1963, 178) observes that "old age deathed" or "having old age for its extreme limit (*maryā*)" seem to be the

literal meaning of *jarāmaryam*. The *Jaimini Brāhmaṇa* concurs with this explanation but substitutes *jarāmūrīya* for *jarāmarya*, perhaps under the influence of the *Paṃcaviṃśa Brāhmaṇa* (25:17.3) where *jīrya mūraḥ* occurs in the context of a long lasting sacrificial session extending to a thousand years (*dīrghasattra*, see Bodewitz 1973, 156).

35. See AV 12:3.55; 19:24.4,8; 19:26.1; 2:13.2; 2:28.2,4; 8:2.11.

36. See RV 2:13.2; 2:28.1–2; 8:67.20; 10:18.6.

37. *Trirha vai puruṣo jāyate . . . mṛtyurna mṛiyate'mṛte hyantastasmādana dṛśyate'mṛte hyantah . . .* (ŚB 10:5.1.3). What Shakespeare has to say in this context is also revealing. Death (like old age one might add) is not something that comes only at the last moment of life; it permeates every human act from birth onwards. It is the act of death which gives uniqueness to our separate, disparate acts in life. Only through death immortality is revealed and reached. Death itself thus contains within it the seed of immortality (Shibles 1974, 147–174).

38. This is based on Sāyaṇa's gloss on that passage:

*Mṛtyurūpah puruṣo mṛtyurupe'antara vartate'mṛtyoḥ puruṣasyāmṛtatvam amṛtarūpa.*

Compare this idea to Yeats' contention that in Rilke's view a man's death is born with him and if his life is successful and he escapes mere "mass death", his nature is completed by his final union with death. Rilke gives Hamlet's death as an example (See Wade 1954, 917).

39. *Plavā hyete adrḍhā yajñarūpā aṣṭadaśoktam avaram yeṣu karma etacchreyo ye'bhinandanti mūdhāḥ jarāmṛtyum te punarevāpi yanti* (*Muṇḍaka Upaniṣad* 1:2.7).

40. This estimation of death compares favorably with Wittgenstein's observation that at death the world does not alter, but comes to an end. Death is not an event in life: we do not live to experience death. If we take eternity to mean not infinite temporal duration but timelessness, then eternal life belongs to those who live in the present (see Shibles 1974, 69).

41. Lamotte (1976, 42), for instance, renders *jarāmaraṇa* as *la vieillèsse-mort*.

42. Here the Buddha is in the company of many distinguished philosophers for whom human existence is—Thomas Hobbes has said it—nasty, mean, brutish and short. After Darwin these views were reformulated and morally mitigated, by recognizing that existence is struggle for existence (see Kallen 1972).

43. Compare to Göethe's enigmatic comment that death is Nature's expert contrivance to get plenty of life (quoted in Mukherji 1975, 382–383).

44. This simile also appears in the *Padma Purāṇa* (1:2.66.116) where Mātali (the charioteer of Indra) is describing the viscissitudes of the human body to King Yayāti.

45. These lines are originally pronounced by Schopenhauer (1982) in the context of his reflections on death. They could equally well be put in the mouth of the Buddha.

46. Compare these ideas to Schopenhauer's comments (1982) that the world is bankrupt and life is a business that does not cover the costs and that man's noble vocation is to suffer.

47. In the *Skanda Purāṇa* ("Pūrvārdha") Śiva rejects King Indradyumna's request to make him ageless (*ajara*) and deathless (*amara*), explaining that nobody who bears a name and form can vanquish old age. See also "Umā Saṃhitā", *Śiva Purāṇa* (26:27).

48. A similar discourse is given by Rāma to his younger brother Bharata who has requested Rāma to abandon his life in exile and return to the capital to rule the kingdom of Ayodhyā:

> The human being is not able to do what it wills on this earth. It is fate which moves us around. Whether we saunter or hasten on, life and death pass us by like a flowing river, which never returns to its source. As pieces of drifting wood floating on the ocean come together for a span, so wives, sons, parents, wealth and property remain with us for a while, only to abandon us in the course of time! (Rām 2:98.15,25,26.)

## Chapter 4

1. "*Tatra śarīram nāma cetanādhiṣṭhānabhūtam pañcamahābhūtavikārasamudayātmakam samayogavāhi*" (Ca.Śā. 6:4).

Caraka also argues that everything about the self is established in the body ( . . . *śarīram hyasya mūlam, śarīramūlaśca puruṣo bhavati,* Ca.ni. 6:6).

2. The *Taittirīya Upaniṣad* also correlates *brahman* with the body, on the one hand, and with food, on the other. Verse 2 posits the relation between the body and food in the following tautology:

> Food indeed is life and the eater of food is the body. The body is founded on life and life is founded on the body. In this way food is founded on food.

3. Consider, for instance, this verse from the *Maitrī Upaniṣad* (6:13) translated in Deussen 1980, 1:351:

> Food is what prevents aging,
> Food certainly is what is soothing,
> Food is the life-breath of creatures.
> It is ordained as the oldest,
> It is ordained as medicine.

4. Anaxagoras analyzes the processes of nutrition and embryology in a similar vein. If it appears that food eaten turns into bodily flesh and hair, this is only because flesh, hair, etc. were already present within the food in invisible particles. Food, thus, is nothing other than a microcosm of the macrocosm, containing all parts of the human—or animal or even plant—body within it. Like substance is augmented by like substance (compare to the Āyurvedic doctrine of the *sāmānya* and *viśeṣa*). In the process of nutrition the invisible particles of flesh, hair etc. are detached from their temporary location within bread, sorted out, and joined to the parts of the body to which they properly correspond: particles of flesh going to flesh and so forth (see Lincoln 1986, 77).

5. Consider, for instance, this Atharvan hymn:

> You are a goddess, born upon the divine earth, O plant! We dig you now, you who stretch downward, in order to make the hairs firm. Make the old ones firm; cause to be born those which are [still] unborn; make those which have been born [grow longer] (AV 6:136,137).

Lincoln (1986, 94) sees in this spell a sophisticated application of the anthropogonic aspect of the mythology of creation rather than the mere sympathetic magic seen by most scholars.

6. To a certain extent this concern with the appropriateness of food to be consumed for sustaining the body and to enable the individual to attain liberation is also evident in Buddhist texts (e.g., *Saundarananda* 14:1–19).

7. Mhaskar and Watve (1954, 2:86) argue that all products with the predominance of the *guru* quality prevent the advent of old age in the persons ingesting them.

8. Though in certain Hindu philosophies and sects such as the Haṭha Yoga, the old ideal of bodily immortality is still retained, the majority of them eventually came to accept the Buddhist contention that admittedly the human lifespan is limited and accordingly modified their philosophies of life to reconcile with that fact. Nonetheless, the awareness of the fact that only a quarter of the lifespan may be enjoyed with full physical and mental health continued to haunt them. In the face of this unsa-

17. *Rasahṛdayatantra* (1:13), an old text (ca. 900 CE) of the Siddha system of medicine, boasts that all can be freed from poverty and rendered ageless (*nirjara*) and deathless by the power of the mercury-based preparations (see Ramacandra Rao 1985, 79).

18. Das (1984) in his review of G. U. Thite's *Medicine: Its Magico-Religious Aspects according to the Vedic and Later Literature* (Poona: Continental Prakashan, 1982) has argued that all ancient medicine is essentially divided into three parts: healing through the knife, healing through plants, and healing through words (incantations and the like).

19. The Galenic medicine advocates similar prophylactic measures. Quoting Athenaeos, a Greek physician of first century CE, Galen remarked that application of the hygiene of old age should already start in youth: just as those who wear coats in summer [are forced to] spend winter in worn out [tattered] clothes, so those who in youth waste their vital force endure old age with difficulty (cited in Grmek 1958, 55).

20. See Engelhardt (1979) where the argument is further developed.

## Chapter 5

1. See Roșu (1978, 80). He also observes that, "*Il n'y a pas pour Caraka, de clivage entre la condition humaine et l'horizon métaphysique* (81), and "*Investigation medicale (śārīravicaya), aboutit a une anthropologie qui engage une vision de la nature de l'être (puruṣavicaya)*" (138).

2. Caraka (Ca.sū. 1:52) explains that the *karma* (active potential) present in the substance is conducive to growth or loss in the composite body. This property of *karma* is *sui generis* and needs no other cause for it.

3. In the *Atharva Veda* (8:7.22), *amṛta* is understood as an elixir of long life. AV 18:3.62 expresses the hope that deathlessness may replace death and decay. *Amṛtatva* in such passages means the deliverance of the liberated self from dying. But in Western tradition, immortality connotes indestructibility by death. The equivalent concept in Indian tradition is *vyatireka* (reaching beyond the body) (see Deussen 1972, 1:287).

4. This shift is also suggested by the title of this particular hymn, "To Which Gods?"

5. Geldner 1951–57 has argued that the concept of the golden germ (*hiraṇyagarbha*) is the precursor of the subsequent Hindu cosmology.

6. Compare this account to that in Plato's *Politicos* (269c–274e), where the cosmos is viewed as a sphere, the motion of which alternates between two opposing phases. In the first phase, the cosmic sphere is

guided by God's hand, which spins it in one rotational direction. The world then partakes of both moral and physical well being. This is the paradisal age of *kronos*. But at a certain moment, God releases his hand from the cosmos, and it begins to spin in the opposite direction. This is the age of Zeus when moral and physical conditions deteriorate. The moment of transition from one rotational direction to another is a period of catastrophe where "beginning and end rush in opposite directions" (Lincoln 1986, 134). In the parallel Hindu myth of the churning of the ocean, the birth and the death of the universe is similarly symbolized by the two rotational directions.

7. This is based on Sāyaṇa's gloss who quotes Śaunaka and the *Taittirīya Brāhmaṇa* (1:6.10.5) in support of this particular line of interpretation.

8. . . . *mṛtyurvivasvantam vasta' ityasau vā'dityo vivasvāneṣa . . . sarvato hyanena parivṛto mṛutyorātmā vivasvati . . .*

9. Sāyaṇa's gloss states that the compound *jarāmṛtyu* has a double meaning: freedom from old age and death *or* freedom even from natural death in old age (*jarāmṛtyuvarjita*).

10. The *Bṛhadarāṇyaka Upaniṣad* (1:5.17) provides a similar death-bed ceremony (*saṃpratti*), although it goes further in that it describes how the faculty of speech (*vāc*), mind (*manas*) and the vital principle (*prāṇa*) arise out of the earth, sky and water respectively and enter the dying father after he has bequeathed his power of life to his son.

11. The same dilemma reappears in the legend of Yayāti in various Purāṇas (see below). But the solutions suggested are different.

12. *Genesis* (5:9.29), too, records the lifespans of ten patriarchs who lived before the flood. Their ages ranged from 365 years of Enoch to the 969 years of Methusaleh, whose name has become a byword for longevity in Western culture (Gruman 1966, 25). In Chinese tradition the *hsein* were men who had won eternal life by their mastery of certain techniques of prolongevity. But they are not painted as young and handsome. They are shown as old men, gnarled but shrewd looking and possessing marvelous powers. (Gruman 1966, 39).

13. Compare to the ancient Greek belief that beyond Boreas (the north wind) there is a culture or society whose people enjoy a remarkably long life (Gruman 1966, 22). This theme is also expressed by the myth of the fountain whose waters are purported to rejuvenate (compare to the Ṛgvedic legend of Cyavana).

14. Consider also the legends involving other old sages—Aṅgirasa (1:51.3), Kali (1:112.15; 10:39.8) and Rebha (1:119.6ff; 4:33.3; 36.3).

15. RV 1:116.10. See also 117.13; 118.6.

16. MB 3:122.1–27; 123.1–23. The etymology of Cyavana (the fallen one) is traced to the verb *cyu* meaning to fall. MB 3:122.22,23 seem to refer to Cyavana's lustful (and therefore 'fallen') nature:

> . . . *rūpaudāryamsamāyuktam lobhamohabalātkṛtam. Tāmeva pratigrhyām rājanduhitaram tava kṣamiṣyāmi mahipāla satyametatbravimī te.*

17. 7:2.27–65; 7:3.12–54; 7:4.1–38; 7:5.7–11.

18. RV 1:92.4,10–11; 1:113.13,15; 1:123.2; 1:124.2; 7:18.20.

19. This simile also figures in the *Agni Purāṇa* (161:15–16) where it is observed that the human body, an easy victim of old age, sorrow, and death, is more transient than a dew drop on a blade of grass.

20. *Mṛtyukanyāsutāścaite jarā tasyāśca kanyakā jarā ca bhrātṛbhiḥ sārdham śaśvadbhramatī bhūtale* (*Brahmavaivarta Purāṇa* 1.17.36).

21. *Kālsya duhitā kācittriloki varamicchatī paryaṭantī* . . . (4:27.5).

22. Such moral lapses are said to lead to parallel developments at the cosmic level. The Satya Yuga is equal to childhood, the Tretā Yuga to youth, the Dvāpara Yuga to old age and the Kali Yuga to disease and the end of all ages to death (Ca.śā. 5:5). See also "Āraṇyaka Parvan", *Mahābhārata* (3:188) which features Mārkaṇḍeya's discourse on the relation between moral action and the aging process.

23. The story is told in the *Mahābhārata* ("Ādi Parvan", chapters 70–88), the *Rāmāyaṇa* (1:56ff), the *Matsya Purāṇa* (chapters 32–42), the *Viṣṇu Purāṇa* (4:10.1–32), the *Vāyu Purāṇa* ("Uttarārdha" chapter 30:28ff, chapter 31), and the *Liṅga Purāṇa* (1:67.1–28).

24. In the Purāṇic literature, old age is usually personified as an old woman with wrinkles covering her entire body. She is described as black faced, red eyed and with tawny, coarse hair. She is the antithesis of the goddess Lakṣmī (see *Padma Purāṇa*, "Brahma Khaṇḍa", 9:9.20). Dange (1986, 12) argues that Ālakṣmī is first mentioned in the *Taittirīya Āraṇyaka* (10:1–10). However, there are references to Ālakṣmī in the *Atharva Veda*.

25. See *Matsyapurāṇa* 33:1–23 and Dumézil 1973, 16.

26. Kavi Usan, the Iranian counterpart of Kāvya Uṣanas, is also said to possess both the magical powers of overcoming old age and death: reviving those who had died and curing the implacable malady of growing old. He is said to have erected seven castles: one of gold, two of iron and two of crystal on Mount Elburz. Anyone enfeebled by old age going quickly all about that mountain had his age fade away and his strength and youth returned to him (see Dumézil 1986, 57–69).

27. When Yayāti requests Mātali (Indra's charioteer) to explain the etiology of aging, the latter, too, traces it to the sex drive (*Padma Purāṇa* 1:2.64.64,65–87). A similar motif is also present in the Babylonian epic of Gilgamesh, wherein the indomitable but witless hero Enkidu (like Yayāti) falls an easy prey to death, after he has allowed himself to be seduced by a courtesan of Iṣṭar.

28. "*Rajasvalā ca kulaṭā cāvīrā jarādūtikā śūdrayājakapatnī yā ṛtuhīnā ca yā satī yo hi tāsām annabhojī brahmahatyām labhettu saḥ tena pāpena sārdham sā jarā tam upagacchati*" (1.16.49,50).

Similarly, when Yadu, one of the sons of Yayāti, is asked to exchange his youth for the old age of his father (*Padma Purāṇa*, see above), he pleads inability to bear the burden of old age and quotes a maxim which traces old age to the following five factors: cold [season], time, inferior diet, [sex] with older women and mental adversities: *Śītam adhvā kadannam ca vayotītaśca yoṣitāḥ manasaḥ pratikūlyam ca jarāyāḥ pañca hetavāḥ* (*Padma Purāṇa* 1:2.78.29).

29. *Pāpānām vyādhibḥi sārdham mitratā satatam dhruvam pāpam vyādhijarābījam vighnabījam ca niścitam* (1.16.51).

30. When Mātali, the charioteer of Indra, is requested by King Yayāti to explain the etiology of aging (*Padma Purāṇa* 1:2.64.64), he, too, attributes aging to *kāma* (1:2.64.80,81,87).

31. Chapter sixteen of the *Brahmavaivarta Purāṇa* (1:16) features an animated discourse on dying to the young queen Mālāvatī, who is grieving over the dead body of her husband, King Upavarahaṇa. The *Garuḍa Purāṇa* 2:1.23–31; 2:2.1–92, too, features an extended dialogue on dying involving god Kṛṣṇa. See also Pārvatī's comiserations with Ratī who laments Śiva's burning to death her husband Kāma, the god of love as described in the *Matsya Purāṇa* (154:289ff).

32. See the dialogue between a wise young brahmin named Sumati, who remembered his former existences, and his father. Sumati explains how death occurs and describes the stages in the life after death (*Mārkaṇḍeya Purāṇa* 10:48–50). See also *Agni Purāṇa* 369:1–10 and *Garuḍa Purāṇa*, "Uttara Khaṇḍa" 21:23–33).

33. *Pañcaitani vilikhyante garbhasthasyaiva dehinaḥ āyuḥ karma ca vidyā ca vittam nidhanameva ca.*

34. *Karmaṇā jāyate pretya mūrtimānṣoḍśātmakaḥ*
*vidyayā jāyate nityamavyayo hayavyayātmakaḥ.*

35. In the *Mahābhārata*, they are variously known as providential and divine acts (*divya kriyā*, 2:42.45ff; 3:2.6; 3:32.40), divine ordinances (*divya vidhi*, 3:31.3ff); fate (*daiva* or *diṣṭi*, 1:84.6–8; 1:89.9), time (*kāla* 2:40.5; 71.42;

72.8–11), death (*mṛtyu, kṛtānta* or *antaka,* 13:1.50ff), nature (*prakṛti,* 11:222–224) and deeds (*karma,* 1:1.188–191; 3:148–154; 12:153:12–13) (see Long 1980).

36. *Mṛtyupāśaḥ* (AV 8.8.16)

37. Compare to Yājñavalkya's exchange with Janaka in BAU 4:3.36. In an interesting commentary on this passage Madhvācārya (ca. 1300) provides a moral causal explanation of the varying lengths of human lifespans in a charming metaphor:

> The fruit of a mango usually falls off the tree long before it gets fully developed; the fruit of Udumbara falls down when fully developed and the fruits of Aśvattha fall down only after they are very ripe. People die in a similar manner. Some in infancy, some in their youth, and still others in their old age. In the Kali Yuga, people die in their infancy like the mango fruit; in the Tretā Yuga, they die in their youth like the Udumbara fruit; and in the Satya Yuga do they die in old age like the fruits of the Aśvattha tree.

38. Ātreya explains to Agniveśa that the genesis of the fetus is attributable to the combination of six different factors (Ca.śā. 3:14).

39. . . . *puruṣo rāśisaṃjñastu mohecchādveṣakarmajaḥ*. The echo of this classification is also to be heard in the *Mahābhāṣya* of Patañjali (3:1.87, quoted in Puri 1957, 221). Here Patañjali mentions the individual self as made of the physical as well as the internal self (*śarīrātman* and *antarātman*). The internal self performs those actions whereby the physical self feels pain and pleasure (*śarīrātmā tat karma karoti yenāntarātmā sukhaduḥkhe'nubhavati*).

40. See also Cakrapāṇi's gloss on Ca.śā. 4:42–45.

41. The "Cūḷakamma Vibhaṅga Sutta" and "Mahākamma Vibhaṅga Sutta" provide the Buddhist version of the attempt to reconcile the inevitable working out of the effects of *kamma* with intentional evil or good acts (*sañcetanika kamma*). The effect of a comparatively weak deed (*dubbala kamma*) may be superceded by the effect of a comparatively strong deed balava kamma) or by the accumulated effects of a series of deeds. Thus, the aging experience of the individual and its quality can be manipulated by his volitional *kamma* (MN 3:202–206, 206–215). To that extent, this line of thought resembles the arguments of Caraka.

## *Conclusion*

1. Aurobindo Ghose (1954 2:6.2) has provided a cogent and modernist expression of this idea. In his view, the dissatisfaction with the aging

body originates in the perception of an actual or potential limitation. However, it acquires spiritual significance only when its cause is perceived "*sub specie aeternitatis*." Suffering, thus, is at once the sign of limitation and the motive for its transcendence.

# *Bibliography*

## *Primary Works and Translations (By Title)*


*Agnimahāpurāṇam*. Edited by R. N. Sharma. Delhi: Nag Publishers, 1985.

*Aitareya Brāhmaṇa* [Of the Ṛgveda]. 1922. Reprint. Translated by Martin Haug. New York: AMS Press, 1974.

*Amarakośa* [With the Unpublished South Indian Commentaries *Amarapadavivṛti* of Liṅgyasūrin & the *Amarapadapārijāta* of Mallinātha]. Critically edited & introduction by A. A. Ramanathan. Adyar, India: The Adyar Library & Research Centre, 1971.

*Aṅguttara Nikāya* [The Book of the Gradual Sayings]. 5 vols. 1951. Reprint. Vols. 1,2 & 5 translated by F. L. Woodward, vols. 3 & 4 translated by E. M. Hare. London: Pali Text Society, 1961.

*Āpastamba Dharma Sūtra* [With the Commentary of Haradatta Miśra]. Edited with Hindi translation by Umeśa Chandra Pāṇḍeya. The Kashi Sanskrit Series, no.93. Varanasi: Chowkhambha Sanskrit Series Office, 1969.

*Aṣṭādhyāyī of Pāṇini*. 2 vols. 1891. Reprint. Edited & translated by S. C. Vasu. Delhi: Motilal Banarsidass, 1962.

*Aṣṭāṅgahṛdayam* [The Core of Octopatrite Āyurveda Composed by Vāgbhaṭa With the Commentaries Sarvāṅgasundarā of Aruṇdatta & Āyurvedarasāyana of Hemādri]. 7th ed. Edited by Harishastri Paradkar. Varanasi: Chaukhambha Orientalia, 1982.

*Atharva Veda (Śaunakīya)* [With the Padapāṭha & Sāyaṇācārya's Commentary. Pt. 2 (*kāṇḍas* 6–10)]. Edited by Vishva Bandhu et al. Hoshiarpur, India: V. V. Research Institute, 1961.

*Atharva Veda Saṃhitā*. 2 vols. 1962. Reprint. Translated with a Critical & Exegetical Commentary by William D. Whitney. Harvard Oriental Series, edited, with Cooperation by Various Scholars, by Charles Lanman, vols. 7 & 8. Delhi: Motilal Banarsidass, 1971.

*Baudhāyana Dharma Sūtra* [With the Vivaraṇa Commentary by Śrī Govinda Swāmī]. Edited with notes, introduction & word index by A. Chinnaswami Sastri. The Kashi Sanskrit Series, no. 104. Karma Kāṇḍa Section, no. 11. Benares: Chowkhamba, 1934.

*Bhāgavata Purāṇa* [With the Commentary of Śrīdhara Svāmin]. Edited by J. L. Shastri. Delhi: Motilal Banarsidass, 1983.

*Brahamasūtra Śāṅkara Bhāṣyam*. Pt.2. Edited with *Tippanī* by S. Ṙ. Krishnamurthi. Madras: Madrapuri Sanskrit Vidyȧ Śamitī, 1979.

*Brahmavaivarta Purāṇam*. 4 vols. Translated by R. N. Sen. Sacred Books of the Hindus Series, no. 24. Allahabad: Panini Office, 1920.

*Bṛhadāraṇyaka Upaniṣad* [With the Commentary of Madhvācārya]. Translated by S. C. Vasu. Sacred Books of the Hindus Series, no. 14. Allahabad, Panini Office, 1916.

*Bṛhaddevatā* [Attributed to Śaunaka]. 1904. Reprint. Translated by Arthur J. Macdonell. Harvard Oriental Series, no. 7, 2nd issue. Delhi: Motilal Banarsidass, 1965.

*Buddhacarita* [Or Acts of the Buddha, Cantos 1–14]. 1936. Reprint. Complete Sanskrit Text with English translation by E. H. Johnston. Delhi: Motilal Banarsidass, 1972.

*Caraka Saṃhitā* [With the *Āyurveda Dīpikā* Commentary of Cakrapāṇidatta]. Bombay: Nirṇaya Sāgar Press, 1952.

*Chāndogya Upaniṣad* [With the Commentary of Madhva]. 1910. Reprint. Translated by B. D. Basu. New York: AMS Press, 1974.

*Devī Bhāgavata*. Pt. 2. 3rd rev. ed. Edited by Śrīrāma Śarmā. Bareli, India: Samskrit Saṃsthāna, 1977.

*Dhammapāda* [A Collection of Verses translated from Pali by F. Max Müller]. 1881. Reprint. Sacred Books of the East series, translated by various oriental scholars and edited by F. Max Müller, no. 10, Pt. 1. Delhi: Motilal Banarsidass, 1973.

*Dīgha Nikāya* [Dialogues of the Buddha]. 3 Parts. Translated by T. W. Rhys-Davids. Sacred Books of the Buddhists translated by various scholars and edited by T. W. RhysDavids, vols. 2–4. London: Pali Text Society, 1965.

*Garuḍa Purāṇa*. 2 Parts. Translated by G. V. Tagare. Ancient Indian Tradition & Mythology Series, translated and annotated by Various Scholars and edited by J. L. Shastri, no. 12. Delhi: Motilal Banarsidass, 1979.

*Gautama Dharma Sūtram* [With Maskarī Bhāṣya]. Critically edited by Veda Mitra. Delhi: Veda Mitra & Sons, 1969.

*Īśa, Kena, Kaṭha, Praśna, Muṇḍaka and Māṇḍukya Upaniṣads*. 1911. Reprint. Edited by B. D. Basu. New York: AMS Press, 1974.

*Jaiminīya Brāhmaṇa* [1.1–65. (*Agnihotra & Prāṇāgnihotra*)]. Translated & Commentary by H. W. Bodewitz. Leiden: E. J. Brill, 1973.

*Jātakas* [Together with its Commentary, being Tales of the Anterior Births of the Buddha]. 7 vols. 1877. Reprint. Translated by V. Fausböll. London: Luzac 1962.

*Kādambarī*. Part 1. Kashi Sanskrit Texts Series, edited by Kṛṣṇamohan Śāstrī, no. 15. Benares: Chowkhamba Sanskrit Series, 1953.

*Kālasamuddeśa* [Chapter Three of Bhartṛhari's Vākyapadīyam, with Helārāja's commentary]. Translated from the Sanskrit by Peri Sarvesvara Sharma. Delhi: Motilal Banarsidass, 1972.

*Kāmasūtram* [With the commentary *Jayamaṇgalā*]. Edited by Sri. Goswami Damodara Shastri. Benares: Chowkhamba, 1929.

*Kauṣītaki Upaniṣad*. 1925. Reprint. Translated by S. C. Vidyaranya & M. L. Sandal. New York: AMS Press, 1974.

*Kirātārjunīyam*. 6 Parts. Edited by Janārdana Śāstrī. Delhi: Motilal Banarsidass, 1965.

*Kūrma Purāṇa* [With English Translation]. Translated by Abhibhushan Bhattacarya et al. Edtited by Anand Swarup Gupta. Varanasi: The All India Kashiraj Trust, 1972.

*Liṅga Purāna* [With the Commentary Śivatoṣiṇī]. Edited by Jagadīśa Śāstrī. Delhi: Motilal Banarsidass, n.d.

*Mahābhārata*. 30 vols. Critically edited by V. S. Sukhthankar et al. Poona: Bhandarkar Oriental Research Institute, 1933–1960.

*Mahābhāṣya* [Of Patañjali]. See below *Vyākaraṇa-Mahābhāṣya*.

*Maitrī Upaniṣad*. Translated by S. C. Vidyaranya & M. L. Sandal. Sacred Books of the East Series, no. 31. Pt. 2. Allahabad: Panini Office, 1926.

*Majjhima Nikāya* [The Collection of the Middle Length Sayings]. 3 vols. Reprint. Translated by I. B. Horner. Pali Texts Translation Society Series, no.s 29, 30, 31. London: Luzac & Co, 1954–1959.

*Manu Smṛti* [With the Commentary *Mānavārtha Muktāvalī* of Kulluka]. 10th ed. Edited by Narayana Ram Acharya, Kavyatirtha. Bombay: Nirnaya Sagar Press, 1946.

*Mārkaṇḍeyamahāpurāṇa*. 3 vols. Edited Sanskrit text with Hindi translation by Satyavrata Singh. Sitapur, U.P., India: Institute for Puranic & Vedic Research, 1984.

*Matsya Purāṇa* [Text in Devanāgarī] Pt.1. Translation and notes in English by S. S. Singh. Delhi: Nag Publishers, 1983.

*Milindapañha* [The Questions of King Milinda]. 2 vols. 1890. Reprint. Translated by T. W. RhysDavids. Sacred Books of the East Series, translated by various scholars and edited by F. Max Muller, nos. 35, 36. Delhi: Motilal Banarsidass, 1969.

*Mṛchhakaṭika* [Of Śūdraka]. 1924. Reprint. Edited with the Commentary of Pṛthvīrāja by M. R. Kale. Bombay: Booksellers Publishing Co., 1962.

*Muṇḍaka Upaniṣad* [In *Eight Upaniṣads* With the Commentary of Śaṅkara]. 3rd Impression. Translated by Swami Gambhirananda. Calcutta: Advaita Asrama, 1973.

*Nārada Purāṇa*. 5 Parts. Translated by G. V. Tagare. Ancient Indian Traditions and Mythology Series, translated by Various Scholars and edited by J. L. Sastri, nos. 15–19. Delhi: Motilal Banarsidass, 1981–1982.

*Nirukta of Yāska* [With the Vivṛti]. 1930. Reprint. Critically edited by Mukund Jha Bakshi. Panini Vaidika Granthamala no. 12. New Delhi: Panini, 1982.

*Padma Purāṇa* [*Khaṇḍa* 1 & 2]. Edited by Raosaheb Mandalik & M. C. Bhate: Ānandāśrama Sanskrit Texts Series, vol. 131. Pune: Ānandāśrama Press, 1893.

*Pañcaviṃśa Brāhmaṇa* [The *Brāhmana* of Twenty-five Chapters]. Translated by W. Caland. Calcutta: Asiatic Society of Bengal, 1931.

*Raghuvaṃśa of Kālidāsa*. 4th ed. Edited with translation and notes by G. R. Nandargikar. Delhi: Motilal Banarsidass, 1971.

———. [A Mahākāvya with 19 Cantos with the Commentary of Mallinātha Sūri, edited by Vāsudeva Śāstrī Paṇaśīkar with critical & explanatory notes of the text & an essay on the life & writings of the poet]. Translated by K. M. Joglekar. Bombay: Pandurang Javji, 1925.

*Rāmāyaṇa*. 15 vols. Critically edited by G. H. Bhatt and Other Scholars. Baroda: Oriental Research Institute, 1958–

*Ṛgveda Saṃhitā* [With the commentary of Sāyaṇa]. 4 Pts. Edited by N. S. Sontakke et al. Poona: Vaidika Samshodhan Mandal, 1936–1946.

*Rig-Veda [Der]: Aus Dem Sanskrit Im Deutsche Übersetzt.* 4 vols. Translated by Karl Friedrich Geldner. Harvard Oriental Series, edited by Charles Lanman. nos. 33–37 Cambridge, Mass.: Harvard Univ. Press, 1951–1957.

*Saṃyutta Nikāya* [The Book of the Kindred Sayings]. 5 vols. Translated by C. A. F. RhysDavids & F. L. Woodward. London: Pali Text Society, 1951–1956.

*Śārṅgadharasaṃhitā* [Of Śrī Śārṅgadharācārya]. Edited by Dayashankar Pandeya. The Haridasa Sanskrit Series, no. 151. Varanasi: Chowkhamba Sanskrit Series Office, 1976.

*Śatakatrayam of Bhartṛhari* [The Southern Archetype of the Three Centuries of Epigrams ascribed to Bhartṛhari]. Critically edited by D. D. Kosambi with an anonymous Sanskrit Commentary edited by K. V. Krishnamoorthy Sharma. Bharatiya Vidya Series, no. 9. Bombay: Bharatiya Vidya Bhavan, 1946.

*Śatapatha Brāhmaṇa* [of the Mādhyandīna Śākhā]. 1849. Reprint. 2d ed. Edited by Albrecht Weber. The Chowkhambha Sanskrit Series, no. 96. Varanasi: Chowkhambha, 1964.

———. [According to the Text of the Mādhyandīna School]. 5 Pts. 1900. Reprint. Translated by Julius Eggeling. Delhi: Motilal Banarsidass, 1963.

*Saundarananda* [of Aśvaghoṣa]. 1925. Reprint. Critically edited and translated by E. H. Johnston. Delhi: Motilal Banarsidass, 1975.

*Siddhānta Kaumudī* [Of Bhaṭṭojī Dīkṣita]. 2 vols. 1906. Reprint. Edited and translated by S. C. Vasu. Delhi: Motilal Banarsidass, n.d.

*Śiva Purāṇa*. 4 Parts. 1969. Reprint. Translated by a Board of Scholars. Delhi: Motilal Banarsidass, 1982.

*Subhāṣita Ratnabhāṇḍāgāra* [Gems of Sanskrit Poetry: A Collection of Witty, Epigrammatic, Instructive and Descriptive Verses with their Sources]. 8th ed. Enlarged and re-edited by Narayana Ram Acharya. Bombay: Nirnaya Sagar Press, 1952.

*Suśruta Saṃhitā* [With the Commentary of Ḍalhaṇa]. Bombay: Nirnaya Sagar Press, 1948.

*Sutta-Nipāta* [A Collection of Discourses]. 1958. Reprint. Translated from Pali by V. Fausböll. The Sacred Books of the East Series, no. 10. Pt. 2. Delhi: Motilal Banarsidass, 1973.

*Taittirīya Upaniṣad*. 1925. Reprint. Translated by S. C. Vidyaranya & M. L. Sandal. New York: AMS Press, 1974.

*Upadeśasāhasrī* [In Śrī Śāṅkaragranthāvaliḥ, Complete Works of Śrī Śaṅkarācārya in the Original Sanskrit]. vol. 3. 1910. Reprint. Madras: Samata Books, 1983.

*Upaniṣad Saṃgraha* [Containing 188 Upaniṣads]. 1970. Reprint. Edited with introduction by J. L. Shastri. Delhi: Motilal Banarsidass, 1980.

*Vākyapadīyam* [Of Bhartṛhari, Part 3. With the Commentary "Prakāśa" by Helārāja]. 2 vols. Edited by Bhagiratha Prasada Tripathi. Saraswati Bhavan Granthamala no. 91. Varanasi: Sampurnananda Samskrit Visvavidyalaya, 1977. See also *Kālasamuddeśa* above.

*Vāyumahāpurāṇa*. Reprint. Delhi: Nag Publishers, 1983.

*Viṣṇupurāṇam* [With Sanskrit Commentary of Śrīdharācārya]. 2 vols. Edited by Thanesh Chandra Upreti. Parimal Sanskrit Texts, no. 21. Delhi: Parimal Publications, 1987.

*Viṣṇudharmottara Purāṇa* [Third Khaṇḍa]. 2 vols. Critically edited with notes by Priyabala Shah.Gaekwad's Oriental Series, nos. 130, 137. Baroda: Oriental Institute, 1958.

*Viṣṇu Smṛti* [Institutes of Viṣṇu]. Translated by Julius Jolly. Sacred Books of the East Series, edited by Max Müller, no. 7. Oxford: Clarendon Press, 1880.

*Vyākaraṇa-Mahābhāṣya* [Of Patañjali]. 3 vols. 1880. Reprint. Edited by F. Kielhorn. 3rd ed. Revised by K. V. Abhyankar. Poona: Deccan College, 1958–72.

*Yājñvalkya Smṛti* [The Institutes of Yājñavalkya together with the Commentary called Mitākṣarā by Śrī Vijñāneśvara]. Edited by J. R. Gharpure. The Collections of Hindu Law Texts, no.1. 1st ed. Bombay: J. R. Gharpure, 1914.

*Yogadarśanam* [Yoga Sūtra of Patañjali with the Yoga Bhāṣya of Vyāsa, the Tattva Vaiśāradī of Vācaspati Miśra and the Yoga Vārtika of Vijñāna Bhikṣu]. Varanasi, India: Bharatiya Vidya Prakashan, 1971.

*Yoga System of Patañjali* [The]. 1914. Reprint. Translated by James H. Woods. Harvard Oriental Series, no. 17. Delhi: Motilal Banarsidass, 1966.

*Pātañjala Yoga Sūtras* [Sanskrit Sūtras with Transliteration]. Translation & Commentary by P. V. Karambelkar. Lonavla, India: Kaivalyadham, 1985.

*Yogavāsiṣṭha of Vālkimi* [with the Commentary Vāsiṣṭhamahārāmāyaṇa Tātparyaprakāśa, Pt. 1]. Edited by Wāsudev Laxman Śāstrī Paṇaśīkar. 3rd rev. ed. Edited by Narayana Ram Acarya. Bombay: Nirṇaya Sāgar Press, 1937.

## Secondary Works

Agrawala, V. S. 1963. *India as Known to Pāṇini: A Study of the Cultural Material in the Aṣṭādhyāyī*. 2d ed., rev. & enl. Varanasi: Prithivi Prakashan.

———. 1969. *The Deeds of Harsha: Being a Cultural Study of Bāṇa's Harshacharita*. Edited by P. K. Agrawala. Varanasi: Prithivi Prakashan.

Aiyangar, K. V. Rangaswami. 1949. *Aspects of the Social & Political System of Manusmṛti (Radhakumud Mookerji Lectures, 1946)*. Lucknow: Univ. of Lucknow.

Aiyangar, Narayana. 1983. *Ancient Hindu Mythology*. 1897. Reprint. Delhi: Deep & Deep Publications.

Amoss, Pamela T. & Steven Harrell, eds. 1981. *Other Ways of Growing Old: Anthropological Perspectives*. Stanford, Ca.: Stanford University Press.

Arapura, John G. 1973. *Religion as Anxiety & Tranquility: An Essay in Comparative Phenomenology of Religion*. Religion & Reason Series, vol. 5. The Hague: Mouton.

Banerji, Sures Chandra. 1962. *Dharma-Sūtras: A Study in their Origin & Development*. Calcutta: Punthi Pustak.

Barua, Benimadhab. 1970. *A History of Pre-Buddhistic Indian Philosophy*. 1921. Reprint. Delhi: Motilal Banarsidass.

Beer, John. 1979. *Wordsworth in Time*. London: Faber & Faber.

Bhagat, M. G. 1976. *Ancient Indian Asceticism*. New Delhi: Munshiram Manoharlal.

Bhargava, P. L. 1971. *India in the Vedic Age: A History of Aryan Expansion in India*. 2d rev. ed. Lucknow: The Upper Indian Publishing House.

Biardeau, Madeleine. 1981. *L'Hindouisme: Anthropologie d'une Civilisation*. Paris: Flammarion.

Bloomfield, Maurice. 1964. *A Vedic Concordance*. 1906. Reprint. Edited by Charles Lanman. Harvard Oriental Series, vol. 10. Delhi: Motilal Banarsidass.

Bodewitz, H. W. 1973. See Primary Works & Translations, s.v. "Jaiminīya Brāhmaṇa".

Bosch, F. D. K. 1960. *The Golden Germ: An Introduction to Indian Symbolism.* Indo-Iranian Monographs, vol. 2. 's-Gravenhage: Mouton & Co.

Breystpraak, Linda M. 1984. *The Development of Self in Later Life.* Boston: Little, Brown & Co.

Brock, Heyward D., ed. 1984. *The Culture of Biomedicine.* Studies in Science & Culture, vol. 1. Newark, N.J.: Univ. of Delaware Press.

Burghart, Richard & Audrey Cantlie, eds. 1985. *Indian Religion.* Collected papers on South Asia, vol. 7. London: Curzon Press.

Chaitanya, Krishna. 1975. *A New History of Sanskrit Literature.* 1962. Reprint. Westport, Conn.: Greenwood Press.

Chakraborti, Haripada. 1973. *Asceticism in Ancient India in Brahmanical, Buddhist, Jaina & Ajivika Societies: From the Earliest Times to the Period of Sankaracarya.* Calcutta: Punthi Pustak.

Chaudhuri, Sukomal. 1976. *Analytical Study of the Abhidharmakośa.* Calcutta Sanskrit College Research Series no. 114. Calcutta: Sanskrit College.

Cole, Thomas R. & Sally A. Gadow, eds. 1986. *What Does It Mean to Grow Old?: Reflections from the Humanities.* Durham, N.C.: Duke Univ. Press.

Comfort, Alex. 1985. "Geriatrics in India." *Journal of the Indian Anthropological Society* 20, Special no., 3 (November): 303–304.

Coomarswami, Ananda K. 1935. "Chāyā." *Journal of the American Oriental Society* 55: 278–283.

———. "Saṃvega, Aesthetic Shock." 1942–1943. *Harvard Journal of Asiatic Studies* 7: 174–179.

Cowgill, Donald O. & Lowell D. Holmes, eds. 1972. *Aging & Modernization.* New York: Meredith Corporation.

Cumming, Elaine & William E. Henry. 1961. *Growing Old: The Process of Disengagement.* New York: Basic Books.

Dange, Sadashiv Ambadas. 1986. *Encyclopaedia of Purāṇic Beliefs & Practices.* vol. 1 (A-C). New Delhi: Navarang.

Das, Rahul Peter. 1984. Review of G. U. Thite, *Medicine: Its Magico-Religious Aspects according to the Vedic and Later Literature.* Poona: Continental Prakashan, 1982. *Indo-Iranian Journal* 27, 3 (July): 232–244.

Das, Veena. 1982. *Structure & Cognition: Aspects of Hindu Caste & Ritual.* Delhi: Oxford Univ. Press.

———. 1985. "Paradigms of Body Symbolism: An Analysis of Selected Themes in Hindu Culture." In *Indian Religion,* edited by Richard Burghart & Audrey Cantlie, 180–207. Collected Papers on South Asia, vol. 7. London: Curzon Press.

Dasgupta, Surendranath. 1968. *A History of Indian Philosophy.* vol. 2. Cambridge: Cambridge University Press.

Defourny, Michel. 1978. *Le Mythe de Yayāti dans la Littérature Épique et Purāṇique.* Bibliothèque de la Faculté de Philosophie et Lettres de l'Université de Liège, Fasc. no. 221. Paris: Les Belles Lettres.

Desai, Gandabhai G. 1967. *Thinking with the Yajurveda.* New York: Asia Publishing House.

Desai, K. G. & R. D. Naik. n.d. *Problems of Retired People in Greater Bombay.* Bombay: Tata Institute of Social Sciences.

Desai, K. G., ed. 1983. *Aging in India.* Bombay: Tata Institute of Social Sciences.

Deshpande, Indu. 1985. "Philosophical Thought in the Āraṇyakas." In *Glimpses of Veda & Vyākaraṇa: Reflections on Some Less Familiar Topics,* edited by G. V. Devasthali, 169–176. Bombay: Popular Prakashan.

de Souza, Alfred., ed. 1975. *Women in Contemporary India and South Asia: Traditional Images & Changing Roles.* New Delhi: Manohar.

———. 1982. *The Social Organization of Aging Among the Urban Poor.* New Delhi: Indian Social Institute.

Deussen, Paul. 1972. *The System of Vedānta.* 1912. Reprint. Translated from German by Charles Johnston. Delhi: Motilal Banarsidass.

———. 1980. *Sixty Upaniṣads of the Veda.* 2 Parts. Translated from German by V. M. Bedekar & G. B. Palsule. Delhi: Motilal Banarsidass.

Devasthali, G. V., ed. 1985. *Glimpses of Veda & Vyākaraṇa: Reflections On Some Less Familiar Topics.* Bombay: Popular Prakashan.

Dumézil, Georges. 1971–1974. *Mythe et Épopeé.* 2 vols. Paris: Bibliothèque des Sciences Humaines.

———. *The Destiny of a King.* 1973. Translated from French by Alf Hiltebeitel. Chicago: The Univ. of Chicago Press.

———. 1986. *The Plight of a Sorcerer.* Edited by Jaan Puhvel and David Weeks. Berekeley, Ca.: Univ. of California Press.

Eggling, J. 1963. See Primary works and Translations, s. v. "Śatapatha Brāhmaṇa."

Eliade, Mircea. 1969. *Yoga: Immortality & Freedom.* 2d ed. Bollingen Series, no. 56. Translated from French by Willard R. Trask. Princeton, N.J.: Princeton Univ. Press.

Engelhardt, H. Tristam. 1979. "Is Aging a Disease?". In *Life Span: Values and Life-Extending Technologies,* edited by Robert M. Veatch, 184–194. New York: Harper & Row.

Fausböll, V. 1962. See Primary Works and Translations, s. v. "Jātakas".

———. 1973. See Primary Works and Translations, s. v. "Sutta-Nipāta".

Feuerstein, Georg. 1979. *The Yoga-Sūtra of Patañjali: A New Translation & Commentary.* Folkstone, England: Wm Dawson & Sons Ltd.

Fox, Michael., ed. 1980. *Schopenhauer: His Philosophical Achievement.* Toronto: Barnes & Noble.

Frayser, Suzanne G. 1985. *Varieties of Sexual Experience: An Anthropological Perspective on Human Sexuality.* New Haven, Conn.: HRAF Press.

Fry, Christine & Contributors. 1980. *Aging in Culture & Society: Comparative Viewpoints & Strategies.* New York: Praeger Publishers.

Gadow, Sally. 1986. "Frailty & Strength." In *What Does It Mean to Grow Old?: Reflections from the Humanities,* edited by Thomas R. Cole & Sally A. Gadow, 237–243. Durham, N. C.: Duke Univ. Press.

Geldner, Karl Friedrich. 1951–1957. See Primary Works and Translations, s. v. "Rig-Veda."

George, K. N. 1981. "Problems of the Aged: Findings of a Survey in Madras City." Paper presented at the National Seminar on Aging in India. Tata Institute of Social Sciences, Bombay, September 24–26.

Ghose, Aurobindo. 1954. *Sāvitrī* [Followed by the Author's Letters on the Poem]. Pondicherry, India: Sri Aurobindo Ashram.

Ghurye, G. S. *Vedic India.* 1979. Bombay: Popular Prakashan.

Gokhale, Balkrishna Govind. 1980. "The Image-World of the *Nikāyas.*" *Journal of the American Oriental Society* 100, no.4 (October-December): 445–452.

Gombrich, Richard. 1985. "The Vessantara Jātaka, the Rāmāyaṇa and the Daśaratha Jātaka." *Journal of the American Oriental Society* 105, no. 3, (July-September): 427–437.

vory aspect of the human condition the medical tradition prescribed such therapies which promised to retain youth and delay the onset of old age ranging from a few years to immortality.

9. See AV 1:4.4; 1:5.4; 1:6.2; 3:7.5, and, in particular, Sāyaṇa's gloss on 1:4.4.

10. Sharma (1987) has observed that the concept of *rasa* covers more than forty ideas—including liquid, sap, nutrient fluid, the first essence or part of anything, mercury, seminal fluid of the god Śiva, any mineral or metallic salt, etc.

11. The *Amarakośa* explicitly links old age with decrepitude (*visrasājarā* 2:6.40). Liṅgyasūrin's gloss, in explaining *visrasā*, attributes the eventual falling apart (or breaking down) of the body to old age (*visraṃsate adhaḥ patati śarīramanayeti visrasā*). Mallinātha's gloss further explains that old age refers to the ripening of the body caused by the final phase of age (*caramavayaḥ kṛtaśarīraparipāka nāmani*). The feminine substantive *jarā* based on the root *jṛ* has come to mean decrepitude, infirmity and general debility consequent on old age (See also chapter three).

12. According to Sāyaṇa's gloss, Rohaṇī is urged to restore to normalcy the organ/member of the body that had lost blood (*sṛtaraktam angam prarohaya*).

13. *Pūrve vayasi madhye vā manuṣyasya rasāyanam prayuñjīta bhiṣak prājñaḥ* . . . (Su.ci. 27:3).

14. A legend in the *Padma Purāṇa* narrates how King Yayāti spurns Indra's invitation to go to heaven and become immortal claiming that old age and death are caused by sin (1:2.72.11). He then boasts that by following a moral code of behavior (akin to that prescribed by Caraka) he will keep his body youthful and free from diseases while inhabiting the earth (1:2.72.17).

15. *"Vyāyāmanityāḥ strīnityā madyanityāśca ye narāḥ nityam māṃsarasāhārā nāturāḥ syurna durbalāḥ"*(Ca.sú. 27:315).

According to Caraka (sū. 27:288), in ancient times, even the demons became free of old age, disease and fatigue by regularly undergoing oil massage.

16. Compare to the more recent attempts to stimulate the activities of the gonads of the elderly by irritation in order to produce rejuvenatory effects, or the use of sex hormones to stimulate failing libido and revive mental faculties. Grmek (1958, 46–48) notes that such effects are nonetheless irregular and of short duration. This is by no means a rejuvenation in the literal sense of the word, but rather a kind of erotization.

Gonda, J. 1975a. *A History of Indian Literature: Vedic Literature (Saṃhitās & Brāhmaṇas)*. Wiesbaden: Otto Harrassowitz.

———. 1975b. *Selected Studies: History of Ancient Indian Religions*. vol. 4. Leiden: E. J. Brill.

———. 1979. *The Medium in the Ṛgveda*. Leiden: E. J. Brill.

Grant, Richard. 1967. "Concepts of Aging: An Historical Review." *Perspectives in Biology & Medicine* (Summer): 449–475.

Greene, David. 1983. "Aeschylus: Myth, Religion & Poetry." *History of Religions* 23:1–17.

Grmek, M. D. 1958. *On Ageing & Old Age: Basic Problems & Historic Aspects of Gerontology & Geriatrics*. Monographiae Biologiae, edited by F. S. Bodenheimer & W. W. Weisbach. vol. 5. no. 2. Den Haag: Uitgeverij Dr. W. Junk.

Gruman, Gerald G. 1966. *A History of Ideas about the Prolongation of Life: The Evolution of Prolongevity Hypothesis to 1800*. Transactions of the American Philosophical Society, New Series, vol. 56. pt. 9. Philadelphia: The American Philosophical Society.

Gubrium, Jaber F., ed. 1976. *Time, Roles & Self in Old Age*. New York: Human Sciences Press.

Hall, David A. 1984. *The Biomedical Basis of Gerontology*. Bristol: Wright. PSG.

Haug, Marie et al., eds. 1985. *The Physical & Mental Health of Aged Women*. New York: Springer Publishing Co.

Heesterman, J. C. 1982. "Householder and Wanderer." In *Way of Life: King, Householder, Renouncer: Essays in Honor of Louis Dumont*, edited by T. N. Madan, 251–271. New Delhi: Vikas Publishing House.

Heine, Steven. 1985. *Existential & Ontological Dimensions of Time in Heidegger & Dögen*. Albany, N.Y.: SUNY Press.

Herman, A. L. 1976. *Introduction to Indian Thought*. Englewood Cliffs, N.J.: Prentice Hall.

Hiebert, Paul G. 1981. "Old Age in South Indian Village." In *Other Ways of Growing Old*, edited by Pamela T. Amoss & Steven Harrell, 211–227. Stanford, Ca.: Stanford University Press.

Hill, Christopher. 1961. *The Century of Revolution 1603–1704*. Edinburgh: Thomas Nelson & Sons.

Hindery, Roderick. *Comparative Ethics in Hindu & Buddhist Traditions*. Delhi: Motilal Banarasidass.

Hopkins, Thomas J. 1971. *The Hindu Religious Tradition*. Encino, Calif.: Dickenson Publishing Co.

Jaini, Padmanabh S. 1980. "Karma & the Problem of Rebirth in Jainism." In *Karma & Rebirth in Classical Indian Traditions*, edited by Wendy D. O'Flaherty, 217–238. Berkeley, Ca.: Univ. of California Press.

Jennings, J. G. 1974. *The Vedāntic Buddhism of the Buddha: A Collection of Historical Texts translated from the Original Pali & edited*. 1947. Reprint. Delhi: Motilal Banarsidass.

Johnson, Willard. 1980. *Poetry & Speculation of Ṛgveda*. Berkeley, Ca.: Univ. of California Press.

Joshi, Lalmani. 1967. *Studies in the Buddhistic Culture of India (During the 7th & 8th Centuries A.D.)*. Delhi: Motilal Banarsidass.

Kallen, Horace M. 1972. "Philosophy, Aging & the Aged." *The Journal of Value Inquiry* 6 no. 1 (Winter): 1–22.

Kane, P. V. 1968–1976. *History of Dharmaśāstra: Ancient & Mediaeval Religious & Civil Law*. 5 Vols. Government Oriental Series Class B, no. 6. Poona: Bhandarkar Oriental Research Institute.

Kapani, Lakshmi. 1976. *Garbhopaniṣad*. Les Upaniṣad Texte et Traduction, no. 21. Paris: Adrien Maissoneuve.

Karambelkar, V. W. 1961. *The Atharvaveda & The Āyurveda*. Nagpur: Vidarbha Samsodhan Mandal.

———. 1985. See Primary Works and Translations, s.v. "Pātañjala Yoga Sūtras".

Karunaratna, W. S. 1979. "Change." In *Encyclopaedia of Buddhism*, vol. 4, Fasc. 1. Edited by Jotiya Dhirasekera, 115–123. Colombo: Govt. of Sri Lanka.

Karve, Irawati. 1965. *Kinship Organization in India*. 2nd rev. ed. Bombay: Asia Publishing House.

Kastenbaum, Robert., ed. 1981. *Old Age on the New Scene*. The Springer Series on Adulthood & Aging, no. 9. New York: Springer Publishing Co.

Keith, A. Berriedale. 1922. "The Period of the later Saṃhitās, the Brāhmaṇas, the Āraṇyakas, and the Upaniṣads." In *The Cambridge History of India*. vol. 1, edited by E. J. Rapson, 114–149. Cambridge: Cambridge Univ. Press.

Keith, Jennie. 1982. *Old People as People: Social & Cultural Influences on Aging & Old Age*. Boston: Little Brown & Co.

King, Helen. 1986. "Tithonos & Tettix." *Arethusa* 19, no. 1 (Spring): 15–37.

Kleinman, Arthur. 1980. *Patients & Healers in the Context of Culture: An Exploration of the Borderland between Anthropology, Medicine & Psychiatry*. Comparative Studies of Health Systems & Medical Care, vol. 3. Berkeley, Ca.: Univ. of California Press.

Knox, Israel. 1980. "Schopenhauer: Aesthetic Theory." In *Schopenhauer: His Philosophical Achievement*, edited by Michael Fox, 132–146. Toronto: Barnes & Noble Books.

Kohn, Robert. 1971. *Principles of Mammalian Aging*. Englewood Cliffs, New Jersey: Prentice Hall.

Kurian, George. 1972. "Aging in India & Canada: A Comparative Perspective." *Social Action* 22 (July-September).

Lamotte, Étienne. 1976. *Histoire du Bouddhisme Indien: Des Origines â l'Ere Śaka*. Publications de l'Institut Orientaliste de Louvain, no. 4. Louvain-La-Neuve: Institut Orientaliste.

Lannoy, Richard. 1971. *The Speaking Tree: A Study of Indian Culture & Society*. London: Oxford Univ. Press.

Larson, Gerald. 1987. "Āyurveda & the Hindu Philosophical Systems." *Journal of Philosophy East & West* 37, no. 3 (July: 245–259).

Lasch, Christopher. 1978. *The Culture of Narcissism: American Life in an Age of Diminishing Expectations*. New York: W. W. Norton & Co.

Leslie, Charles. 1976. *Asian Medical Systems: A Comparative Study*. Berkeley, Ca.: Univ. of California Press.

Limaye, V. P. 1974. *Critical Studies in Mahābhāṣya*. Vishveshvarananda Indological Series, no. 49. Hoshiarpur, India: V. V. Research Institute.

Lincoln, Bruce. 1980. "The Ferryman of the Dead." *The Journal of Indo-European Studies* 8, nos. 1 & 2 (Spring/Summer): 41–61.

———. 1986. *Myth, Cosmos & Society: Indo-European Themes of Creation & Destruction*. Cambridge, Mass.: Harvard Univ. Press.

Long, Bruce. 1980. "The Concepts of Human Action & Rebirth in the Mahābhārata." In *Karma & Rebirth in Classical Indian Traditions*, edited by Wendy D. O'Flaherty, 38–60. Berkeley, Ca.: Univ. of California Press.

Lüth, Paul. 1965. *Geschichte der Geriatrie: Dreitausend Jahre Physiologie, Pathologie und Therapie des Älten Menschen*. Stuttgart: Ferdinand Enke Verlag.

Madan, T. N., ed. 1982. *Way of Life: King, Householder, Renouncer: Essays in Honor of Louis Dumont*. New Delhi, Vikas Publishing House.

Maduro, Renaldo. 1981. "The Old Man as Creative Artist in India." In *Old Age on the New Scene*, edited by Robert Kastenbaum, 71–101. New York: Springer Publishing Co.

Maslow, Abraham. 1970. *Motivation & Personality*. 2d ed. New York: Harper & Row.

Maves, P. B. n.d. "Research in Religion in Relation to Aging." Proceedings of Seminars 1961–1965. Durham, N.C.: Council on Gerontology, Duke University.

Macdonell, Arthur A. & Arthur O. Keith. 1967. *Vedic Index of Names & Subjects*. vol. 1. 1912. Reprint. Delhi: Motilal Banarsidass.

McDermott, James P. 1980. "Karma and Rebirth in Early Buddhism." In *Karma & Rebirth in Classical Indian Traditions*, edited by Wendy D. O'Flaherty, 165–192. Berkeley, Ca.: Univ. of California Press.

McKee, Patrick L., ed. 1982. *Philosophical Foundations of Gerontology*. New York: Human Sciences Press.

Mehta, P. M. 1978. "Verses on Old Age from Subhāṣita Ratna Bhāṇḍāgāram." *Indian Journal of History of Medicine* 3, no.1 (June): 7–11.

Mhaskar, K. S. and N. S. Watve. 1954. *Health & Longevity in Āyurveda* [in Sanskrit, Hindi and English]. Vol. 2. Bombay: Board of Research in Āyurveda.

Miller, Jeanine. 1974. *The Vedas: Harmony, Meditation & Fulfilment*. London: Rider & Co.

———. 1985. *The Vision of Cosmic Order in the Vedas*. London: Routledge & Kegan Paul.

Misra, G. S. P. 1972. *The Age of Vinaya*. New Delhi: Munshiram Manoharlal.

Mitchell, Carol O. 1985. "Nutrition as Prevention & Treatment in the Elderly." In *The Physical & Mental Health of Aged Women*, edited by Marie R. Haug et al, 187–193. New York: Springer Publishing Co.

Mitra, Veda. 1965. *India of Dharma Sūtras*. New Delhi: Arya Book Depot.

Mizruchi, Ephraim H., Barry Glassner & Thomas Pastorello. 1982. *Time & Aging: Conceptualization in Sociological & Gerontological Research.* New York: General Hall Inc.

Mukherji, Jugal K. 1975. *The Destiny of the Body: The Vision & the Realisation in Sri Aurobindo's Yoga.* Pondicherry, India: Sri Aurobindo International Centre of Education.

Nakamura, Hajime. 1983. *A History of Early Vedānta Philosophy.* Translated by Trevor Leggett et al. Religions of Asia Series, edited by Lewis R. Lancaster & J. L. Shastri. no. 1, Pt. 1. Delhi: Motilal Banarasidass.

Nespor Karell and R. H. Singh. 1986. "The Experiences with Ayurvedic Psychotherapy "Sattvāvajaya" in Europe." *Ancient Science of Life* 5, no. 3 (January): 154–155.

Obeyesekere, Gananath. 1981. *Medusa's Hair: An Essay on Personal Symbols and Religious Experience.* Chicago: Univ. of Chicago Press.

O'Flaherty, Wendy D. 1973. *Asceticism & Eroticism in the Mythology of Śiva.* London: Oxford Univ. Press.

———. 1976. *The Origins of Evil in Hindu Mythology.* Berkeley, Ca.: Univ. of California Press.

———., ed. 1980. *Karma & Rebirth in Classical Indian Traditions.* Berkeley, Ca.: Univ. of California Press.

———. 1980a. *Sexual Metaphor & Animal Symbols in Indian Mythology.* Delhi: Motilal Banarsidass.

———. 1984. *Dreams, Illusions & Other Realities.* Chicago: Univ. of Chicago Press.

———. 1985. *Tales of Sex & Violence: Folklore, Sacrifice & Danger in the Jaiminīya Brāhmaṇa.* Chicago: Univ. of Chicago Press.

Olivelle, Patrick. 1978. "The Integration of Renunciation by Orthodox Hinduism." *Journal of the Oriental Institute* 27, no. 1 (September): 27–36.

———. 1981. "Contributions to the Semantic History of Saṃnyāsa." *Journal of the American Oriental Society,* 101, no. 3 (July-September): 265–275.

Organ, Troy Wilson. 1970. *The Hindu Quest for the Perfection of Man.* Athens, Ohio: Ohio Univ. Press.

Pande, G. C. 1974. *Studies in the Origins of Buddhism.* 2d ed. Delhi: Motilal Banarsidass.

Pandey, R. C. 1963. *Problems of Meaning in Indian Philosophy.* Delhi: Motilal Banarsidass.

Panikkar, Raimundo with the collaboration of N. Shanta et al., ed. trans. with intro. & notes. 1977. *Vedic Experience: Mantra Mañjarī, An Anthology of the Vedas for the Modern Man & Contemporary Celebration.* Berkeley, Ca.: Univ. of California Press.

Paul, Diana [With Contributions from Frances Wilson]. 1979. *Women in Buddhism: Images of the Feminine in Mahāyāna Tradition.* Berkeley, Ca.: Asian Humanities Press.

Prasad, Hari Shankar. 1984. "Time & Change in Sāṃkhya-Yoga." *Journal of Indian Philosophy* 12: 35–49.

Prasad, Mantrini. 1975. *Language of the Nirukta.* Delhi: D. K. Publishing House.

Pilkington, J. G., trans. 1927. *The Confessions* [of Augustine]. New York: Boni & Liveright.

Puri, Baij Nath. 1957. *India in the Time of Patañjali.* Bombay: Bharatiya Vidya Bhavan.

Rabelais, François. 1893. *The Five Books & Minor Writings.* 2 vols. Translated from French by W. F. Smith. London: Alexander Watt.

Rabuzzi, Kathryn A. 1984. "Humpty Dumpty: A Literary Challenge to the Concept of Personality Integration." In *The Culture of Biomedicine,* edited by D. Heyward Brock, 187–193. Studies Science & Culture, vol. 1. Newark, N.J.: Univ. of Delaware Press.

Ramachandra Rao, S. K., ed. 1985. *Encyclopaedia of Indian Medicine,* vol. 1 "Historical Perspective." Bombay: Popular Prakashan.

Ramacandran, C. K. 1985. "Gerontology in Āyurveda." *Ancient Science of Life* 5, no. 1 (July): 5–8.

Rapson, E. J., ed. 1922. *The Cambridge History of India.* vol. 1. Cambridge: Cambridge Univ. Press.

Renou, Louis. "Védique nirṛti." *Indian Linguistics* 16 (1955): 11–14.

RhysDavids, T. W. 1965. See Primary Works and Translations, s. v. "Dīgha Nikāya."

———. 1969. See Primary Works and Translations, s. v. "Milindapañha".

Roşu, Arion. 1978. *Les Conceptions Psychologiques dans les Textes Medicaux Indiens.* Paris: Institut de Civilisation Indienne.

Sahni, Ashok. 1981. "Health Services for the Aged in India: An International Perspective." Paper presented at the National Seminar on Aging in India, Tata Institute of Social Sciences, Bombay, September 24–26.

Sarao, K. T. S. 1987. "Who and What Originated Buddhism?" Paper presented at the Seventh World Congress of Sanskritists, Leiden; Netherlands, August 23–29.

Schopenhauer, Arthur. 1982. "Stages in Life" In *Philosophical Foundations of Gerontology*, edited by Patrick L. McKee, 196–219. New York: Human Sciences Press.

Sebeok, Thomas A., ed. 1977. *A Perfusion of Signs*. Bloomington, Indiana: Indiana Univ. Press.

———. 1986. *I think I am a Verb: More Contributions to the Doctrine of Signs*. New York: Plenum Press.

Sharma, Hariprasad. 1987. "Development of Rasaśāstra in Medieval Period." *Ancient Science of Life*. 4, no. 3 (January): 158–164.

Sharma, Priyavrat. 1975. *Scientific History of Āyurveda* [in Hindi]. Varanasi: Chowkhambha.

Sharma, P. S. 1972. See Primary Works and Translations, s.v. "Kālasamuddeśa".

Sharma, P. V. 1972. *Indian Medicine in the Classical Age*. Chowkhamba Sanskrit Series, vol. no. 85. Varanasi: Chowkhamba.

Shibles, Warren. 1974. *Death: An Interdisciplinary Analysis*. Whitewater, Wis.: The Language Press.

Sinha, Braj M. 1983. *Time & Temporality in Sāṃkhya-Yoga & Abhidharma Buddhism*. New Delhi: Munshiram Manoharlal.

Soodan, Kirpal Singh. 1975. *Aging in India*. Calcutta: Minerva Associates.

Spicker, Stuart, Kathleen Woodward and David van Tassel, eds. 1978. *Aging & the Elderly: Humanistic Perspectives in Gerontology*. Atlantic Highlands, New Jersey: Humanities Press.

Stewart, Garrett. 1984. *Death Sentences: Styles of Dying in British Fiction*. Cambridge, Mass.: Harvard Univ. Press.

Swami Nikhilananda. 1963. *The Upaniṣads*. Translated & abridged edition. London: Allen & Unwin.

Tagare, G. V. 1981–1982. See Primary Works and Translations, s. v. "Nārada Purāṇa".

Tatz, Mark., trans. 1985. *Buddhism and Healing: Demiéville's Article "Byō" from Hobōgirin*. Lanham, Md.: University Press of America.

Thapar, Romila. 1978. *Ancient Indian Social History: Some Interpretations*. New Delhi: Orient Longman.

———. 1982. "The Householder and the Renouncer in the Brahmanical and Buddhist Traditions." In *Way of Life: King, Householder, Renouncer: Essays in Honor of Louis Dumont*, edited by T. N. Madan, 273–298. New Delhi: Vikas Publishing House.

———. 1984. *From Lineage to State: Social Formation in the Mid-First-Millenium BC in the Ganga Valley*. Bombay: Oxford Univ. Press.

Upadhyaya, Govind Prasad. 1979. *Brāhmaṇas in Ancient India: A Study in the Role of the Brāhmaṇa Class from C.200 BC to C. A. D. 500*. Delhi: Munshiram Manoharlal.

van Tassel, David D., ed. 1979. *Aging, Death, & the Completion of Being*. Philadelphia: Univ. of Pennsylvania Press.

Varma, Vishvanath Prasad. 1973. *Early Buddhism & Its Origins*. Delhi: Munshiram Manoharlal.

Vatuk, Sylvia, 1975. "The Aging Woman in India: Self-Perceptions & Changing Roles." In *Women in Contemporary India & South Asia: Traditional Images & Changing Roles*, edited by Alfred de Souza, 142–163. New Delhi: Manohar.

———. 1980. Withdrawal & Disengagement as a Cultural Response to Aging in India." In *Aging in Culture & Society: Comparative Viewpoints & Strategies*, Christine L. Fry & Contributors, 126–148. New York: Praeger Publishers.

Veatch, Robert M., ed. 1979. *Life Span: Values and Life-Extending Technologies*. New York: Harper & Row.

Verdu, Alfonso. 1979. *Early Buddhist Philosophy in the Light of the Four Noble Truths*. Washington, DC.: University Press of America.

Vishva Bandhu. 1975. *Vedic Textuo-Linguistic Studies*. Edited & introduction by K. V. Sarma. Hoshiarpur, India: V. V. Research Institute.

Wade, Allan. 1954. *The Letters of W. B. Yeats*. London: Rupert-Davis.

Wayman, Alex. 1963. "The Stages of Life according to Varāhamīhira." *American Oriental Society Journal* 83, no. 3 (August-September): 360–361.

———. 1984. *Buddhist Insight*. Edited with an introduction by George Elder. Religions of Asia Series, edited by Lewis R. Lancaster & J. L. Shastri, no. 5. Delhi: Motilal Banarsidass.

Weiss, Mitchell G. 1980. "*Caraka Saṃhitā* on the Doctrine of Karma." In *Karma & Rebirth in Classical Indian Traditons,* edited by Wendy D. O'Flaherty, 90–115. Berkeley, Ca.: Univ. of California Press.

———. 1987. "Karma and Āyurveda." *Ancient Science of Life*. 6, no.3 (January): 129–134.

Werner, Karel. 1978. "The Vedic Concept of Human Personality & Its Destiny." *Journal of Indian Philosophy* 5: 275–289.

Woodruff, Diana & James E. Birren, eds. 1983. *Aging: Scientific Perspectives & Social Issues*. 2d ed. Monterey, Ca.: Brooks/Cole Publishing Co.

Woods, James H. 1914. See Primary Works and Translations, s.v. "Yoga System of Patanjali."

Yeats, W. B. *The Poems of W. B. Yeats: A New Edition*. 1983. Edited by Richard J. Finneran. New York: Macmillan Publishing Co.

Young, Katherine. 1981. "Why are Hindu Women Traditionally Oriented to Rebirth rather than Liberation (*mokṣa*)?" In *Proceedings of the Third International Symposium on Asian Studies,* 937–945. Hong Kong: Asian Research Service.

———. Forthcoming. "Euthanasia: Traditional Hindu Views & the Contemporary Debate." In *Purity, Abortion & Euthanasia: The Hindu View of Ethical Issues,* by Harold Coward, Julius Lipner & Katherine Young. Albany, N.Y.: SUNY Press.

Zimmer, Stefan. 1985. "Tod Und Sterben im Ṛgveda." *Indo-Iranian Journal* 28, no. 3 (July): 189–199.

Zimmerman, Francis. 1980. "Ṛtu-Sātmya: The Seasonal Cycle and the Principle of Appropriateness." *Social Science and Medicine* 14B: 99–106.

Zysk, Kenneth. 1985. *Religious Healing in the Veda: With Translations and Annotations of Medical Hymns from the Ṛgveda and the Atharvaveda and Renderings from the Corresponding Ritual Texts.* Transactions of the American Philosophical Society, vol. 75, Pt. 7. Philadelphia: The American Philosophical Society.

# *Subject Index*


*A*

Aging:

—universal characteristics of: ix, 2, 3, 131–32; circumscribed by life and death, 81; conducive to growth and maturity, 3, 159, 161; confers minority status, 4; and death inherent at conception, 2; contributes to class awareness, 4; historical dialectic on, 15–41; ideas on, shared and participated, 132; marker of life's journey, 159; patterns of, experience, 161; produces uniquely personal and universal experiences, 5

—in Vedas: 16–21; theoretical discussion of, avoided, 20; evidence of earliest documented views on, 16; relative lack of reference to lived experience of, 20

—in Upaniṣads: treated with dread, 26; source of sorrow, 22; Vedic views on, redefined, 22

—in Buddhism: 24–34, 85; continuous with suffering, 33; impediment to spiritual liberation, 9; inherent in all component things, 29; campaign of dread against, 31

—in Hinduism: 34–41

—Āyurveda: labeles, as disease, 128–29

—Dharma Śāstras: emphasize developmental dimension of, 43–44; foster care and culture of, 158; judge, to be goal-directed, 44; see, as promoting relaxation and warmth in elderly women, 40; see, as revealing authentic modes of being, 96

*B*

Body: face and front of self, 52; substratum for sacrifices, 57; system of meanings, 51

—in Vedas: physiology of, 57; structure of 54–58;

—in Buddhism: abode of old age, 30; critique of, 58–63; denigrated on account of perishable condition of, 60; ephemeral nature

of, stressed, 59–60; genesis of, 68; *nirvāṇa* does not prevent aging of, 61; premature revulsion toward, 47; sphere and origin of suffering, 60; tolerated for didactic and hermeneutic purposes only, 58–59
—in Hinduism: condition of 70; Rāma's discourse on, 70; response to, 63–80; source of bliss, 70
—in Āyurveda: collection of elements, 63, 67; function of humors, *guṇas* and elements, 65; genesis of, 68; growth and decline of, 78; passes through phases, 68; substratum for conscious self, 111; woman's, pathogenic changes in, 76
—in Dharma Śāstras: denigration and disgust of, 38, 46; impediment to spiritual liberation, 69; infused with ultimate reality, 58; knowledge of, needed for cultivating dispassion toward, 69; ripened by power of deeds, 69

## C

Codes of behavior. *See also* Sadvṛtta and Svasthavṛtta: 8; 123–26
Coping with the stress of aging: 4, 8, 114–29; strategies in *Yoga Sūtra* for, 96

## D

Death:
—general remarks: cannot be attributed to aging, 97; category in *Amarakoṣa,* 98; elusive rhetoric of, 97–98; end product of aging, 97; aging and, 97–109; natural process, 2; semantic of, 98
—in Vedas: 99–102; and aging, transitory forms of matter, 113; associated with old age, 100; does not die, 101; is accidental and in middle of life, 101; never final but repeated, 56, 61, 99; permeates human moments in life and act, 101; ritually recurring act, 99; shadow of immortality, 135; transcended by sacrifices, 136; unseen comrade and companion, 101
—in Upaniṣads: as dancer, 102; old age and, speculations on, 101–103; with old age, seen as twin terrors, 102; Vedic notion of, is reversed, 53
—in Buddhism: break up of five aggregates, 103; conquest of, principle aim, 103; is evil, 107, 150; identified with Māra, 103; old age and, fear of, 62; sole purpose of life process, 105; repudiation of, 103–105
—in Hinduism: *bhakti,* antidote of, 106; knowledge, antidote of, 105; life, mere deviation of, 107–108; response to, 105–109; substratum of sentient beings, 107–108; vanquished by mercury-based medicines, 127

## E

Etiology of aging: 2, 3, 153–56; glossed over in many texts, 135; initiated and sustained by time, 118; linked to divine action, intervention, and time, 149, 185n.35; linked to impaired body

## M



## O

# *Author Index*

# Primary Works Index

# *Sanskrit Terms and Proper Names Index**

## *A*



*Proper names are capitalized.

## U



## V



## Y